Lecture Notes in Business Information Processing   233

More information about this series at http://www.springer.com/series/7911

Narjès Bellamine Ben Saoud · Carole Adam
Chihab Hanachi (Eds.)

Information Systems for Crisis Response and Management in Mediterranean Countries

Second International Conference, ISCRAM-med 2015
Tunis, Tunisia, October 28–30, 2015
Proceedings

 Springer

Editors
Narjès Bellamine Ben Saoud
Institut Supérieur d'Informatique
University of Tunis El Manar
Tunis
Tunisia

and

RIADI Laboratory
Ecole Nationale des Sciences de
l'Informatique
University La Manouba
Manouba
Tunisia

Carole Adam
Grenoble Informatics Laboratory
Université Grenoble-Alpes
Saint-Martin-d'Hères
France

Chihab Hanachi
University of Toulouse 1
Toulouse
France

ISSN 1865-1348   ISSN 1865-1356 (electronic)
Lecture Notes in Business Information Processing
ISBN 978-3-319-24398-6   ISBN 978-3-319-24399-3 (eBook)
DOI 10.1007/978-3-319-24399-3

Library of Congress Control Number: 2015948717

Springer Cham Heidelberg New York Dordrecht London

Printed on acid-free paper

Springer International Publishing AG Switzerland is part of Springer Science+Business Media
(www.springer.com)

Preface

Welcome to the Second International Conference on Information Systems for Crisis Response and Management in Mediterranean Countries (ISCRAM-med 2015), held in Tunis, Tunisia, October 28–30, 2015. The first edition of the ISCRAM-med conference was successfully held in Toulouse, France, October 15–17, 2014.

The objectives of the ISCRAM-med conference are to provide an outstanding opportunity and an international forum for local and international researchers, practitioners, and policy makers to address and discuss new trends and challenges in the area of Information Systems for Crisis Response and Disaster Management.

Similarly to the international ISCRAM conference (its 12th edition was held in May 2015 in Norway), the aim of ISCRAM-med is to focus on crises and disasters (natural or man-made) and the solutions (computer-based or not) required to be effective and efficient according to the disaster phases, types, and scales. A special focus on Mediterranean-related experiences has been considered. In fact, many crises have occurred in recent years around the Mediterranean Sea. Also, the shared history between the Mediterranean countries and common geopolitical issues has led to solidarity among people and cross-country interventions. This observation proves the importance of the need to enhance multi-disciplinary collaborations. Crises in this region should be studied in a participatory way following a holistic and systemic approach at a Mediterranean level, rather than as isolated phenomena. Researchers concerned with crises in Mediterranean countries have often limited their work to a country or to a class of crises. Now it becomes appropriate to exchange and share information and knowledge about the course and management of these crises and also to get the point of view of stakeholders, practitioners, and policy makers.

We received 41 papers involving around 115 authors from 21 countries and 4 continents. The submissions to the conference covered a broad area of topics and attracted many south Mediterranean researchers. In fact, 19 papers were submitted involving 45 researchers from Morocco, Algeria, Tunisia, Egypt, and Senegal. Each submission received at least three review reports from Program Committee members. Fifty-six researchers, from 23 countries and 4 continents, kindly accepted to serve on the Program Committee. The reviews were based on five criteria: relevance, contribution, originality, validity, and clarity of the presentation. Using these, each reviewer provided a recommendation from which we selected 14 full papers (of about 12 pages each) for publication and presentation at ISCRAM-med. Accordingly, the acceptance rate of ISCRAM-med 2015 for full papers is about 34 %. In addition, these proceedings also include four short papers (eight pages each), which were presented at ISCRAM-med 2015.

The 18 selected papers (involving 66 authors from 16 countries and 4 continents) are related to the preparedness and response phases of a disaster management lifecycle and are organized according to five main topics: social computing, modelling and simulation, information and knowledge management, engineering of emergency management systems, and decision support systems and collaboration.

Furthermore, invited keynote talks were given by Mauro Dolce (General Director of the Department of Civil Protection, President of the Council of Ministers, Rome, Italy) on "Civil Protection Achievements and Critical Issues in Seismology and Earthquake Engineering Research." Nissaf Bouafif Ben Alaya (Associate Professor of Preventive Medicine and Epidemiology, Faculty of Medicine of Tunis and General Director of the Observatory of New and Emerging Diseases, Tunis, Tunisia) gave a keynote talk on Early Warning Systems in Tunisia: Evolution, Challenges, and Place of Environment and Modelling.

Consequently, during this three-day conference, attendees were invited to present and discuss their experiences, their recent research results, best practices, and case studies. Tool demonstrations relating to the social, technical, and practical aspects of current or future ICT systems for all phases of management of emergencies, disasters, and crises, were given. By organizing the conference in Tunis, on the southern side of the Mediterranean Sea, we attracted many researchers from African countries and provided the ISCRAM community with the opportunity to expand the influence of the conference, to favor community building and knowledge sharing with the participants coming from these regions.

Last, but not least, we hope that this international "new born" event organized in Mediterranean countries will grow and continuously lead to creating a great Mediterranean multidisciplinary network tightly connected to and active with the international ISCRAM community to manage disasters.

Acknowledgments

We gratefully thank all members of the Steering Committee, members of the Program Committee, as well as all external referees for their work in reviewing and selecting the contributions.

Special thanks to Julie Dugdale and Henda Hajjami Ben Ghézala, the conference co-chairs.

Moreover, we wish to acknowledge the scientific and/or financial support of:

- The International ISCRAM Association,
- From France, the IRIT laboratory of Toulouse, all the Universities of Toulouse, and the LIG Laboratory of Grenoble,
- From Tunisia, the RIADI laboratory, the National School of Computer Science (Ecole Nationale des Sciences de l'Informatique, ENSI, Tunisia), the Higher School of Computer Science (Institut Supérieur d'Informatique, ISI, Tunisia), the University of Manouba, the University of Tunis El Manar, ACEUT Association, STICODE doctoral school, and the Ministry of Higher Education and Scientific Research.

For the local organization of the conference, we gratefully acknowledge the help of Mehrez Essafi, Chahrazed Labba, Malika Charrad, Moncef Gafsi, Nesrine Ben Yahia,

Rahma Amri, Ahmed Maalel, Inès Thabet, Wided Mathlouthi, Maroua Kessentini, Fadoua Ouamani, Wala Rebhi, and Riadh Hadj'Mtir.

Finally we would like to thank Christine Reiss and Ralf Gerstner from Springer for their cooperation in the preparation of this volume.

October 2015   Narjès Bellamine Ben Saoud
                                                                  Carole Adam
                                                               Chihab Hanachi

Organization

Conference Co-chairs

Narjès Bellamine Ben Saoud   Institut Supérieur d'Informatique, University of Tunis El Manar - RIADI Laboratory, Ecole Nationale des Sciences de l'Informatique, University La Manouba, Tunisia

Chihab Hanachi   University Toulouse 1, IRIT Laboratory, France

Julie Dugdale   Université Pierre-Mendès-France – LIG, Grenoble, France

Program Co-chairs

Henda Hajjami Ben Ghézala   Ecole Nationale des Sciences de l'Informatique - RIADI Laboratory, University La Manouba, Tunisia

Carole Adam   University Grenoble-Alpes and Grenoble Informatics Laboratory, Grenoble, France

Steering Committee

Chihab Hanachi   University Toulouse 1, IRIT Laboratory, France

Frédérick Benaben   Ecole des Mines Albi Carmaux, France

François Charoy   University of Lorraine, France

Narjès Bellamine Ben Saoud   Institut Supérieur d'Informatique (ISI) & RIADI Laboratory, Tunisia

Julie Dugdale   Université Pierre-Mendès-France & Laboratoire d'Informatique de Grenoble, France

Tina Comes   University of Agder, Norway

Victor Amadeo Banuls Silvera   Pablo de Olavide University, Spain

Program Committee

Adam Widera   University of Muenster, Germany

Andrea Omicini   Università di Bologna, Italy

Athman Bouguettaya   RMIT University, Melbourne, Australia

Baghdad Atmani   LIO, Faculté des Sciences Exactes & Appliquées, Université d'Oran, Algeria

Benoit Gaudou   University Toulouse 1, IRIT Laboratory, France

Cen Li   Middle Tennessee State University, USA

Chantal Bonner Cherifi   University Lyon 2, France

Christophe Claramunt	Naval Academy Research Institute, Brest, France
Elise Beck	Université Joseph Fourier, Grenoble, France
Elyes Lamine	Ecole des Mines d'Albi, France
Eric Andonoff	University of Toulouse 1 Capitole, France
Erwan Tranvouez	Aix Marseille University, Marseille, France
Esma Aïmeur	University of Montreal, Canada
Fiona McNeill	Heriot-Watt University, UK
Francis Rousseaux	University of Reims, France
François Pinet	Irstea, Clermont-Ferrand, France
François Charoy	University of Lorraine, France
Frederic Amblard	University of Toulouse 1 Capitole, France
Frédérick Benaben	Ecole des Mines Albi Carmaux, France
Ghassan Beydoun	University of New South Wales, Australia
Hajer Baazaoui	University of Manouba, Tunisia
Hamid Mcheick	University Québec at Chicoutimi, Canada
Hocine Cherifi	Laboratoire Electronique, Informatique et Image, France
Inès Thabet	University of Jendouba, Tunisia
Ioannis Dokas	Democritus University of Thrace, Greece
Ismail M. Romi	Palestine Polytechnic University, Palestine
Jean Marie Dembele	Gaston Berger University, Saint-Louis, Senegal
Jens Pottebaum	Universität Paderborn, C.I.K, Germany
Jose J. Gonzalez	University of Agder, Norway
Lamjed Ben Said	University of Tunis, Tunisia
Laurent Franck	Télécom Bretagne, France
Lotfi Bouzguenda	University of Sfax, Tunisia
Malika Charrad	University of Gabès, Tunisia
Marouane Kessentini	University of Michigan, USA
Matthieu Lauras	Ecole des Mines d'Albi, France
Mohamed Erradi	ENSIAS, Rabat, Morocco
Monica Divitini	Norwegian University of Science and Technology, Norway
Muhammad Imran	Qatar Computing Research Institute, Qatar
Paloma Diaz Perez	Universidad Carlos III de Madrid, Spain
Pascal Salembier	Université de Technologie de Troyes, France
Ricardo Rabelo	Federal University of Santa Catarina, Brazil
Rim Faiz	Institut des Hautes Etudes Commerciales, University of Carthage, Tunisia
Robert Power	Digital Productivity Flagship, CSIRO, Australia
Rui Jorge Tramontin Jr.	Santa Catarina State University, Brazil
Serge Stinckwich	IRD, France
Shady Elbassuoni	American University of Beirut, Lebanon
Silvia Ciotti	Eurocrime, Italy
Tim Grant	Netherlands Defence Academy, Retired But Active Researchers (R-BAR), The Netherlands
Valentina Emilia Balas	Aurel Vlaicu University of Arad, Romania

Yiannis Verginadis   National Technical University of Athens, Greece
Youcef Baghdadi   Sultan Qaboos University, Oman

External Reviewers

Chahrazed Labba   RIADI Laboratory, Tunisia
Fadoua Ouamani   RIADI Laboratory, Tunisia
Hai Dong   RMIT University, Melbourne, Australia
Hanene Lejmi   SOIE Laboratory, Tunisia
Houda Benali   University of Gafsa, Tunisia
Lassaâd Mejri   University of Bizerte, Tunisia
Mohamed Ramzi Haddad   University of Tunis El Manar, Tunisia
Nesrine Ben Mustapha   RIADI Laboratory, Tunisia
Nesrine Ben Yahia   University of Manouba, Tunisia
Sajib Kumar Mistry   University of Dhaka, Bangladesh
Yahya Benkaouz   ENSIAS, UM5S, Morocco

Abstracts of Invited Talks

Civil Protection Achievements and Critical Issues in Seismology and Earthquake Engineering Research

Mauro Dolce

Director general
Department of Civil Protection
Presidency of the Council of Ministers
Via Ulpiano, 11
00193 Rome – Italy
mauro.dolce@protezionecivile.it

Abstract. A great complexity characterizes the relationships between science and civil protection. Science attains advances that can allow civil protection organizations to make decisions and undertake actions more and more effectively. Provided that these advances are consolidated and shared by a large part of the scientific community, civil protection has to take them into account in its operational procedures and in its decision-making processes, and it has to do this while growing side by side with the scientific knowledge, avoiding any late pursuit.

The aim of the talk is to outline the general framework and the boundary conditions, to describe the overall model of such relationships and the current state-of-the-art, focusing on the major results achieved in Italy and on the many criticalities, with special regards to research on seismc risk.

Among the boundary conditions, the question of the different roles and responsibilities in the decision-making process will be addressed, dealing in particular with the contribution of scientists and decision-makers, among the others, in the risk management. In this frame, the different kinds of contributions that civil protection receives from the scientific community will be treated. Some of them are directly planned, asked and funded by civil protection. Some contributions come instead from research that the scientific community develops in other frameworks. All of them represent an added value from which civil protection wants to take advantage, but only after a necessary endorsement by a large part of the scientific community and an indispensable adaptation to civil protection utilization. This is fundamental in order to avoid that any decision and any consequent action, which could in principle affect the life and property of many citizens, be undertaken on the basis of non-consolidated and/or minor and/or not shared scientific achievements.

Early Warning System in Tunisia: Evolution, Challenges and Place of Environment and Modelling

Nissaf Bouafif Ben Alaya

Associate Professor of Preventive Medicine and Epidemiology,
Faculty of Medicine of Tunis, Tunisia
General Director of the Observatory of New and Emerging Diseases,
National Observatory of New Emerging Diseases, Tunis, Tunisia
5-7, Rue Khartoum, Complexe Diplomat,
bloc 4, 13ème étage, Le Belvédère, 1002, Tunis
nissaf.bouafif@rns.tn

Abstract

National public health surveillance serves two main objectives:

- Measure disease burden, including monitoring morbidity/mortality trends, to effectively guide control programs and the corresponding allocation of resources; and
- Detect as early as possible any public health events requiring rapid investigation and response to minimize the negative health consequences to the affected population.

Early Warning and Response (EWAR) is the organized mechanism to detect as early as possible all public health events requiring rapid investigation and response. These events are either unusual events or abnormal patterns in the usually observed morbidity/mortality trends.

The objective of this talk is to present the Implementation of an Early Warning and Response system in Tunisia by integration of Event-Based Surveillance to the traditional surveillance system, Emergency and General practitioners networks, environmental data integration and mathematical modelling using time series analysis.

Contents

Social Computing

Semantic Visualization of Twitter Usage in Emergency and Crisis Situations

Teresa Onorati[(✉)] and Paloma Díaz

Universidad Carlos III de Madrid, Avda de la Universidad 30, 28911 Leganés, Spain
{tonorati,pdp}@inf.uc3m.es

Abstract. In the last decade, social networks have become an important and popular communication channel for accessing to a great variety of data. It is common that people share what they are feeling or some event that has caught their attention in any kind of situation including disasters. For example, during the Hurricane Sandy in 2012 Twitter generated more than 20 million of tweets in just one week. In order to take advantage of this huge quantity of data, it would be useful to be able to have a quick view of the most relevant information, which facilitates situational awareness and decision taking processes, with the possibility to ask for more details when needed. In this paper, we propose a semantic mechanism for collecting, categorizing and visualizing Twitter data about emergency and crisis situations. The categorization is based on a knowledge model of the emergency domain and it consists of grouping information depending on their semantic similarity with such knowledge. Moreover, we propose a visualization of such categorization based on the co-occurrence of information in the collected tweets.

Keywords: Information visualization · Information categorization · Emergency management · Semantic modeling · Ontologies

1 Introduction

Nowadays, social networks represent one of the most important and used channel for communicating a great variety of information. People use them to share their feelings or opinions about different kinds of events, both personal or of public interest, at anytime from anywhere. Indeed, thanks to the technological advances of these last decades, smart devices are becoming more and more accessible for the general public. According to a 2012 of ICT penetration worldwide, there are far more mobile subscriptions than wired subscriptions [1, 7]. This means that more and more people do have the possibility to own a device with a wide range of capabilities, as a camera, an audio or video recorder and a quite fast Internet connection. In this way, they can share their posts or access to published ones. As stated by Westlund in [2, 8], *"mobile devices are used for reporting live from both everyday life events and more significant events"* allowing the growth of the so called *citizen journalism*. Following this idea, citizens are actively involved in sharing news and creating a continuous flow of information. This is particularly

© Springer International Publishing Switzerland 2015
N. Bellamine Ben Saoud et al. (Eds.): ISCRAM-med 2015, LNBIP 233, pp. 3–14, 2015.
DOI: 10.1007/978-3-319-24399-3_1

true when an emergency situation occurs and the citizen participation becomes critical for the involved agencies and organizations [3, 9].

In several emergency cases, including natural disasters or large-scale accidents, social media have been widely used for seeking help or accessing to useful information like evacuation routes or dangerous areas. For instance, on the 2nd of November 2012, the official Twitter account posted that *"people sent more than 20 million Tweets about the storm between Oct 27 & Nov 1"*. Counted tweets were tracked looking for the words "hurricane" and "sandy", as well as the hashtags #hurricane and #sandy. In that situation, many people had no power and they started to use Twitter as the only communication channel still available thanks to the battery and the Internet connection of their mobile phone [4, 10]. Another interesting example is given by the accident of the Germanwings Flight 9525 of the 24th of March 2015. The H + K Belgium team has analyzed the online communication activities and in particular the Twitter usage [5, 11]. One of the most interesting results is that during the first 60 min after the disaster, almost 60 thousands Tweets have been published using the hashtag #Germanwings.

As shown by these examples, the volume of generated information (e.g. published tweets) could grow exponentially. The management of this kind of data is a complex task that could require an extra effort for collecting and analyzing them. It is worth to note that in many cases, tweets have irrelevant, inaccurate or false information that difficult sense making processes. It is crucial to provide a mechanism for accessing and analyzing such data in a way that makes it possible to extract relevant information for other citizens or even for emergency operators.

In literature, several solutions have been already proposed as it will be discussed in Sect. 3. They basically aim at analyzing and visualizing the number of posted messages and trending topics, but it is still missed a concrete focus on the emergency domain that could help to identify meaningful data. To cover this lack, our approach consists of adding semantics to the collected tweets so they can be understood in terms related to the domain of application: the crisis. In this way, the most relevant terms can be extracted and visualized and such relevance will be measured according to their relation with the crisis situation. Moreover, we introduce a categorization of extracted terms from the tweets in seven main topics: *emergency*, *evacuation*, *media*, *place*, *time*, *hashtags* and *general*. The aim of this categorization is to make it easier for users to identify the main topics of interest and eventually access to the related information. This approach is based on several data mining techniques for computing the semantic similarity between terms and categories using existing knowledge representations as an ontology and two taxonomies. We also present a real use case as an example of the applicability of this approach to semantically visualize the tweets collected about the Nepal Earthquake of April 25, 2015.

In Sects. 2 and 3, the most relevant contributions about the usage of social networks in emergency management and their visualization are summarized. In particular, we are going to present both practical and theoretical related works as the basis of our proposal. In Sect. 4, the semantic approach for visualizing emergency information is described in a detailed way, while Sect. 5 is about the Nepal Earthquake use case. Finally, some conclusions and future works are drawn.

2   Social Networks in Crisis

Thanks to the technological advances that make it possible to connect different kinds of devices all over the world through the Internet, the concept of social network has been translated from the physical communities to the virtual ones. Following the same principles of the social interactions among humans, virtual networks aim to offer a technological platform for allowing people to be in contact for both personal and business purposes. In this way, it is possible to establish a new communication channel where users can share a great variety of data (e.g. photos, videos or links) reaching many people geographically distributed in just few moments.

A consequence of this information spread has been pointed out in [6, 12] as an epidemic wave that could influence the personal behavior and thinking of people. Other social researchers have been collecting data from different social networks in order to study how users interact among them and which effects these behaviors have on political and social changes, as shown in [13]. This phenomenon is clearly observed for example during political elections, where candidates use social networks as an important part of their campaign to share slogans, photos or videos.

Another recurring topic that generally generates a great amount of shared messages is related to critical events, including natural disasters, accidents or terrorist attacks. People tend to share their own experience and their feelings about the situation, or repost what others have written about it. In [14], the analysis of this sharing activity identified seven different usages of social networks in emergencies: *listening to public debate, monitoring situations, extending emergency response and management, crowd-sourcing and collaborative development, creating social cohesion, furthering causes (including charitable donation)* and *enhancing research*. Given the huge quantity of user-generated data, there are some limitations to consider when trying to use them to support decision making processes, such as the lack of specific policies or the reliability of collected information (as discussed in [15, 16]). Nevertheless, it is crucial that the process adopted for managing critical situations takes into account data coming from social networks as a direct communication channel with citizens.

A similar conclusion has been also discussed in [17] after an extensively review of the literature about how social networks have been used during the crisis occurred in the last ten years. One of the first considered cases is the terrorist attacks of 9/11 (September 11th, 2001), when citizens used wikis for retrieving any useful detail about missing people. After this, researchers have observed a similar behavior in many other situations concluding that during these events people communicate or search for information through social networks, such as Twitter, Facebook, YouTube or Flickr. In the same work, authors also propose a classification of the usage of social networks for managing crisis based on the literature review. In particular, they define a bidirectional communication between a receiver and a sender. The receiver and the sender can be both official organizations and common citizens, and depending on their role, a different type of communication is defined. For example, we speak about an *Integration of Citizen Generated Content* if the official organizations are acting as receiver and the general public as sender. Otherwise, the official organization is the sender and the citizens are the receivers in case of a *Crisis Communication*. This classification aims at clarifying how the interaction among users in social networks works when an emergency occurs.

3 Social Network Visualization in Crisis

To take advantage of the messages published on the social networks during a crisis, several researchers have been studying the application of information visualization techniques. Among available social networks, contributions mostly focus on the usage of Twitter thanks to the possibility to have texts with a limit of 140 characters, easy to manage and analyze. Moreover, Twitter has about 302 million of monthly active users and an average of 500 million of tweets sent per day [18].

In 2012, Yin et al. analyzed the correlation between Twitter traffic and emergency management activities [19]. Their aim was to understand how information collected from general public can improve the overall situation awareness. Within this scope, they propose an intelligent system for capturing automatically any burst on Twitter that generates a large number of posts. Collected data are then clustered depending on the topic and related with real events occurred at the same time in the same place. Finally, some visualization tools are offered to users for a better understanding of the situation awareness. The first one is a map where tweets are grouped depending on their geographical localization. The second one is a tag cloud with a time slider where users can access to the most frequent terms depending on the chosen time range.

Another interesting example of intelligent system developed for analyzing and visualizing tweets related to an event is TweetXplorer by Morstatter et al. [20]. The purpose of this system is not specific for crisis, but it has been already applied in this area. For example, in [21] authors have included it within their theoretical framework about how emergency information is propagated through social media. TweetXplorer has been designed as a solution for the questions that an analyst would ask working with social media: *when*, *who*, *what* and *where*. The system provides a different functionality and visualization for each question. Considering for example the localization of the tweets, a heat map is used with circles of different colors over a map. The colors and the size of each circle depend on the number of tweets co-located in the same place.

Despite other interesting systems developed for visualizing social media information, several researchers have been working also at proposing general design findings and recommendations about how to manage emergency information collected from social media. An example is given by Carter et al. in [22]. In this work, authors have conducted different studies about how the social media are used for searching keywords, monitoring conversations and analyzing their semantic meaning. Their final proposal is a set of three recommendations for establishing an effective communication channel between emergency operators and citizens. The first one is about the kind of content of shared posts, mainly news report or photos. The second one concerns the creation of ad-hoc hashtags to facilitate the search of information. The last recommendation is more related to the general need of a deeper involvement of official emergency agencies in sharing information on social media.

On the same line of the findings proposed by Carter et al. [22], Calderon et al. [23] have conducted a detailed review of main contributions in literature about social media visualizations in emergency management [23]. Their contribution mainly focuses on providing a design solution for improving the real-time animation of tweets. In particular, they have evaluated their proposal with a streamgraph of the tweets related to the Hurricane Sandy, grouped by their sentiment content. As a result, they have pointed out three main findings about emergency practitioners' needs: avoiding manual analysis of social network messages, rapid understanding of the most relevant information from available data, and understanding citizens' feelings and moods.

These last two contributions show a growing attention to understanding how to design the social interaction among citizens and emergency operators. In this paper, we are going to take in mind them as theoretical motivation of our proposal. Nevertheless, from the contributions already analyzed, we have extracted some useful features that an effective visualization has to provide. The first one is about the geo-localization of tweets to relate each message with a specific point of the emergency area. The second one is the possibility to apply different visualization techniques depending on the purpose to achieve. For example, in case of real-time analysis it would be better to use a streamgraph where each stream represents a different topic. Finally, not only the number of tweets matters, but also their content is crucial for understanding the information flow. In this case, it would be useful to identify most relevant terms, to extract photos or to analyze sentiments. The content analysis allows to filter the collected information depending on its meaning and its semantic value respect to the domain of application.

4   A Semantic Similarity-Based Approach for Twitter

The mechanism we are going to present here aims at analyzing tweets related to a specific event. The choice of Twitter is related to both practical and theoretical reasons. From a practical point of view, tweets are short messages with a limit of 140 characters. In this way, users have to be concise in order to express their opinions or feelings, reducing the number of used words. From a theoretical point of view, Twitter is the most studied social network in the emergency area and it is also the most popular. Indeed, during the Hurricane Sandy of 2012 people shared 20 million of tweets in just one week.

The approach is based on computing the semantic similarity of the words contained in each tweet with existing ontologies and taxonomies for their categorization. It consists of four main steps, as shown in Fig. 1. The first step (a in Fig. 1) is a query on Twitter for some specific keywords (e.g. "Nepal", "earthquake", "hurricane", "Sandy") through the Search API available as part of the Twitter's v1.1 Rest API. The result is a set of tweets containing the considered keywords. It is also possible to choose a date range for limiting the search to a specific period of time.

The second step (b in Fig. 1) is the syntactic analysis of collected tweets using an algorithm called POS (Part Of Speech). The POS tagger associates each word with its syntactic function (e.g. noun, verb, adjective) and it has been developed by the Stanford Natural Language Processing Group [24]. From the tagged tweets, we extract both proper and common nouns in their root form, as for example *disaster, help* or *China*. Considering the limitation of 140 characters for each tweet, people have to be concise in their posts using few words to express their opinions. Among these words, the most

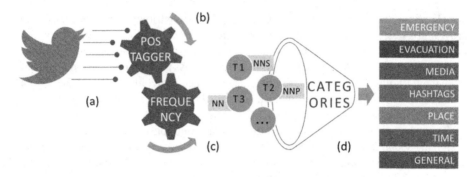

Fig. 1. A schema for the proposed semantic approach

meaningful ones are the nouns and for this reason we decide to dismiss the other parts of speech. Nevertheless, in future works it would be interesting to include also verbs, adverbs and adjectives and compare with the current approach.

The number of obtained terms after this second step can vary depending on the number of tweets that have been collected. In order to filter them and select the most relevant ones, we compute the frequency of each term as how many times it occurs over collected tweets (step c in Fig. 1). As discussed in [25], in general the most frequent words are also the most relevant ones respect to the analyzed text. To reduce the list already ordered by frequencies, we apply the Zipf's law stating that the less frequently a word is used, the less meaning it carries [26]. The threshold is decided depending on the particular use case and observing obtained nouns.

In the fourth step (d in Fig. 1), the terms previously filtered are semantically related to some fixed categories. Considering the scope of this work, the chosen categories of meanings are the following: *emergency, evacuation, media, place, time, hashtags* and *general*. All of them come from the "Five Ws and one H" formula of the journalistic style: who did that (*general* and *emergency*), what happened (*hashtags, emergency* and *evacuation*), where did it take place (*place*), when did it take place (*time*), why did that happen (*emergency*) and how did it happen (*emergency*). In particular, the *emergency* and *evacuation* categories are related to the scope of this work and the kinds of event queried on Twitter. The *hashtags* category groups the hashtags used in the tweets, where a hashtag is composed by a sharp symbol (#) followed by one or more words. The *general* category is for all that words that are not semantically related to the other categories.

In order to identify which is the most related category for each term, we have compared their semantic similarity. To do so, we use different knowledge representations. The first one is an existing ontology called SEMA4A (Simple EMergency Alerts 4[for] All) that has been developed for correlating users' needs, technologies and relevant information about emergency situations [27]. In particular, SEMA4A is organized into four classes of concepts: *emergency, evacuation, accessibility* and *communication*. Each concept has a set of meanings and it is related to others through ad-hoc relations depending on considered domains. For example, *evacuation* has an *include* relation with *map* or *typhoon* has a *kind of* relation with *emergency*.

The terms to categorize are searched directly into SEMA4A. If they are found, the categories are decided depending on the belonging class. Otherwise, we verify if they can be still related to one of the ontology concepts as synonyms. For this purpose, we use an existing taxonomy of words called WordNet, containing for each word its meanings, synonyms and other semantic relations [28]. If we obtain a negative result from WordNet, we can conclude that the term is not semantically similar to any concept of SEMA4A.

Following with the categorization, a part from SEMA4A we have also employed two different taxonomies containing words related with time and place. The first one has about 150 time expressions[1] like *day*, *after* and *later*. The second is an open source list of all countries in the world[2]. Also in this case, we search directly for the terms and if they are not included into one of the taxonomies, we try with their synonyms extracted from WordNet. The terms that cannot be related semantically to the *time* or *place* category are finally included into the *general*.

Once the terms are filtered and grouped into the seven categories, the final step of our approach proposes a visualization that could represent both the categorization and the co-occurrences of the terms in the same tweet. The categorization is shown as a hierarchical representation visualized as a tree. The co-occurrences are weighted edges between two nodes where the weight depends on the number of times that the two terms co-occur in a tweet. Combining these two visualization techniques, we finally decide for the Hierarchical Edge Bundle (see Fig. 2 for an example). In particular, the tree is a circle where the elements with the same parent node are adjacent, while the edges are modeled as a B-spline curve and grouped together if they have the same source and final nodes.

In the following section, we present the results obtained from applying our approach to a real use case.

5 Semantic Visualization for Twitter Usage: A Use Case

On April 25, 2015 an earthquake of magnitude 7.8 hit the central area of Nepal. The count of victims reached 8000 in few days and the material damages were invaluable. From the very first hours, people started to post messages on Twitter with the hashtag #NepalEartquake. Considering the large scope of this disaster, we decided to take it as a use case for the proposed semantic visualization.

Between the 25 and the 28 of April, we have collected 822 tweets containing the words "Nepal" and "Earthquake" or the hashtag "#NepalEarthquake". Following the approach previously described (see Fig. 1), the words contained into each tweet have been tagged with the part of speech syntactic function and the common and proper nouns as well as the hashtags have been extracted.

After the extraction, the frequencies of the nouns have been computed counting how many times each one of them appears in the analyzed tweets. The resulting list consists of 1262 terms, where the most frequent one is *earthquake* with 326 occurrences. In order

---

[1] http://www.enchantedlearning.com/wordlist/time.shtml.

[2] https://openconcept.ca/blog/mgifford/text-list-all-countries-world.

Fig. 2. Semantic visualization for Nepal earthquake tweets (Color figure online)

to filter this list, we apply the Zipf's law for identifying and cutting off the less mean-ingful terms. In this particular case, we have excluded nouns or hashtags with a frequency of less than five. This limit has been defined experimentally, observing the list of terms and identifying which ones have a less frequent and less relevant respect to the specific topic, like *activity* or *diplomacy*. The filtered list contains about 116 words and 9 hashtags.

While the hashtags have been directly grouped in the *hashtags* category, the following step of the proposed approach concerns the semantic association of the terms with one of the others among *emergency*, *evacuation*, *media*, *general*, *place* and *time*. To do so, first of all we have looked for them or their synonyms in the SEM4A ontology. As a result, the term *video* has been automatically included into *media*, while *earthquake* and *magnitude* with other 26 terms have been collected into *emergency*. Moreover, the *evacuation* class contains 10 nouns as for example *shelter* and *building*. About the *place* category, countries like *Nepal* and *China* and three more have been retrieved, while *time* has 17 expressions as *hour*, *day* or *moment*. Finally, the other 53 terms are into *general*.

About the visualization part, Fig. 2 shows the obtained Hierarchical Edge Bundle. The categories are coded with a specific color, as shown by the legend in the upper part of Fig. 2: orange for *emergency*, blue for *evacuation*, green for *media*, purple for *hashtags*, yellow for *place*, sky-blue for *time* and gray for *general*. Moreover, the terms are related depending on their co-occurrences in the same tweet and the paths are light-blue if not selected, green otherwise.

Observing the semantic visualization for the Nepal earthquake, we can point out some interesting issues. First of all, the circle put the categories on the same level but it is easy to recognize which one has more terms: *general* followed by *emergency* in this use case. Moreover, the weight of the edges among nodes gives us an idea about which occurrences are the most common over the collected tweets. In this particular case, we can recognize the hashtag #neaplearthquake and the nouns *aid*, *earthquake*, *people*, *Nepal* and *relief* among others. They represent a summary of the most discussed topics in Twitter during the first four days after the disaster. Coming back to the tweets containing these words, effectively they content general data about the earthquake and how to help affected people. Finally, the proposed visualization is able to guide the attention of the user from the individual terms to their relations in order to understand how the information flows from a category to another.

One more interesting issue is related to the running time. The semantic visualization can be both dynamic and static. In the first case, the proposed mechanism is executed real-time during the first moments after the occurred event as part of the emergency response phase. This means that each time a new tweet is published about the event, extracted terms have to be added and the visualization can change. The emergency operators can take advantage of this dynamism for improving their understanding of the situation and supporting the decision making process. In the static case, the entire mechanism is executed once the crisis has been solved and the emergency operators are working at the recovery phase. The proposed visualization can be used for a post-crisis analysis of the information flow. In particular, it is possible to have a more clear idea about how citizens participate and which topics are the most discussed.

6   Conclusions and Future Works

The technological advances of these last decades have changed the way in which people interact with information. Nowadays, they have the possibility to access to big sources of data, at anytime and from anywhere. Consequently, in order to know more about an event it is possible to find quickly updated information looking for it in any web search engine. Related to this idea, social media represent an important innovation for the so called citizen journalism [2, 8] a practice that also appears in crisis and emergency situations. Citizens are actively involved in the information flow, sharing and posting a great variety of data. This activity gets more intense when a large-scale event occurs, as for example a natural disaster or a terrorist attack.

In literature, there are already several contributions aimed at analyzing messages published in social media during critical events. Their scope stands mainly on the role of citizens, how their active participation can influence the emergency management process and how the collected data can be included into current notification systems.

Moreover, other related works focus on how the social interaction between citizens and emergency operators can be designed. From their analysis, we have extracted three main issues to take into account for following up with this research line: geo-localization of messages, adaptation of visualization techniques to specific objectives, and a semantic analysis of the messages. This paper mainly contributes to these two last aspects, proposing a semantic visualization for Twitter usage during critical situations.

The proposed approach takes advantage of several data mining techniques to extract and then categorize the most frequent words from a collection of tweets. The categorization is an automatic mechanism based on the usage of semantic resources that categorize the domain of application and they include an ontology called SEMA4A [2, 8] and two taxonomies about the countries in the world and the most common time expressions. After extracting proper and common nouns from the tweets, their frequency is computed in order to exclude the less frequent and consequently less meaningful ones. After that, the categorization consists in looking for the semantic similarity of terms with each one of the categories through the considered knowledge representations.

Looking at the obtained list of terms, we can conclude that the categorization has achieved a quite good result even if a more detailed evaluation is needed. In fact, as a future work we are planning to involve emergency experts to verify the consistency of proposed categorization. Moreover, we are also thinking about how to improve the adopted method, for example looking for different methods for computing the semantic similarity.

Based on the categorization, we have also proposed a semantic visualization implementing a Hierarchical Edge Bundle. This technique combines a circle tree and a weighted edge between nodes. Observing the result, it is possible to easily distinguish among the seven categories and identify the most common terms. Moreover, the edges between nodes are designed as B-spline curves to create a sort of information flow among the different terms. Users can also navigate the visualization, select a node and visualize its co-occurrences in the tweets. Future works will include the possibility to visualize the original tweets and some kind of animation for highlighting the most relevant nouns. Based on the analyzed literature, we are also considering other visualization techniques to be combined with the Hierarchical Edge Bundle, like a tree map or a heat map. In any case, the selection of the visualization technique depends on the task being performed with the data, for which further studies on the expectations of emergency operators or citizens when looking at twitter during a disaster are required.

Acknowledgments. This work is supported by the project emerCien grant funded by the Spanish Ministry of Economy and Competitivity (TIN2012-09687).

References

1. Smith, T.F., Waterman, M.S.: Identification of common molecular subsequences. J. Mol. Biol. **147**, 195–197 (1981)
2. May, P., Ehrlich, H.C., Steinke, T.: ZIB structure prediction pipeline: composing a complex biological workflow through web services. In: Nagel, W.E., Walter, W.V., Lehner, W. (eds.) Euro-Par 2006. LNCS, vol. 4128, pp. 1148–1158. Springer, Heidelberg (2006)

3. Foster, I., Kesselman, C.: The Grid: Blueprint for a New Computing Infrastructure. Morgan Kaufmann, San Francisco (1999)
4. Czajkowski, K., Fitzgerald, S., Foster, I., Kesselman, C.: Grid information services for distributed resource sharing. In: 10th IEEE International Symposium on High Performance Distributed Computing, pp. 181–184. IEEE Press, New York (2001)
5. Foster, I., Kesselman, C., Nick, J., Tuecke, S.: The physiology of the grid: an open grid services architecture for distributed systems integration. Technical report, Global Grid Forum (2002)
6. National Center for Biotechnology Information. http://www.ncbi.nlm.nih.gov
7. Measuring the Information Society. http://www.itu.int/ITU-D/ict/publications/idi/
8. Westlund, O.: Mobile news: a review and model of journalism in an age of mobile media. Digit. J. **1**, 6–26 (2013)
9. Díaz, P., Aedo, I., Romano, M., Onorati, T.: Supporting citizens 2.0 in disasters response. In: 7th International Conference on Methodologies, Technologies and Tools enabling e-Government, pp. 1–10 (2013)
10. Hurricane Sandy and Twitter. http://www.journalism.org/index_report/hurricane_san-dy_and_twitter
11. Germanwings 9525: an analysis of the evolving role of digital technology on crisis communications. http://www.hkstrategies.com/blogs/crisis/germanwings-9525-analysis-evolving-role-digital-technology-crisis-communications
12. Kleinberg, J.: The convergence of social and technological networks. Commun. ACM **51**(11), 66–72 (2008)
13. Agrawal, D., Budak, C., El Abbadi, A., Georgiou, T., Yan, X.: Big data in online social networks: user interaction analysis to model user behavior in social networks. In: Madaan, A., Kikuchi, S., Bhalla, S. (eds.) DNIS 2014. LNCS, vol. 8381, pp. 1–16. Springer, Heidelberg (2014)
14. Alexander, D.E.: Social media in disaster risk reduction and crisis management. Sci. Eng. Ethics **20**(3), 717–733 (2014)
15. Hiltz, S.R., Kushma, J., Plotnick, L.: Use of social media by US public sector emergency managers: barriers and wish lists. In: 11th International Conference on Information Systems for Crisis Response and Management, pp. 602–611. The Pennsylvania State University, USA (2014)
16. Díaz, P., Aedo, I., Herranz, S.: Citizen participation and social technologies: exploring the perspective of emergency organizations. In: Hanachi, C., Bénaben, F., Charoy, F. (eds.) ISCRAM-med 2014. LNBIP, vol. 196, pp. 85–97. Springer, Heidelberg (2014)
17. Reuter, C., Marx, A., Pipek, V.: Crisis management 2.0: towards a systematization of social software use in crisis situations. Int. J. Inf. Syst. Crisis Response Manag. **4**(1), 1–16 (2012)
18. Twitter. http://about.twitter.com/company
19. Yin, J., Lampert, A., Cameron, M., Robinson, B., Power, R.: Using social media to enhance emergency situation awareness. IEEE Intell. Syst. **27**(6), 52–59 (2012)
20. Morstatter, F., Kumar, S., Liu, H., Maciejewski, R.: Understanding twitter data with tweetxplorer. In: 19th ACM SIGKDD International Conference on Knowledge Discovery and Data Mining, pp. 1482–1485. ACM, New York (2013)
21. Pohl, D., Bouchachia, A.: Information propagation in social networks during crises: a structural framework. In: Krol, D., Fay, D., Gabryś, B. (eds.) Propagation Phenomena in Real World Networks, vol. 85, pp. 293–309. Springer, Switzerland (2015)
22. Carter, L., Thatcher, J.B., Wright, R.: Social media and emergency management: exploring state and local tweets. In: 47th Hawaii International Conference on System Sciences, pp. 1968–1977. IEEE Press, New York (2014)

23. Calderon, N.A., Arias-Hernandez, R., Fisher, B.: Studying animation for real-time visual analytics: a design study of social media analytics in emergency management. In: 47th Hawaii International Conference on System Sciences, pp. 1364–1373. IEEE Press, New York (2014)
24. Toutanova, K., Manning, C.D.: Enriching the knowledge sources used in a maximum entropy part-of-speech tagger. In: Joint SIGDAT Conference on Empirical Methods in Natural Language Processing and Very Large Corpora held in Conjunction with the 38th Annual Meeting of the Association for Computational Linguistics, pp. 63–70, Morristown, New Jersey (2000)
25. Ihara, S.: Information Theory for Continuous Systems. World Scientific, New Jersey (1993)
26. Zipf, G.K.: Human Behaviour and the Principle of Least-Effort. Addison-Wesley, Cambridge (1949)
27. Onorati, T., Malizia, A., Diaz, P., Aedo, I.: Modeling an ontology on accessible evacuation routes for emergencies. Expert Syst. Appl. **41**(16), 7124–7134 (2014)
28. Miller, G.A., Beckwith, R., Fellbaum, C., Gross, D., Miller, K.J.: Introduction to WordNet: an on-line lexical database. Int. J. of Lexicogr. **3**(4), 235–244 (1990)

A Comparative Study of Microblogs Features Effectiveness for the Identification of Prominent Microblog Users During Unexpected Disaster

Imen Bizid[1,2]([✉]), Nibal Nayef[1], Oumayma Naoui[2],
Patrice Boursier[1,3], and Sami Faiz[2]

[1] L3i Laboratory, University of La Rochelle, La Rochelle, France
{imen.bizid,patrice.boursier,nibal.nayef}@univ-lr.fr
[2] LTSIRS Laboratory, Tunis, Tunisia
sami.faiz@insat.rnu.tn
[3] IUMW, Kuala Lumpur, Malaysia
patrice@iumw.edu.my

Abstract. This paper presents a learning-based approach for the selection of relevant feature categories in the context of information retrieval from microblogs during unexpected disasters. Our information retrieval strategy consists of identifying prominent microblog users who are susceptible to share relevant and exclusive information in a disaster case. To identify these users, we evaluate the effectiveness of the state-of-the-art features characterizing microblog users for the identification of prominent users in a specific context. We experimented with a different sets of feature categories to determine those that discriminate prominent users sets from non-prominent ones interacting in Twitter during the 2014 Herault floods that occurred in France. The achieved results show that on- and off-topical user activities features are the most representative features for identifying prominent users in a disaster context. We also note that SVM outperforms the ANN learning algorithm for this classification context especially when it is trained with additional spatial features.

Keywords: Effectiveness of feature categories · Prominent microblog users · Disaster management

1 Introduction

The climate change unleashes a multitude of unexpected disaster characteristics and effects that have never been perceived in our planet. Heat waves in summer, winter without snow, climate disruption, floods in some regions of Europe while other neighboring regions suffer from terrible droughts. Climate change manifests itself in diverse unexpected forms. Such phenomena still turn into disasters, causing irreversible damages in many places of our planet.

The challenges of managing such disasters are related especially to situation awareness and real-time information collection. The need for emergency teams to

N. Bellamine Ben Saoud et al. (Eds.): ISCRAM-med 2015, LNBIP 233, pp. 15–26, 2015.
DOI: 10.1007/978-3-319-24399-3_2

go on the disaster affected zones, risking their lives, in order to collect information about what is taking place diminishes greatly. People from surrounding areas can provide nearly real-time observations about disaster scenes by interacting in microblogs. Citizens in the affected zones can share information about what they are experiencing; watching or hearing during a disaster. These microblogging platforms represent a rich source of information fundamental to have an accurate insight into what is happening on the ground in order to efficiently manage these unexpected disasters.

Although these microblogs such as Twitter provide many specificities (e.g. number of favorites, number of retweets of a tweet, etc.) reflecting other microblog users feedback regarding the shared information, it is still challenging to retrieve relevant and exclusive information from the huge amount of shared data. These microblogs specificities remain inaccurate as they refer mostly to the information shared by popular users independently of the relevance and freshness of their content. Therefore, it is more rational to associate the relevance and the quality of the shared information with user's prominence during the disaster.

By tracking prominent microblog users who are sharing relevant and exclusive information during an unexpected event, emergency first responders can have a real-time global view of what is happening in the threatened or affected areas. The identification of these key users have been widely explored in the context of influencers and domain experts identification. However, it has never been explored in the context of prominent users identification during unexpected disasters.

Prominent users, in the context of this paper, refer to microblog users who are susceptible to share exclusive and relevant information during a given unexpected event. Finding such users depends generally on the effectiveness of the selected categories of features describing these microblog users according to the specific context.

In this paper, we aim at evaluating the effectiveness of both the state-of-the-art and our prior proposed features describing microblog users for the identification of prominent microblog users in the context of unexpected disasters. This study focuses on the selection of the most descriptive categories of features that may lead us to the identification of these microblogs key users during disasters.

The rest of this paper is organized as follows. Section 2 reviews related works for identifying prominent microblog users. Section 3 describes the different categories of features evaluated in this paper. Experimental results are presented in Sect. 4. The experiments are discussed in Sect. 5. Finally, we conclude this paper with direction to future work in Sect. 6.

2   Related Work

Current Information retrieval systems in microblogs for disaster management are mostly based on the content analysis of microbogs posts. Tweak the tweet system [1] provided a hashtag based syntax to make text mining of the huge amount of information shared in microblogs during disasters easily processed.

Imran et al. [2] proposed a classification model for disaster-related information extraction by analyzing tweets text content. MicroFilters system [3] extracted the valuable disaster-related-images shared in microblogs based on image analysis techniques. These systems have yielded promising results for the identification and classification of disaster-related-content. However, they are computationally expensive, on the one hand, and they are still sensitive to redundant and outdated information on the other hand. Moreover, it is more logical to identify prominent users that may share relevant and exclusive information during the disaster and track them in order to access in real time to their shared disaster-related-information.

To the best of our knowledge, the issue of prominent users' identification has never been studied in the context of disasters. However, it has been widely explored in the different contexts defining key users as influential users in the network or as domain experts who are active and popular in a specific topic or domain [4–6].

Existing approaches for the identification of social media influencers are based on standard centrality measures such as eigenvector centrality and its variants HITS [7] and PageRank [8]. These adapted measures to microblogs specificities (e.g. number of tweets, mentions, retweets ...) are computationally expensive and sensitive to well-connected users (e.g. celebrities, communication channels...) [6]. Therefore, these approaches could not be used in real time scenarios, on the one hand, and they could not lead us to identify users sharing fresh information during unexpected disasters on the other hand.

Apart from the above research studies, domain experts identification has been explored using supervised and unsupervised learning techniques based on a set of features describing the activities of users regarding only the particular analyzed topics [9–11]. IA-Rank [12] ranked users based on the features characterizing how the user name is amplified via mentions, replies or retweets by other users. Pal et al. [9] proposed a new identification model using a set of features characterizing microblog users according to the different nature of their activities and their social position in the network. Xianlei et al. [10] proposed a Gradient Boosted Decision Tree to identify domain experts in Sina Microblog based on profile and tweeting behavior features.

These features have yielded promising results in the identification of domain experts. However, they have never been explored in the context of the identification of prominent users during disasters. Hence, in this paper, we evaluate the effectiveness of the different categories of both state-of-the-art features and our prior proposed features [13,14] in a disaster context.

3   User Modeling Using Microblogs Features

The identification of prominent users problem in the context of disasters can be casted into a binary classification problem. Many supervised learning algorithms can be used to learn the classification model for this purpose. The performance of the used algorithms is potentially associated to the strength of the selected features to model the user behavior in a disaster context. The more the features are representative for the prominent and non-prominent users behavior during a disaster the more the learned classifiers are efficient.

To learn the classification model, we study a large set of the state-of-the-art features and some new features proposed in our prior work [13,14]. The listed features may reflect the behavior and the importance of each user interacting about the disaster. We have split these features into five broad categories: profile features (PrF), on-topical features (OnAF), off-topical features (OfAF), spatial features (SpF) and social network structure features (SnF). The rest of this section describes in depth these main categories of user features.

3.1   Profile Features

Profile Features (PrF) characterize the user profile description. This description is registered by the user himself (e.g. location, domains of interest...) or generated automatically by the microblogging service in order to report the user activeness rate in the network (e.g. Number of collected favorites, Number of followers...). Table 1 presents the set of user profile features. These features are extractable from any user profile using Twitter APIs.

Table 1. Profile Features (PrF) from the microblogging platform Twitter.

Name	Features
P1	Certified user [10]
P2	Enabled geolocation [14]
P3	Protected [10]
P4	Number of produced tweets [10]
P5	Number of collected favorites [14]
P6	Creation date of the Twitter account [14]
P7	Number of followers [10]
P8	Number of followees [10]

PrF give a general representation of each user independently of his activeness rate during the disaster. At the first sight, we can note that P2 and P1 may be descriptive for prominent users during disasters. P2 refers to the user information precision during the disaster where the geographic information is important. P1 can be used as a strong proof or indicator to evaluate the veracity of the information shared by each user. P7 and P8 are generally used in order to detect celebrities and domain experts. These features are evaluated in order to study if there is a correlation between the user's popularity in the network and their prominence during unexpected disasters. Moreover, P4 and P5 which refer to the user activeness in the network are studied in order to evaluate if users who are generally active in the network may be prominent during unexpected disasters or not and vice versa.

3.2   User Activity Features

Microblog users can express what they are seeing, hearing and experiencing during a disaster using different nature of tweets:

User's own produced tweets are original tweets shared by the profile owner. These tweets are expressed by a simple content which do not include any retweet or mention symbols.

Mention tweets are tweets destined specially to particular users to make them aware about a particular information. These tweets include the @ symbol followed by the name of users to whom the tweet content is destined.

Repeated tweets are original tweets posted by someone else and rebroadcasted by the user in order to share it with his followers. These tweets are informally called retweets and can be identified by the RT@username label that is automatically inserted at the beginning of the tweet.

All these three TYPES of tweets can refer to valuable contents that are indispensable to manage unexpected disasters. Hence, we need to analyze any nature of tweets shared by users interacting during a disaster in order to identify the prominent ones.

Moreover, in order to differentiate prominent users activities from non-prominent ones, we analyze both the user's on-topic tweets related to the disaster and the off-topic ones. The categorization of on and off-topic user activities was proposed in our prior work [14] under the assumption that users affected by the disaster would be interested only by the disaster news and would neglect any other off-topical information diffused in the network.

Thus, we divide the different user activities features during the disaster into two categories On-topic Activities Features (OnAF) and Off-topic ones (OfAF). These feature categories are measured respectively according to the user on-topic and off-topic activities:

On-topic an activity is considered on-topic when it contains a subset of a list of keywords and hashtags which are defined to describe the unexpected disaster under consideration

Off-topic an off-topic activity refers to any activity that was not recorded as an on-topic one

Additionally, in this paper we assume that tweets referring to the disaster and including at least one keyword reflecting non-serious or non-valuable contents (e.g. advertising or joke words and symbols such as sale, rent, pub, lol and so on), it will be directly recorded as an off-topic one. Thus, users who share non valuable contents could be penalized.

Our rationale behind the extraction of on-topic and off-topic activities is based on penalizing users who are toggling among several topics, and who may share outdated information. Using this strategy, users are evaluated based on their impact on the analyzed disaster, and on the strength of their attachment to that disaster. For example, Top news outlets sharing news about several topics are penalized as they do not focus mainly on the analyzed disaster.

Table 2. On-topic User Activities Features (OnAF) and Off-topic User Activities Features (OfAF) in Twitter.

Name	Features	On	Off
Original tweets			
T1	Number of original tweets [9, 10, 14]	+	+
T2	Number of links shared [14, 15]	+	+
T3	Number of keyword and hashtags [9, 14]	+	−
T4	Number of favorites of original tweets [14]	+	+
Retweets			
T5	Number of retweets of other's tweets [10, 14, 16]	+	+
T6	Number of unique users retweeted by the user [14]	+	+
T7	Number of retweets of author's tweets [14]	+	+
T8	Number of unique users who retweeted author's tweets [14, 16]	+	+
Mentions			
T9	Number of mentions of other users by the author [9, 14, 17]	+	+
T10	Number of unique users mentioned by the author [9, 14, 17]	+	+
T11	Number of mentions by others of the author [9, 14, 17]	+	+
T12	Number of unique users mentioning the author [9, 14, 17]	+	+

Table 2 presents both the state-of-the-art features characterizing user activities during the disaster and our prior proposed features.

On- and Off-topical user activity features will be studied separately in this paper in order to estimate the effect of each category of features in the identification of prominent users in the context of unexpected disasters.

3.3   Spatial Features

Spatial Features (SpF) characterize microblog users according to their assigned location and geolocation regarding the threatened disaster zone. Such features may be essential to determine which are the users geolocated in the disaster zone and who may play the role of sensors to diffuse information about what is really happening on the ground. The following spatial features described in Table 3 are studied in the context of disasters:

Table 3. Spatial Features (SPF) characterizing the geographic position of microblog users regarding the disaster.

Name	Features
S1	User location [13]
S2	Shared geo-coordinates [13]

S1 indicates if the location indicated in the user profile has been stricken by the disaster or not.

S2 measures the inclusion rate of the geo-coordinates related to the user shared tweets are included in the territory threatened by the disaster or not.

3.4 Network Structure Features

Many works have explored the microblogs structure features in order to identify mostly influential and popular users. However, all of these works have used mainly time consuming algorithms that are not feasible in real time and unsuitable for the disaster context. Moreover, the used profile features referring to the number of user's followers and followees may promote popular users who are toggling between several topic and who are sharing outdated information and neglect real prominent users having a small number of connections in the network. Thus, in this category of features, we focus only on the user followers and followees who are interacting about the disaster. Table 4 presents the network structure features studied in this paper.

4   Experiments and Results

4.1   Dataset

To conduct experimental performance evaluation on real data, we collected most of the tweets shared during the floods that have occurred from 29th to 30th September 2014 in the Herault area, situated in the south of France. The flooded area witnessed record-shattering 252 mm of rainfall in just three hours, causing important damages estimated between 500 and 600 million Euros. Data collection was processed using our multi-agent System called MASIR [18]. At the lowest level, the system detects the different users who have shared at least one on-topic tweet (i.e. talking about the floods) during the analyzed period. On-topic tweets are detected using the hashtags and keywords: #Hérault, #Herault, #intempéries, #crues, #flooding, #Montpellier, #Alert, #Inondations, #RedAlert, which were employed by Twitter users to share information about

Table 4. Network Structure Features (SnF) characterizing the social position of microblog users.

Name	Features
NS1	Number of user's topical followers [9, 13]
NS2	Number of user's topical followees [9, 13]
NS3	Number of user's topical followers adjusted by the total number of followers [13, 14]
NS4	Number of user's topical followees adjusted by the total number of his followees [13, 14]

the disaster. The system then crawls all the on-topic and off-topic tweets shared by the detected users from 29th September at 00:00AM to 1st October at 00:00AM. We collected 60195 tweets composed of on and off-topic tweets shared by 3332 users during the two days of the disaster.

Ground Truth: For the purposes of training and evaluation, users tracked in our dataset have to be assigned labels indicating whether they are prominent users or not. We have asked some volunteers from our laboratory to classify the tracked users according to the relevance and exclusivity of their tweets during the event. The number of users to be labeled varied from 66 to 200 users per volunteer.

These volunteers labeled each user as one of the two classes: C1 for prominent users, or C2 for non-prominent ones. The labeling is based on the subjective study of the tweets' content of each user (varying from 1 to 82 tweets per user). According to this study, 90 users have been classified as C1, and 3242 users have been classified as C2.

4.2   Evaluation Tools and Metrics

We describe in this section the methodologies used to evaluate the effectiveness of the different categories of features for identifying prominent microblog users in a disaster context.

Features Categories Selection Approaches. We studied the effectiveness of the different feature categories in a disaster context with two learning algorithms. Support Vector Machine (SVM) [19] and Artificial Neural Networks (ANN) [20] are used for this study. Using these algorithms, we tested all the combination of feature categories that may represent prominent microblog users interacting during a disaster.

SVM is used in order to learn a linear SVM model for the identification of microblog prominent users in a disaster case based on different feature categories.

ANN is used in order to train and test a multi-layer ANN classification model by experimenting several combination of feature categories representative to microblog users.

In order to deal with the unbalanced data classification problem, we gave a more important weight to the class C1 of prominent users ($W_1 = 10$) than the class C2 of non prominent users ($W_2 = 1$). These parameters were set experimentally in the training phase of SVM.

As there is no parameters to tune the class weights using ANN, we have duplicated the dataset of prominent users by 30 in order to balance the two datasets of prominent and non prominent users in the training phase of ANN.

Experimental Setup and Evaluation Metrics. For experimental set-up, we randomly sampled 60 % of both prominent and non-prominent labeled users datasets as training data for learning the classification and ranking models based on different feature categories, and the remaining 40 % as test data to test the efficiency of the learned model (Table 5).

Table 5. Training and test datasets description

	Training dataset (60 %)	Test dataset (40 %)
Number of prominent users	54	36
Number of non-prominent users	1945	1297

Through the different experiments conducted to evaluate the efficiency of the different feature categories for the classification of microblog users, we have used standard precision, recall and F1-score (i.e. F-measure) evaluation metrics.

$$\text{Precision} = \frac{\#\text{Correctly classified prominent users}}{\#\text{Users classified as prominent users}}$$

$$\text{Recall} = \frac{\#\text{Correctly classified prominent users}}{\#\text{Ground truth prominent users}}$$

$$\text{F1-score} = \frac{2 \times \text{Precision} \times \text{Recall}}{\text{Precision} + \text{Recall}}$$

4.3   Feature Categories Effectiveness

In order to select the most representative feature categories for microblog prominent users in a disaster, we evaluate the effectiveness of each category of the state-of-the-art features separately. Table 6 reports the experimental results evaluating the effectiveness of each category of features using two different learning algorithms.

According to the test results returned by both the learned SVM and ANN models, the category of features characterizing the on-topical user activity in microblogs during the disaster (OnAF) is the most representative category for prominent users in a disaster context. The remaining categories of features have yielded poor results and failed to identify microblog prominent users. However, these categories may yield improvement in terms of precision and recall if they are combined with other categories. Therefore, we study the effectiveness of these categories when they are combined with the OnAF feature category. Table 7

Table 6. Effectiveness of each feature categories for prominent users identification in terms of Precision, Recall and F1-score evaluation metrics.

Feature categories	N⁰ of features	SVM			ANN		
		Precision	Recall	F1	Precision	Recall	F1
OnAF*	12	0.43	0.86	0.57	0.29	0.80	0.42
OfAF	11	0	0	0	0.04	0.33	0.07
PrF	8	0	0	0	0.01	0.33	0.03
SnF	4	0.05	0.02	0.03	0.09	0.61	0.15
SpF	2	0	0	0	0	0	0

Table 7. Effectiveness of each pair of feature categories (OnAf, An additional Feature Category) for prominent users identification in terms of Precision, Recall and F1-score evaluation metrics.

Feature categories	Nº of features	SVM			ANN		
		Precision	Recall	F1	Precision	Recall	F1
OnAF+OfAF*	23	0.47	0.75	0.58	0.43	0.80	0.56
OnAF+PrAF	20	0.42	0.86	0.56	0.36	0.86	0.51
OnAF+SnF	16	0.40	0.86	0.55	0.24	0.66	0.35
OnAF+SpF	14	0.43	0.86	0.57	0.39	0.88	0.54

reports the results of the different pairs of categories used to learn the ANN and SVM models for the prominent user identification.

We note that combining the two categories of features OnAF and OfAF improves the identification results using both ANN and SVM. Thus, these two categories are more efficient for the identification of microblog prominent users in the context of disasters when they are combined. Regarding the other combinations, we observe that they have a negative effect when they are combined with the OnAF category. Thus, we select the most efficient combination (OnAF+OfAF) in order to enrich it with the remaining categories of features. The identification of prominent users results using the new categories of features combination are reported in Table 8.

According to these results, there is no significant enhancements when adding a third category of features to OnAF and OfAF. Only the spatial category of features slightly improves the identification results obtained by learning the SVM model. However, training an ANN classification model based on these same categories, decreases the identification performance compared to the previous resulted ANN learned based on OnAF and OfAF categories.

We experiment in Table 9 OnAF OfAF and SpF categories with additional categories in order to evaluate the effectiveness improvement rate using our two learning approaches.

We notice that all the trained combinations reported in Table 8 have failed to improve prominent users identification effectiveness.

Table 8. Effectiveness of 3 combined feature categories (OnAf, OfAF, An additional Feature Category) for prominent users identification in terms of Precision, Recall and F1-score evaluation metrics.

Feature categories	Nº of features	SVM			ANN		
		Precision	Recall	F1	Precision	Recall	F1
OnAF+OfAF+SpF	25	0.48	0.75	0.60	0.41	0.80	0.54
OnAF+OfAF+PrAf	31	0.43	0.72	0.54	0.32	0.75	0.45
OnAF+OfAF+SnF	27	0.45	0.75	0.56	0.36	0.77	0.50

Table 9. Effectiveness of 4 combined feature categories (OnAf, OfAF, SpF, An additional Feature Category) for prominent users identification in terms of Precision, Recall and F1-score evaluation metrics.

Feature categories	№ of features	SVM			ANN		
		Precision	Recall	F1	Precision	Recall	F1
OnAF+OfAF+SpF+SnF	29	0.45	0.75	0.56	0.38	0.80	0.52
OnAF+OfAF+SpF+PrAf	33	0.42	0.72	0.53	0.30	0.77	0.43

5   Discussion

The obtained results in this study have led us to conclude on the importance of using the on-topical and off-topical activities features categories and the spatial features category to learn an efficient classification SVM model identifying prominent microblog users during real-time disasters. On- and off-topical features are extremely useful in disaster management scenarios where prominent users focus mainly in sharing disaster-related information. Thus, using off-topical activity features, users toggling between different topics will be penalized. In addition, referring to the on-topical activities features, users focusing potentially on the unexpected disaster will be promoted. Such a property has shown that users faced by a disaster would share mainly on-topical information and neglect the other topics-related information. Moreover, we showed that users geolocated in the disaster area are more susceptible to share fresh and relevant information about what is happening around them than the others. These results have been validated using the Herault Floods database. An open access to Twitter would be necessary to evaluate these features using more microblogs disasters databases which could not be afforded.

6   Conclusion and Future Work

In this paper, we analyzed the effectiveness of different state-of-the-art categories of features and the additional categories of features proposed in our prior work in the context of microblog prominent users identification during unexpected disasters. We tested different combinations that may lead to an efficient classification model using two different learning algorithms ANN and SVM. We found that on-topic activities category of features and the off-topic one are almost the only categories that can differentiate microblog prominent users from non prominent one in a disaster context. Moreover, we noted that the SVM algorithm is more suited to identify prominent users especially when it is learned based on the spatial, on- and off-topic categories of features.

For future work, we aim to analyze the effectiveness of each feature characterizing prominent users independently of their category using different feature selection algorithms. Moreover, we wish to propose additional engineered features which are more representative for active microblog users in the context of disaster management.

References

1. Starbird, K., Stamberger, J.: Tweak the tweet: leveraging microblogging proliferation with a prescriptive syntax to support citizen reporting. In: 7th International ISCRAM Conference (2010)
2. Imran, M., Castillo, C., Lucas, J., Meier, P., Rogstadius, J.: Coordinating Human and Machine Intelligence to Classify Microblog Communications in Crises, pp. 712–721. The Pennsylvania State University (2014)
3. Ilyas, A.: Microfilters: harnessing twitter for disaster management. In: GHTC, pp. 417–424 (2014)
4. Weng, J., Lim, E.P., Jiang, J., He, Q.: Twitterrank: finding topic-sensitive influential twitterers. In: WSDM, pp. 261–270. ACM (2010)
5. Zhang, M., Sun, C., Liu, W.: Identifying influential users of micro-blogging services: a dynamic action-based network approach. In: Seddon, P.B., Gregor, S. (eds.) PACIS, p. 223 (2011)
6. Silva, A., Guimarães, S., Meira, Jr., W., Zaki, M.: Profilerank: finding relevant content and influential users based on information diffusion. In: SNAKDD, pp. 2–9. ACM (2013)
7. Agichtein, E., Castillo, C., Donato, D., Gionis, A., Mishne, G.: Finding high-quality content in social media. In: WSDM, pp. 183–194 (2008)
8. Kwak, H., Lee, C., Park, H., Moon, S.: What is twitter, a social network or a news media? In: WWW, pp. 591–600 (2010)
9. Pal, A., Counts, S.: Identifying topical authorities in microblogs. In: WSDM, pp. 45–54. ACM, New York (2011)
10. Xianlei, S., Chunhong, Z., Yang, J.: Finding domain experts in microblogs. In: WEBIST (2014)
11. Ghosh, S., Sharma, N., Benevenuto, F., Ganguly, N., Gummadi, K.: Cognos: crowdsourcing search for topic experts in microblogs. In: SIGIR, pp. 575–590 (2012)
12. Cappelletti, R., Sastry, N.: Iarank: ranking users on twitter in near real-time, based on their information amplification potential. In: SOCIALINFORMATICS, pp. 70–77 (2012)
13. Bizid, I., Boursier, P., Morcos, J., Faiz, S.: A classification model for the identification of prominent microblogs users during a disaster. In: ISCRAM (2015)
14. Bizid, I., Nayef, N., Boursier, P., Faiz, S.: Prominent users detection during specific events by learning on- and off-topic features of user activities. In: ASONAM (2015, to appear)
15. Java, A., Kolari, P., Finin, T., Oates, T.: Modeling the spread of influence on the blogosphere. In: WWW (2006)
16. Boyd, D., Golder, S., Lotan, G.: Tweet, tweet, retweet: conversational aspects of retweeting on twitter. In: 43rd Hawaii International Conference on System Sciences (HICSS), pp. 1–10 (2010)
17. Honey, C., Herring, S.: Beyond microblogging: conversation and collaboration via twitter. In: 42nd Hawaii International Conference on System Sciences, pp. 1–10 (2009)
18. Bizid, I., Boursier, P.G., Morcos, J., Faiz, S.: Masir: a multi-agent system for real-time information retrieval from microblogs during unexpected events. In: 9th International KES Conference on Agents and Multi-Agent Systems: Technologies and Applications. KES-AMSTA-15, pp. 3–13 (2015)
19. Osuna, E., Freund, R., Girosi, F.: Support vector machines: training and applications. Technical report, Cambridge (1997)
20. Zhang, G.P.: Neural networks for classification: a survey. In: Cybernetics - Part C: Applications and Reviews (2000)

Recognizing Information Spreaders in Terrorist Networks: 26/11 Attack Case Study

Imen Hamed[1]($\boxtimes$) and Malika Charrad[1,2,3]

[1] RIADI Lab, La Manouba University, Manouba, Tunisia
imen.hamed@outlook.com
[2] University of Gabes, Zrig Eddakhlania, Tunisia
[3] MSDM Team, Cedric Lab, CNAM, Paris, France
malika.charrad@riadi.rnu.tn

Abstract. Terrorism is a man-made hazard characterized by its uncontrollability and unpredictability. In fact, terrorist cells are covert networks where secrecy is the prime concern during the operation. To disrupt these inhuman operations, it is crucial to reveal this secrecy and identify the responsible key actors. Therefore, a new research area emerges. Investigative Data Mining (IDM) is the study of terrorist networks using Social Network Analysis (SNA). It involves graph theory to analyze networks. Among analysis techniques, network metrics defined as centrality measures have been successfully involved in terrorist networks destabilization methods. In this paper, we propose another disruption strategy of terrorist network using the percolation centrality metric. This measure allows to conduct a dynamic analysis of terrorist network on one hand. On the other hand, it identifies information spreaders in the network. We experiment on the Mumbai 26/11 attack data set, the proposed approach recognizes the information spreaders involved in this incident.

Keywords: Social network analysis · Terrorist network · Percolation centrality

1 Introduction

The world has witnessed many terrorist attacks in the past few years such as Casablanca, Morocco (May 16, 2003), Russia (September 1–3, 2004) and Tunisia (Chaambi mount terror operations and the Bardo museum attack on March 2015). The consequences of these attacks in terms of number of lives lost and the infrastructure damage appeal for an urgent remedy. Thinking the crisis management at macro level, it is necessary to isolate terrorist group components and prevent or (at least) limit the impact of such crisis.

Several important works propose different techniques to disrupt the terrorist cells. SNA techniques are prominent among them. SNA can be used to identify, measure, visualize and analyze the ties among people, groups and organizations.

© Springer International Publishing Switzerland 2015
N. Bellamine Ben Saoud et al. (Eds.): ISCRAM-med 2015, LNBIP 233, pp. 27–38, 2015.
DOI: 10.1007/978-3-319-24399-3_3

Information about terrorists is usually transformed into network structure in which nodes represent the terrorists and the links are the connections between these individuals. SNA can provide useful information about these terror groups through the study and analysis of the network evolution, the node position in the graph and the connections between different individuals.

Terrorist networks are complex adaptive systems [5]. In fact, they are composed of dynamic autonomous cells which are widely dispersed and typically covert. Given that individuals play different roles in their cells [6], the illegal activities of the terrorists are split among them. Therefore, isolation of terrorist cells requires the identification of important actors and respectively their different roles.

To analyze terrorist networks, it is fundamental to measure network density and centrality. Various behaviors of individuals are significantly influenced by their positions in networks [1]. Therefore, it is required to determine the dominant roles and to reveal the key players in the network through centrality measures. Throughout this paper, we review different destabilization algorithms based on centrality measures (Sect. 3). Then, we introduce a new network destabilization method based on percolation centrality. We analyze the terror attacks in Mumbai on November 26, 2008 to illustrate the feasibility of our approach (Sect. 4). Our contributions may be summarized as follows:

– We visualize the network of the 26/11 hijackers using the statistical and mining tool R. The produced graph helps to do further interpretation and analysis.
– We explain how the percolation centrality metric can be incorporated in terrorist cells destabilization strategy. Traditional disruption methods rely on the identification of central node. We illustrate the flaws of these methods. Thereby, we introduce our strategy based on identifying information spreaders in the network.

2   Preliminaries

We design the terrorist graph as G. G consists of a pair (N,E) where N is the set of nodes and E is the set of edges that connect different nodes. For any finite network G of N vertices, we denote the sets of vertices and edges by V(G) and E(G) respectively:

$$V(G) = v_i | i = 1...N, |V(G)| - \text{size of network G- N, .} \tag{1}$$

$$E(G) = e_{ij} | i, j = 1...N, e(G) - |E(G)| - \text{number of network edges, .} \tag{2}$$

An edge e_{ij} represents opportunities for flow between vertices i and j. A path between two nodes is the set of edges connecting those two nodes. Once this set is minimized, the path is called the shortest path. This latter may also be called the geodesic distance between given nodes. The Adjacency matrix, $A \in M_{nn}(\Re)$, of network G is defined such that each matrix element, a_{ij}, indicates if G contains an edge e_{ij} connecting vertex v_j to v_i [3].

$$a_{ij} = \begin{cases} 1 & \text{if there is an edge connecting } v_i \text{ to } v_j \\ 0 & \text{otherwise.} \end{cases} \tag{3}$$

A host of centrality measures have been proposed to analyze complex networks. A centrality measure of a vertex or edge gives a numerical qualification of that element's relative network importance [3]. Betweenness centrality is prominent among different centrality measures.

This well known measure aims to quantify a node's importance as a conduit of information flow in a network. Formally, it is defined as:

$$BC(v) = \frac{1}{(N-1)(N-2)} \times \sum_{s \neq v \neq t} \frac{\sigma_(s,t)(v)}{\sigma_(s,t)} . \tag{4}$$

So, it is expressed as the fraction of shortest paths between source node s and target node t that pass through a given node v: $\sigma_{s,t}$ (v), averaged over all pairs of node in a network $\sigma_{s,t}$. N is the number of nodes in the network.

3   Related Work

SNA offers a branch of techniques to study terrorist networks. Different works emerge to propose methods to disrupt terrorist cells.

The authors in [10] propose a new centrality measure: network flow centrality Load. The objective of their work is to identify vertices to remove from the network in such a way as to force more flow through a critical vertex. Thus, the information flow is forced to pass through this vertex. Hence, it becomes possible to measure the activity of that node through quantifying how much flow must pass through it.

The authors in [13] introduce a new method to destabilize terrorist networks. This method consists in comparing different centrality values of different nodes to recognize nodes that are powerful, influential or worthy to neutralize.

The works in [11] analyzes the attacks of 26/11 using a set of centrality measures namely degree, betweenness, eigenvector and closeness. The degree of a node is the number of neighbors it has. The closeness measures the average shortest path length between the node and all other nodes in the graph. Eigenvector defines the influence of a node on its neighboring nodes. Based on these indices, the authors deduce the hierarchy of the terrorist network and recognize the most influential node. In [13], the authors propose two steps approach to achieve the destabilization. First, they define an algorithm that converts the undirected graph to a directed one using the degree and eigenvector centralities. Then, the second step is to construct a tree from the dependence centrality measure. So, the destabilization is reached.

As an attempt to improve the previous approach, the authors in [12] used two measures Katz centrality and PageRank centrality. Instead of running the two algorithms separately, the authors introduce a single step approach. Katz centrality can be viewed as a variant of eigenvector centrality. The aim of Katz is to measure the influence of a given node on the rest of nodes. Indeed, it counts the number of walks starting from a node or ending on a node, providing penalties to longer walks. The PageRank metric defines the influence of a node. It is an enhanced version of in-degree centrality. The computing of PageRank and Katz centralities reduce the time and space complexities.

The algorithm proposed in [9] relies on three centrality measures: degree centrality, closeness centrality and betweenness centrality. The authors claim that the financial manager is the most central node which is closest to other nodes. So these dark cells may be disrupted when the financial manager is isolated.

The authors in [8] propose a new centrality measure for destabilization purposes namely influence index. This measure is based on three degree of influence rule: A node is influenced by other nodes that lie at three degree of separation but not by those beyond. The influence index method consists of internal influence (itself) and external influence (from others'). The approaches presented above adopt traditional centrality measures such as betweenness, eigenvector and closenes. They define an influential node as a topologically central node holding multiple connections.

In this paper we propose a single step approach consisting in the computation of a single metric and adopting a different definition of influential nodes.

4   Proposed Approach

4.1   What Is Percolation

The percolation aspect in complex networks occurs in many scenarios: Viral content or rumors spread over contact networks. In a network of towns, the spread of disease and the contagious infections are considered as typical scenarios of percolation. Besides, computer viruses can divide over computer networks (Fig. 1).

The aforementioned schema illustrates the percolation process. At t = 1, the state of node A changes. Given that node A is related to node B, the state of node B changes also at t = 2. So, the contagion alters the state of the node as it spreads. A percolated node percolates its neighbors over time. The state of a node can be binary (such as received/not received a piece of news), discrete (susceptible/infected/recovered) or even continuous (such as the proportion of infected people in a town) as contagion spreads [4].

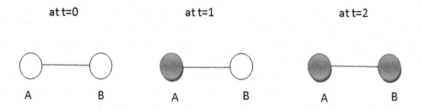

Fig. 1. The percolation process

The percolation centrality measures the importance of a node in terms of aiding the percolation through the network. While current centrality measures focus on purely topological importance of a node, the percolation measure combines the topological importance of the node in the graph and the node state (percolated/non-percolated/partially percolated). So, this measure copes very well with the network dynamics. Formally, the percolation centrality denoted PC is defined as:

$$PC^t(v) = \frac{1}{(N-2)} \times \sum_{s \neq v \neq r} \frac{\sigma_{s,r}(v)}{\sigma_{s,r}} \times \frac{x_s^t}{[\sum x_i^t] - x_v^t} . \tag{5}$$

x_s^t is denoted to the percolation state of the node s at time t.
x_i^t represents the percolation state of any node i at time t.
x_v^t is the percolation state for the node v to which the percolation centrality is computed.

PC determines at any time how important is the node to the overall process of percolation. Formally, the percolation centrality measure adopts the betweenness centrality measure logic since it relies on the number of shortest paths in the network. There are two extreme cases where the percolation centrality is trivially equal to the betweenness centrality: Given a single percolated node in the network; if we iterate over all possible percolated nodes one by one and then average over all the scenarios then we get:

$$PC^t(v) = \frac{1}{(N-1)(N-2)} \times \sum_{s \neq v \neq r} \frac{\sigma_{s,r}(v)}{\sigma_{s,r}} = BC(v). \tag{6}$$

So, the percolation centrality is reduced to betweenness centrality. Another scenario leads to the reduction of percolation centrality to the betweenness one is when all the nodes of the network are fully percolated:

$$\frac{x_s^t}{[\sum x_i^t] - x_v^t} = \frac{1}{(N-1)} . \tag{7}$$

Hence:

$$PC^t(v) = \frac{1}{(N-1)(N-2)} \times \sum_{s \neq v \neq r} \frac{\sigma_{s,r}(v)}{\sigma_{s,r}} = BC(v). \tag{8}$$

That is the percolation centrality starts as betweenness centrality and then it evolves and finally reduces to end as betweenness centrality again.

4.2 Why Percolation Centrality in Terrorist Network

The SNA defined centrality measures have been successfully incorporated in the destabilization of terrorist networks by determining the dominant role(s) from the network [12]. To sustain a successful attack operation, the terrorists tend to play different roles. A terrorist network is led by a leader who mostly acts as a mentor and only provides guidance on how to organize and motivate the group operatives [9]. The finance manager is the one who occupies the most central and active role in a decentralized terrorist network.

The majority of works focus on recognizing the leader of the terrorist cell. SNA can locate the true points of vulnerability in the network rather than simply the apparent leadership [7]. The best node to attack is not always that which has the most connections [7]. Dynamic analysis based on changing time and place can dig out more useful information that classical methods could not find [8]. It can also provide a clear picture of how information flows in the network [7].

In this paper, we aim to identify the information spreaders in the terrorist cell. We adopt a dynamic analysis based on the percolation centrality. The traditional centrality measures quantify the importance of a node in purely topological terms. The advantage of the percolation centrality is the consideration of the network dynamics. The important node is no longer the most central one, but the node which contributes more in the percolation process. Therefore, we propose a new method to destabilize the terrorist network. The nodes that spread the information in the terrorist network are important nodes. The identification of such nodes may disrupt the network. The authors in [7] claim that the leader in the network is not the most central node or the node that held many connections. Accordingly, the removal of key personnel, such as the most central node, will not necessarily collapse the network.

4.3   Terrorist Network Visualization

As a case study in this paper, we analyze the 26/11 attacks in Mumbai using the public data that were available in [11]. As a first experimentation, we considered a static terrorist network. In future work, we aim to consider dynamic network. So, we perform further analysis.

Figure 2 represents the hijackers of the Mumbai attacks on 26/11/08. Three among the thirteen terrorists were handling the operation simultaneously from Pakistan. The others were dispersed in different regions in Mumbai. The network depicted in Fig. 2 is not complete. In fact, some links are missing probably or a part of the network is still opaque. The terrorist number 12 and 13 are involved in the attack operation. However, they do not yield any connection with the other members. Despite the incompleteness of the network, we still may make some interesting inferences. Node 2 seems to be an important node. He has many connections with nodes in different regions in Mumbai. As shown in Table 1, the node 2 has the highest betweenness centrality in the network.

The authors in [11] conclude that he is the responsible for the attack operation. Given that the terrorist organizations have quite organizational roles to conduct successful operations, computing betweenness centrality does not provide a clear insight into the hijackers' roles since it reveals the most central node in the network. We wonder what are the roles of the individuals with 0 betweenness centrality score. Therefore, we propose to apply the percolation centrality metric.

The first step in our approach consists in computing the percolation centrality for each node at different time steps then iterating over the 13 nodes at different

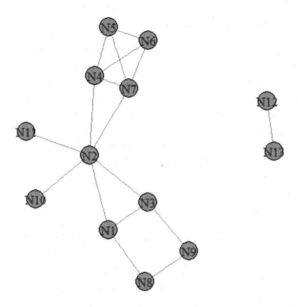

Fig. 2. 26/11 terrorist network

Table 1. Nodes betweenness centrality

Nodes N	Betweenness centrality
N1	7.5
N2	33
N3	7.5
N4	7
N5	0
N6	0
N7	7
N8	0.5
N9	0.5
N10	0
N11	0
N12	0
N13	0

time steps. We consider a binary percolation state: received/not received a piece of information. In addition, the percolation is not random .i.e. the terrorists follow a well organized strategy to spread information in the network. The second step consists in studying the impact of the percolated node on the other nodes and identifying nodes which are central in terms of their impact.

4.4 Interpretation and Discussion

To maintain clear interpretation of the experimental analysis, we divide the nodes into peripheral nodes and non peripheral nodes. A node i in a graph is called peripheral if there is a node j in the graph such that the distance d ij equals the diameter of the graph [15]. The percolation centrality illustrated in the following graphs represents the impact of the percolated node on the other nodes. The node which highly impacts the other nodes is considered as an information spreader. Due to space restriction, we can not represent a graph per node. So, we have combined the impact of 3 or 4 nodes on the other nodes in each graph.

The process of percolation is explained as follows:

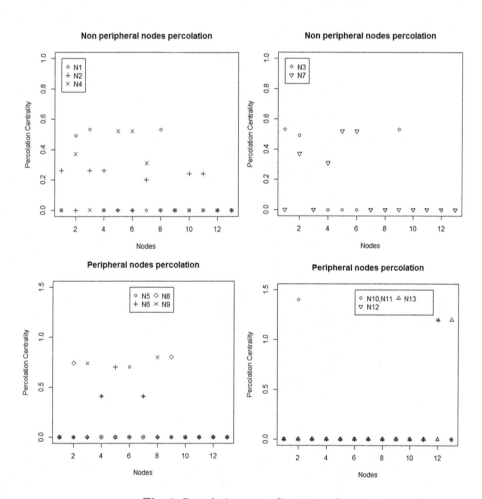

Fig. 3. Percolation centrality at t = 2

- At t = 1, one node is percolated. As discussed in previous section, when a single node is percolated in the network, the percolation centrality is equivalent to betweenness centrality.
- At t = 2, each node percolates its neighbors. Indeed, all the paths connecting the percolated node with its neighbors become percolated. The information starts to spread in the network. For example, node 1 is percolated. Consequently, it percolates its neighbors: node 2, 3 and 8. All the scenarios of percolation are presented in the following figures.
- At t = 3, the nodes continue to percolate the rest of the network as shown in Fig. 4 At t = 3, the node 2 percolates the entire network. The percolation centrality of nodes 10 and 11 decreases significantly. Nodes 12 and 13 maintain the same score given that they are isolated from the rest of the network.

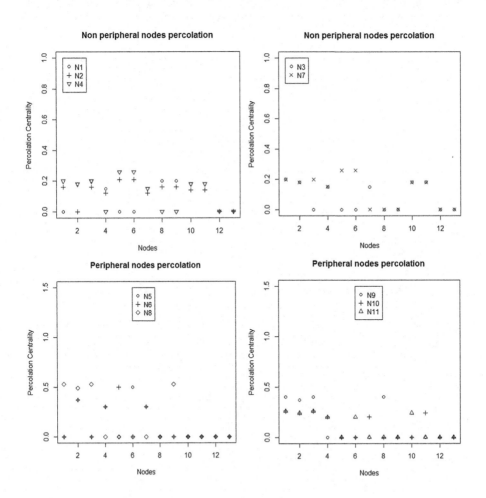

Fig. 4. Percolation centrality at t = 3

So, the percolation process for this couple of nodes stops at t = 2. These nodes preserve slightly high scores when nodes 8 and 9 are percolated.
 – At t = 4, almost the entire network gets percolated for different scenarios.

We may notice that non peripheral nodes are speedier in percolating the network rather than the peripheral nodes. For example, node 2 percolates the entire network in 3 time steps. However, some other nodes such as nodes 8 and 9 need 5 time steps to percolate all the other nodes. In t = 4, we notice that the nodes have higher percolation centrality when nodes 5 and 6 are considered the source of percolation. However nodes 8 and 9 lose their importance in the percolation process.

When all nodes are percolated, the percolation centrality becomes the same regardless to the initially percolated node. As shown in Figs. 3, 4 and 5, nodes 5 and 6 held the higher percolation centrality at t = 4. Nodes 8 and 9 are also

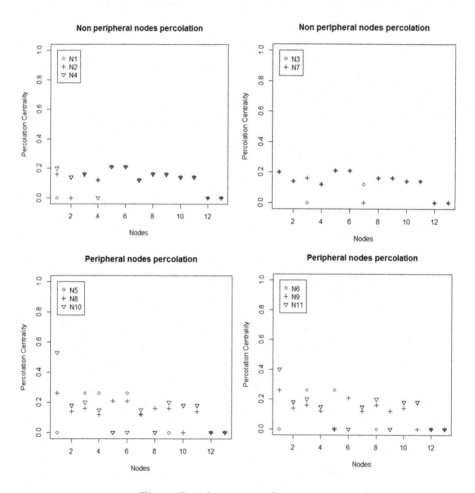

Fig. 5. Percolation centrality at t = 4

considered of higher score of percolation centrality at t = 2 and t = 3. Thus, it is clear that the peripheral nodes are the most important nodes in the process of information spread.

The obtained results illustrate that the nodes are shown to have a high percolation centrality when nodes 8, 9, 10 and 11 are percolated. Also, nodes 12 and 13 are shown to have a high score as well. We may conclude that these nodes are the most important in the spreading process. At this time step, they are considered as the information spreaders.

As depicted in the presented figures, we considered all the possible scenarios. Each node is susceptible to be the information spreader. At each time step, we measure the effect of the percolated node on the rest of nodes. The percolation centrality decreases considerably when the number of neighbors increases. Peripheral nodes tend to have higher percolation centrality, although they spend more time to percolate the entire network. Percolation centrality scores start to stabilize over time.

The dynamic aspect of the percolation centrality measure provides better understanding of how information flows in the network even though the network is static. The percolation centrality may be calculated in O(NM) time. So, there is no significant increase in time complexity compared to betweenness centrality.

As indicated in [14], nodes 5, 6, 8 and 9 were exchanging information with the three handlers in Pakistan by phone calls. These information confirm the retrieved results with the proposed approach. The destabilization strategy of this dark network can take place by isolating those node spreaders.

5   Conclusion

In this paper, we propose a dynamical analysis of the Mumbai terrorist incident. Based on percolation centrality metric, we reveal the information spreaders in the dark network through different time steps. The proposed approach may aid the law enforcement agencies to track the terrorists and develop stronger disruption strategies.

Future work consists in considering large and dynamic networks. Furthermore, we tend to combine the percolation centrality metric with other metrics to develop more robust destabilization method.

References

1. Eom, Y.H., Jo, H.H.: Generalized friendship paradox in complex networks: the case of scientific collaboration. J. Sci. Rep. **4**, Article No. 4603 (2014)
2. Krebs, V.E.: Mapping networks of terrorist cells. J. Connect. **24**, 43–52 (2002)
3. Newman, M.: Networks: An Introduction. Oxford University Press, Oxford (2010)
4. Piraveenan, M., Prokopenko, M., Hossain, L.: Percolation centrality: quantifying graph-theoretic impact of nodes during percolation in networks. J. PLoS One **8**, 53–95 (2013)
5. Ilachinski, A.: Self-organized terrorist-counterterrorist adaptive coevolutions, part 1: a conceptual design. Technical report (2005)

6. Shaikh, M.A., Wang, J., Yang, Z., Song, Y.: Advanced Data Mining and Applications. LNCS(LNAI), vol. 4632, pp. 570–577. Springer, Heidelberg (2007)
7. Lauchs, M.A., Keast, R., Le, V.: Social network analysis of terrorist networks: can it add value? J. Criminol. **3**, 21–32 (2012)
8. Xuan, D., Yu, H., Wang, J.: A novel method of centrality in terrorist network. In: 7th International Symposium on Computational Intelligence and Design (ISCID), pp. 144–149. IEEE Press, China (2014)
9. Berzinji, A., Kaati, L., Rezine, A.: Detecting key players in terrorist networks. In: European Intelligence and Security Informatics Conference (EISIC), pp. 297–302. IEEE Press, Denmark (2012)
10. Martonosi, S., Altner, D., Ernst, M., Ferme, E., Langsjoen, K., Lindsay, D., Plott, S., Ronan, A.S.: A new framework for network disruption. J. ArX. Prep (2011)
11. Azad, S., Gupta, A.: A quantitative assessment on 26/11 mumbai attack using social network analysis. J. Terror. Res. **2**(1) (2011)
12. Chaurasia, N., Tiwari, A.: Efficient algorithm for destabilization of terrorist networks. J. Inf. Technol. Comput. Sci. **5**, 21–30 (2013)
13. Memon, N., Larsen, H.L.: Structural analysis and mathematical methods for destabilizing terrorist networks using investigative data mining. In: Li, X., Zaïane, O.R., Li, Z. (eds.) ADMA 2006. LNCS (LNAI), vol. 4093, pp. 1037–1048. Springer, Heidelberg (2006)
14. Government of India: Mumbai terrorist attack, (26–29 Nov 2008) (2009)
15. Gimes, R.G., Pierce, D.J., Simon, H.D.: A new algorithm for finding a pseudoperipheral node in a graph. J. Matrix Anal. Appl. **11**, 323–334 (1990)

Towards an Intelligent Application of Large Scale Community Detection to Support Collaboration During Emergency Management

Wala Rebhi[1]([✉]), Nesrine Ben Yahia[1], and Narjès Bellamine Ben Saoud[1,2]

[1] RIADI Laboratory, National School of Computer Sciences, University of Manouba, Manouba, Tunisia
Wala.rebhi@gmail.com, Nesrine.benyahia@ensi.rnu.tn,
Narjes.Bellamine@ensi.rnu.tn
[2] Higher Institute of Computer Sciences, University of Tunis El Manar, Tunis, Tunisia

Abstract. During crisis situations, people often use social media to seek for help and to find new collaborators who can help them in emergency management. In this context, we propose an intelligent application to find and recommend potential and relevant collaborators through social media. This application is based on a large scale contextualized community detection to compose dynamic groups. To do so, we propose to reuse a new community detection algorithm that considers simultaneously the network structure (social connections) and profiles homophily (similarities). An application of the proposed solution and a comparison with another community detection algorithm evaluates its performance.

Keywords: Emergency management · Collaboration recommendation · Contextualized community detection · Social media · Large scale · Intelligent application

1 Introduction

On 26 April 2015, a strong earthquake hit Nepal in the area near Barpak, a mountain village between capital Kathmandu and tourist town Pokhara. The earthquake caused extensive damage to buildings and thousands of deaths and injuries and was even felt in Pakistan, India and Bangladesh.The quake was followed by more than 200 aftershocks and another huge earthquake on 12 May 2015 [1].

Following the disaster, different people used social media such as Facebook and Twitter to cover the event, to seek for help and to find new collaborators for emergency management through creating new Facebook pages [2], sharing pictures [3] and exchanging messages regarding the event.

However, with the huge number of social media users, finding rapidly the most relevant collaborators is often difficult. In fact, according to latest statistics [4] market leader Facebook was the first social network to surpass 1 billion registered

© Springer International Publishing Switzerland 2015
N. Bellamine Ben Saoud et al. (Eds.): ISCRAM-med 2015, LNBIP 233, pp. 39–49, 2015.
DOI: 10.1007/978-3-319-24399-3_4

accounts. Tenth-ranked microblogging network Twitter had over 288 million monthly active accounts. Meanwhile, blogging service Tumblr had more than 230 million active blog users on their site. Therefore, one way to help people involved in this disaster is to provide an intelligent application which recommends rapidly the most relevant community according to user' characteristics and preferences during the crisis.

In this context, we propose an intelligent application that supports collaboration seeker in the emergency management process by clustering social media networks (represented by a graph, where nodes represent social media users and edges represent relationships between them) into communities. In order to detect communities with strong connections and homogeneities and to satisfy the user's needs, we propose in this paper, to use a community detection algorithm that combines the network structure (social connections) and profiles homophily (similarities) in one metric. And, to get best clustering rapidly, the algorithm relies on Particle Swarm Optimization (PSO), which represents a fast and computational optimization technique, to maximize the proposed metric [5].

The outline of this paper is as follows. In section two, we present related works that use social media in emergency management. Then, we propose the architecture of the intelligent application which instantiates a generic community detection algorithm to support emergency management process by facilitating the 'collaborators seeking' phase. Finally, we present experimentation and evaluation of the proposed solution.

2   Emergency Management and Social Media

Social media is defined as a group of Internet-based applications that build on the ideological and technological foundations of Web 2.0, and that allow the creation and exchange of user-generated content [6].

The term 'social media' refers to Internet-based applications that enable people to communicate and share resources and information [7]. Some examples of social media include blogs, discussion forums, chat rooms, wikis, YouTube Channels, LinkedIn, Facebook, and Twitter.

Social media are being used more and more for communicating, detecting, tracking, and extracting information about currently occurring or recently passed crises [8]. Due to the popularity of social media, people often use it to communicate about crises [9–11]. In fact, when disasters occur, many members of the public, emergency response agencies, and others use the popular microblogging service Twitter or the social networking website Facebook as a way to quickly disseminate information about the event. One of the earliest known cases of people using Twitter in an emergency was during severe wildfires that took place near San Diego, California (in the United States) in 2007 [10].

As a result, several researches use social media for emergency management. [8] presents the first release of an extensive terminological resource for crisis management in English, which reflects the real, observed linguistic expressions used in Twitter to describe a wide-range variety of crises, and, at the same time, focuses on the information needs of emergency managers. To do so, the terms have been collected from a seed set of terms manually annotated by a linguist and an emergency manager from tweets broadcast during 4 crisis events. A Conditional Random Fields (CRF) method was then applied to tweets from 35 crisis events, in order to expand the set of terms while overcoming the difficulty of getting more emergency managers' annotations [8].

[12] uses microblogs to detect rapidly the sentiment of the crowd towards crises or disasters in order to inform humanitarian efforts, and improve the ways in which informative messages are crafted for the crowd regarding an event. They used 3698 Tweets collected during the September 2010, San Bruno, California gas explosion and resulting fires. Then, this data was manually coded to understand better how people feel.

Social media can also be used for community detection. [13] detects clusters during emergencies especially natural disasters, in order to analyze the behavior of Twitter users. In fact, in their paper Naturel Language Processing (NLP) techniques were used to extract three types of actionable events from 2011 Japan Tsunami and 2012 Hurricane Sandy datasets: receive the warning, seek information or confirmation, and take prescribed action. NLP techniques were used to associate tweets with following attributes- modality and polarity. These attributes provide further insights into the information being shared on Twitter. Additionally, first story analysis demonstrated the amount of unique/new emergency relevant information that was exchanged among the Twitter users. The analysis was also used to trace the information initiators [13].

Inspiring from these solutions using social media to analyze and understand the behavior of citizens, this paper aims to show how social media can be effectively used to engage collaboration during Emergency Response and how generic community detection can be specialized for emergency management. This will be the content of the next section.

3   Architecture of the Intelligent Application to Support Collaboration During Emergency Management

When a disaster occurs, people resort rapidly to social media such as Facebook and Twitter to cover and follow the event, to disseminate information about it, to seek for help and to find new collaborators for emergency management through creating new Facebook pages [2], sharing pictures [3], updating Facebook status and exchanging messages regarding the event. For example, following the earthquake which hit Nepal on 12 May 2015, a citizen of Nepal created a Facebook group named 'Help For Victims Earthquake Nepal 2015 (Ayuda Para Terremoto Nepal 2015)' [14] in order to interact and collaborate with Facebook users who can help him. This group must contain only relevant collaborators. Thus every group member needs a collaboration recommendation tool which must provide rapidly the most relevant community for him.

In this context, we propose a new intelligent application which aims to recommend rapidly the most relevant group for social media users especially Facebook users who are seeking for new collaborators to help them in emergency management.

To do so, the first phase of the proposed application is data preparation. When a Facebook user is seeking for new collaborators, this phase aims to identify the objective and the context of his search. Then it extracts information about it and collects users' profiles who are involved in this context. In this paper, this phase is done manually and should become automatic in future works.

Then, these data are represented by a graph. In fact, each node represents social media user and is characterized by a weight that reflects homophily or similarity between the member who is seeking for collaborators and the others users. As for edge, it represents relationships between users.

This graph is the input of community detection algorithm to find rapidly relevant collaborators.

Finally, we propose to evaluate the detected community in order to improve the quality of community detection. This phase will be based on user tracking.

In Fig. 1, we present a diagram that summarizes the different functional modules of the proposed architecture.

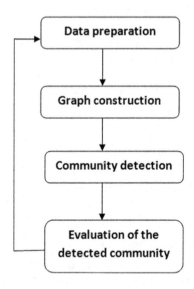

Fig. 1. Architecture of the intelligent application of recommendation

In this paper, we focus on community detection phase. Our aim is to find the appropriate community detection algorithm which can provide rapidly the most relevant community for a member who is seeking for new collaborators. This will be the objective of the next section.

4   Community Detection Phase

Community detection phase is crucial in the proposed application. In fact, the quality of detected community depends on the choice of the algorithm. In this paper, we propose to implement and compare performances of two algorithms: a classical algorithm of Louvain [15] and a combined community detection algorithm for collaboration recommendation [5].

4.1   Louvain Algorithm

The Louvain method is a simple, efficient and easy to implement method for identifying communities in large networks [16].

This algorithm is based on network structure. In fact, it is divided in two phases that are repeated iteratively. In the first phase, each node of the network is considered as a community. Then, for each node i it considers the neighbours j of i and it evaluates the gain of modularity that would take place by moving i from its community to the community of j. The node i is then placed in the community for which this gain is maximum and positive. If no positive gain is possible, i remains in its original community. This phase is repeatedly applied for all nodes until no further improvement can be achieved. The second phase of the algorithm consists in building a new network whose nodes represent the communities of the first phase. And the weights of the edges between the new nodes represent the sum of the weights of the edges between nodes in the corresponding communities [15] (Fig 2).

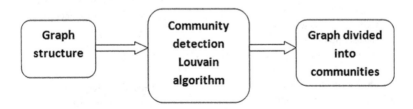

Fig. 2. Input/output of Louvain algorithm

4.2   A Combined Community Detection Algorithm for Collaboration Recommendation

This algorithm combines two community detection approaches [5], modularity optimization which considers only social connections and automatic classification which aims to bring together individuals with the same features, into one approach by proposing a combined metric that considers both social connections and features. This approach can be justified by a phenomenon called homophily which indicates that people tend to collaborate with others who have similar interests and similar demographic characteristics [17]. Then, it relies on a computational optimization technique (i.e. Particle Swarm Optimization) to maximize this combined quality [18].

The proposed metric Q to evaluate community detection quality, given by (1), is based on a weighted combination of two components that must be maximized simultaneously:

$$Q = \alpha M + (1 - \alpha)I \tag{1}$$

The first component concerns the frequency of social interactions between individuals based on the assumption that people who frequently socialize (have interactions between them) are more likely to collaborate together. It relies on the structural quality, thus we propose to reuse the modularity M of Newman for weighted graphs.

The second component concerns the attribute similarity. Thus, we propose to reuse the notion of inertia I [19]. Inertia is a metric that permits to measure the dispersion of a weighted cloud (a set of nodes where each node has a weight).

In Fig. 3, we present a diagram that summarizes the input and the output of the combined community detection algorithm for collaboration recommendation. Contrary to Louvain algorithm, it considers the context which is in this case emergency management in order to find the relevant community for one user.

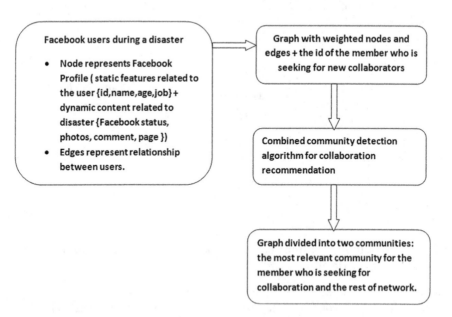

Fig. 3. Input/output of the combined community detection algorithm for collaboration recommendation

4.3 Community Detection Algorithm Used in the Proposed Application

Our aim is to develop an intelligent application that finds rapidly for a Facebook user the most relevant community for him and according to the context of his search.

Between the two algorithms, we propose to reuse the combined community detection algorithm for collaboration recommendation. Although this algorithm is generic, it can be easily specialized for emergency management.

As illustrated in Fig. 4, we notice that for the same person (represented by node 1) who has launched two different searches (for example in graphs 1 and 2 he is seeking for doctors to help victims but in graphs 3 and 4 he is looking for firemen), Louvain algorithm always gives the same community (nodes 3,6 and 8) as the combined community detection algorithm for collaboration recommendation finds community according to the objective of user (nodes 2,4,7 and 8 the community of doctors and nodes 3,6,5 the community of firemen).

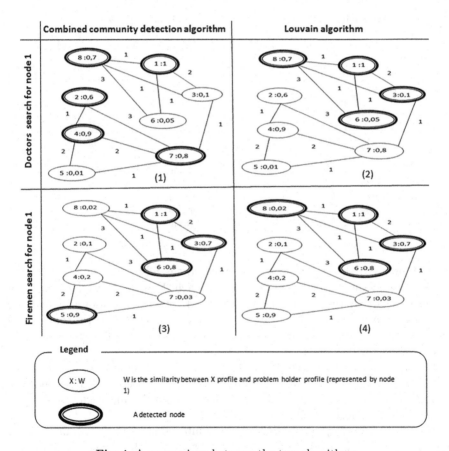

Fig. 4. A comparison between the two algorithms

5   Experimentation and Results

In Table 1, we apply both approaches on Facebook networks. To do, we reuse profile and networks data [20] obtained by [21]. Each Facebook user (static features such as identifier, age, work, education, location, hometown, etc.; and dynamic features such as facebook status, comments, photos, etc.) is represented by a node and edges represent friendship between users.

At each step, we increase the size of the graph and we compare the two algorithms. The comparison between these two approaches is based on communities' number, evaluation of the quality (modularity and inter-classes inertia proportion given separately) and time execution (in milliseconds) for each approach. For our application scenario, we suppose the weighting factor α is equal to 0.5 so we obtain equitability between modularity proportion and inter-classes inertia proportion.

Table 1. Comparison between qualities of clustering

Network components		Louvain algorithm				Algorithm for collaboration recommendation			
Nodes number	Edges number	Time (s)	Detected community modularity	Detected community inertia	Number of detected communities	Time (s)	Detected community modularity	Detected community inertia	Number of detected communities
100	116	0.118	0.10	0.71	21	0.064	0.19	0.96	2
250	3580	4.905	0.06	0.002	19	1.226	0.005	0.85	2
500	8390	39.724	0.05	0.04	34	5.421	0.03	0.91	2
800	14642	124.564	0.03	0.27	5	15.794	0.02	0.9	2
1000	19823	255.850	0.03	0.12	6	22.816	0.01	0.92	2
1175	24742	428.875	0.02	0.08	9	21.150	0.12	0.91	2
1500	37743	1149.638	0.05	0.04	13	48.003	0.006	0.93	2
1600	41797	2143.013	0.01	0.07	15	52.434	0.004	0.92	2
1750	45008	1836.131	0.01	0.02	16	63.173	0.005	0.91	2
2000	54050	1450.954	0.01	0.04	23	87.210	0.004	0.87	2

To better visualize these measures, we build the following three curves.

Concerning the performance of each approach, Fig. 5 illustrates comparison between execution time of clustering obtained by Louvain approach and the combined algorithm for collaboration recommendation. We notice that for all networks, the second algorithm is slightly faster than the other and needs less time to converge.

Considering only the inter-classes inertia proportion, we notice that the combined algorithm for collaboration recommendation gives better results than Louvain approach, Fig. 6. However, for modularity, Louvain approach gives better results for some most tested configurations, see Fig. 7.

It is also interesting to note that for the combined algorithm for collaboration recommendation, the change of nodes ordering does not have a significant influence neither on the obtained quality nor on computation time. On the contrary

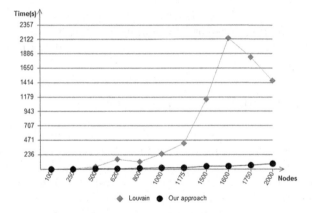

Fig. 5. Comparison between execution times of clustering

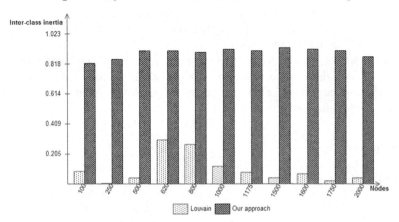

Fig. 6. Comparison between inter-class inertia of clustering

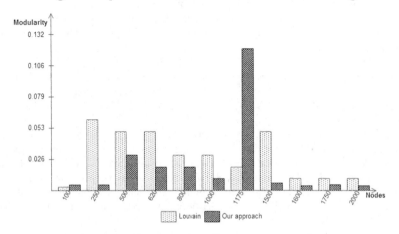

Fig. 7. Comparison between modularity of clustering

for Louvain algorithm, its result depends on the ordering of nodes. In fact, the change of nodes ordering does not have an important influence on the obtained modularity, but it may affect the computation time, and the reasons for this dependence are not clear [15].

6   Conclusion and Further Research

The aim of this paper is to propose architecture of an intelligent application which supports emergency management by recommending relevant collaborators during crisis. This objective is achieved by instantiating a generic community detection algorithm. In fact, in this paper we tested two algorithms the first one is classical and it is based on structure network and the second is based on combining the network structure (social connections) and profiles homophily (similarities) in one metric, then to make community detection as fast as possible, it uses particle swarm optimization to maximize the combined quality.

The experimentation showed that the second algorithm is faster than the first one and gives better results.

In future works, we aim to complete the development of the intelligent application by making data preparation and evaluation automatic. Then, we propose to use this application on others social media and other scenarios to support collaboration recommendation.

References

1. Nepal earthquake. http://www.earthquake-nepal.com
2. Nepal earthquake Facebook page. https://www.facebook.com/pages/Help-Nepal-EarthQuake-Victims-2015/1569266940013121?fref=ts
3. Facebook status. https://www.facebook.com/SMFNepal/posts/790276374413112
4. Social networks statistics. http://www.statista.com/statistics/272014/global-social-networks-ranked-by-number-of-users
5. Ben Yahia, N., Bellamine, N., Ben Ghezala, H.: Community-based collaboration recommendation to support mixed decision making support. J. Decis. Syst. **23**(3), 350–371 (2014)
6. Social Media. http://en.wikipedia.org/wiki/Social_media
7. Lindsay, B.R.: Social Media and Disasters: Current Uses, Future Options, and Policy Considerations. Congressional Research Service, Washington (2011)
8. Temnikova, I., Castillo, C., Vieweg, S.: EMTerms 1.0: A Terminological Resource for Crisis Tweets
9. Blanchard, H., Carvin, A., Whitaker, M.E., Fitzgerald, M., Harman, W., Humphrey, B.: The case for integrating crisis response with social media (2012)
10. Imran, M., Castillo, C., Diaz, F., Vieweg, S.: Processing Social Media Messages Proceedings of Mass Emergency: A Survey (2014). arXiv preprint arXiv:1407.7071
11. Vieweg, S.E.: Situational awareness in mass emergency: A behavioral and linguistic analysis of microblogged communications. Doctoral dissertation, University of Colorado (2012)
12. Nagy, A., Stamberger, J.: Crowd sentiment detection during disasters and crises. In: Proceedings of the 9th International ISCRAM Conference, pp. 1–9 (2012)

13. Missaoui, R., Sarr, I. (eds.): Social Network Analysis-Community Detection and Evolution. Springer, Switzerland (2015)
14. Facebook group. https://www.facebook.com/groups/326049010852461/?fref=ts
15. Blondel, V.D., Guillaume, J.L., Lambiotte, R., Lefebvre, E.: Fast unfolding of communities in large networks. J. Stat. Mech. Theor. Exp. **10**, 10008–10020 (2008)
16. Lancichinetti, A., Fortunato, S.: Community detection algorithms: a comparative analysis. Phys. Rev. E **80**(5), 056117 (2009)
17. McPherson, M., Smith-Lovin, L., Cook, J.M.: Birds of a feather: homophily in social networks. Annu. Rev. Soc. **27**(1), 415–444 (2001)
18. Clerc, M., Siarry, P.: Une nouvelle mtaheuristique pour l'optimisation difficile: la mthode des essaims particulaires [A new metaheuristic for hard optimization : particle swarm method]. Journal l'enseignement des sciences et technologies de l'information et des systmes, **3**(7) (2004)
19. Lebart, L., Maurineau, A., Piron, M.: TraiTement des Donnes Statistiques. Dunod, Paris (1982)
20. Data. http://snap.stanford.edu/data/
21. Leskovec, J., Mcauley, J.J.: Learning to discover social circles in ego networks. In: Advances in Neural Information Processing Systems, pp. 539–547 (2012)

Modelling and Simulation

Modelling the Tactical Behaviour
of the Australian Population in a Bushfire

Carole Adam[1,2]([✉]), Elise Beck[2,3], and Julie Dugdale[1,2,4]

[1] Grenoble Informatics Laboratory, Grenoble, France
{carole.adam,julie.dugdale}@imag.fr
[2] Université Grenoble-Alpes, Grenoble, France
[3] PACTE Laboratory, University of Grenoble, Grenoble, France
[4] University of Agder, Kristiansand, Norway

Abstract. This paper is concerned with the development of an agent-based model of population behaviour during a bushfire, to form the basis of a simulator that will be used as a decision-support tool for emergency managers. To ensure the validity of the simulation results, it is essential that the model, and the underlying agent architecture, are as realistic as possible. After providing some context about recent bushfires in Victoria, Australia, we justify the need for a BDI (belief, desire, intention) agent architecture. Although some tools exist to support the integration of such agents in simulations, they are infrequently used. We therefore show how an existing methodology for modelling military tactics can be adapted to this context. The contribution of this paper is two-fold: providing an agent-based model of population behaviour during bushfires; and presenting a methodology that can be used by other model designers in the field of crisis management.

Keywords: Agent-based modelling and simulation · Agent behaviour models · Multi-agent methodologies · Belief-Desire-Intention architecture

1 Introduction

A recent field of application of particular societal interest for AI techniques concerns Crisis and Disaster Management, where emergency managers need new and improved decision support tools. In particular, computer modelling and simulation offers a powerful tool to evaluate the efficiency of emergency management policies and to tailor them without waiting for a real crisis to occur with human lives at stake. Simulation provides a great degree of control over contextual variables, allowing repeated experimentation using the exact same settings, or the ability to try out different scenarios. Computer based simulators can be an essential companion to the currently run real-life simulation exercises, which are often time-consuming and difficult to organise. However, it is hard to capture the complexity of human behaviours using mathematical models. Conversely, multi-agent models offer a finer level of description of human behaviour

N. Bellamine Ben Saoud et al. (Eds.): ISCRAM-med 2015, LNBIP 233, pp. 53–64, 2015.
DOI: 10.1007/978-3-319-24399-3_5

that can be more faithful to reality. Nevertheless, for the results of such simulations to be valid and therefore useful, the underlying model needs to be very realistic [22], both regarding the environment (requiring spatialised simulation based on real Geographical Information Systems data) and the behaviour of people (necessitating the appropriate level of complexity of agent's cognitive architecture: proactive behaviours, emotional behaviours, etc.). Unfortunately this is often not the case, with many simulations using simple grid environments and/or over-simplified reactive agents, in particular due to the lack of tools to support the integration of more complex agents [1]. Although there are some good models of fire behaviour (e.g. Phoenix, see [19]), models of human behaviour have received less attention. Our approach is to favour a participative design of the behaviour model using visualisation tools that will allow stakeholders to give early feedback and validation. In this paper we focus on the population's decision-making process when facing a bushfire in the state of Victoria in Australia, and draw upon our previous experience designing spatialised models and simulations for crisis management [5, 13, 21]. We show that BDI (belief, desire, intention) agents are advantageous in modelling human behaviour in this context. To address the lack of tools for integrating such complex agents into our simulation, we use a new methodology that was recently designed to model military tactics, and we show how it can be adapted to also model civilian tactical behaviour.

2   Context

2.1   Bushfires in the State of Victoria

Every summer the state of Victoria in Australia is subject to bushfires of varying intensity. On "Black Saturday", the 7th of February 2009, a particularly violent bushfire resulted in 173 fatalities, destroyed many houses and burnt many acres of bush. Despite regular awareness campaigns, the state policy titled "Prepare, Stay and Defend, or Leave Early" was not followed by the population. Reports from the Royal Commission [20] found that most people would still "wait and see" until the fire was too close, waiting for a personal evacuation order; yet the emergency services only broadcast general alert messages. Therefore most victims were people who left it too late to evacuate. Researchers tried to explain this unexpected "wait and see" behaviour and found that information overload had led to "paralysing indecisiveness" [12]. These results suggest that more targeted information and alert messages might help in reducing the casualties. However it is hard to predict their actual impact and effectiveness ahead of time.

Other studies [7, 17] confirm the discrepancy between how the emergency managers expected the population to behave (which is what they use to decide what information to send) and how the population actually behaved (which is what determines what information people really need). As a result many residents dismissed the messages as irrelevant or not making sense to them. The authors of these report identify seven behavioural archetypes and their associated underlying motivations and information needs, and recommend that emergency managers should take these into account when designing their messages.

2.2   Behaviour Profiles

The seven archetypes[1] of population behaviour identified by [7,17] are as follows:

- Can-do Defenders: are determined to protect their house, have good knowledge of the area, possess previous experience and skills, are action-oriented, self-sufficient, and confident;
- Considered Defenders: are strongly committed to stay and defend their house, are aware of the risks and make deliberate efforts to prepare and train;
- Livelihood Defenders: are committed to stay and defend what they consider as their livelihood (farm, hotel, etc.), and so are well-prepared year-round;
- Threat Monitors: do not intend to stay when faced with a serious threat, but do not intend to leave until it feels necessary, will wait and see;
- Threat Avoiders: are conscious of the risk, feel vulnerable, and plan to leave early before any real threat occurs, but have no plan if caught by surprise;
- Unaware Reactors: are unaware of the risk, feel unconcerned by fires, have no knowledge of how to react (e.g. tourists), therefore totally unprepared;
- Isolated and Vulnerable: are physically or socially isolated (e.g. elderly people) which limits their ability to respond safely.

Each archetype has a different behaviour, with its own underlying motivation, level of risk-awareness and knowledge, response strategy, and associated information needs. The authors of the studies also state that these archetypes are not particularly linked to socio-demographic features, and have a dynamic aspect since individuals can change their behaviour depending on the circumstances. For instance a person can start out as a considered defender, before realising that their skills are not sufficient to deal with the fire; or they can change strategy when they have to take care of a vulnerable neighbour. As a result, they do not provide any statistics regarding the repartition of these profiles in the population. We next discuss the type of agent architecture needed to model these behaviours.

3   Agent Architecture

Various architectures can be used in agent-based simulations, of varying complexity, offering different levels of abstraction and several types of reasoning, which have to be adapted to the target application [4]. For our application to crisis management, we need to provide a faithful model of actual population behaviour so that the results of the simulations are valid and trustworthy and will readily support emergency managers' decisions; realism of the model is therefore essential in this case. We will show that a BDI agent architecture is a suitable approach to faithfully model the civilians' behaviours identified above.

---

[1] The authors do not explicitly claim that their list is exhaustive, but we could not identify any other profile from the other surveys that we studied.

3.1   Requirements for the Agent Cognitive Architecture

The seven behaviour archetypes described above differ on a number of features that obviously impact people's decisions and actions during a bushfire, and that should therefore be modelled. Each archetype has a main **intention** (defend or leave) to which they are, more or less strongly, committed. They also have some possibly conflicting **desires** (fight fire but protect lives, escape fire but avoid moving if unnecessary, take shorter route but avoid congested roads, leave early but finish some things before, watch the fire but avoid risk, etc.). Finally each individual has a number of **beliefs** about themselves (self-confidence), about the fire (awareness, previous experience, etc.), about the state of their environment (state of the roads, location of shelters, etc.), and about others (location of family or friends, expected behaviour from firefighters or neighbours, etc.). These beliefs can be incomplete and possibly wrong (false belief of safety, unknown location of shelters, etc.). As a result each archetype needs certain types of information that are relevant to their own intention, such as the progress of the fire, location of shelters, road congestion, etc. Individuals can **react** to stimuli in their environment (fire alert, evacuation order, immediate threat, etc.), or **act proactively** by trying a number of **plans** to achieve their intention. Their behaviour can also be influenced by their **emotions** (paralysing stress, anxiety to lose one's livelihood, irrational hope that the fire will just disappear or avoid the area, fear of fire or that their family is pushing them to leave, etc.). Consequently, an agent cognitive architecture is needed that is able to handle such complexity: the reactive and proactive plan-based behaviour, and reasoning with high-level concepts such as beliefs, desires, intentions and emotions.

3.2   Belief-Desire-Intention (BDI) Agent Architecture

The BDI agent model (Belief, Desire, Intention) is based on folk psychology and designs agents in terms of their Beliefs, Desires and Intentions [16]. It therefore offers realism, as well as the right level of abstraction to easily integrate behavioural data obtained from field studies and from experts, and also to explain the results of the simulations to the emergency managers and the general public. It describes behaviour in terms of different plans, relevant to different contexts, that are applied to reach goals. The classical BDI can also be extended to account for emotions [2]. Cognitive architectures such as SOAR [18] or ACT-R [3] also offer a good level of abstraction, but the more complex underlying concepts make it difficult to explain the generated behaviour, which is a problem for applying this model to decision support. In addition, such cognitive architectures are rule-based, and do not put sufficient emphasis on sociological aspects, collective actions, and social phenomena that are crucial in modelling human group behaviours, so we believe they are less adapted for our application.

The BDI architecture has been extensively used in Agent-Oriented Software Engineering [14,23] but rarely in Agent-Based Modelling and Simulation (ABMS). Despite the fact that some tools do exist that couple BDI and ABMS (*e.g.* CoJACK [8]), they are designed by and for computer scientists, and are therefore rarely used by modelers from other disciplines. Besides, designers usually prefer simpler models for a number of reasons [1]: fear that their complexity will limit the scalability needed to be able to cope with millions of agents; and the lack of tools to support design of such complex models by non-computer scientists. However, these two obstacles can be overcome, for example by using simulation platforms that have been specifically designed to cope with large numbers of agents. The second concern, that of having the right tool to support designing complex models, is the focus of this paper.

4 Methodology and Tools

In this section we address the issue of a tool that can support the design of complex models by describing the Tactics Development Framework (TDF) methodology and tool for developing BDI models for ABMS. We show how this methodology can be adapted from its initial field (capturing military experts knowledge) to our own application domain (modelling population behaviour during a crisis).

4.1 Tactics Development Framework (TDF)

The TDF methodology [10] extends the well-known Prometheus agent-oriented design methodology [14] with the notion of tactics: specific means of achieving a mission, including both reactive and deliberative behaviour. TDF and the associated tool is very useful to help non computer-scientists designing their own models, or at least allow them to participate in the design and give feedback at an early stage. It was designed and previously demonstrated for modelling undersea warfare tactics from interviews with military experts [9]. Following the Prometheus methodology, TDF models are designed via several iterations on three consecutive stages, with progressive validation in-between each phase and each iteration (this methodology is illustrated in Fig. 1):

1. System Specification: identification of system-level artefacts, namely missions, goals, scenarios, percepts, actions, data, actors and roles;
2. Architectural Design: specification of the internal workings of the system, grouping agents into roles, and specifying their interactions (protocols and messages);
3. Detailed Design: definition of the internal workings of the agents (plan diagrams, internal events, messages sent and received, and data used).

We next show that despite being initially devised for eliciting knowledge from military experts, this methodology can also be successfully expanded to cope with integrating other information sources and applied to crisis management.

4.2 Adaptation of Methodology from Military to Civilians

TDF was initially designed for modelling military tactics, which are the means of achieving a specific mission objective. In this paper we want to apply it to

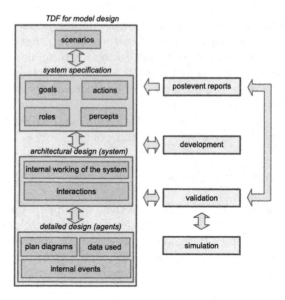

Fig. 1. Methodology

crisis management, in order to model the behaviour of the civilian population in terms of tactics applied and information needed. We explain below the differences between military and civilian tactics modelling, and how to adapt the methodology.

Our goal is not to obtain a prescriptive model of the best tactics for programming an autonomous entity (*e.g.* a drone), but rather to provide a realistic model for simulating a believable population, allowing the validation of emergency management policies. The tactics modelled are the ones actually employed by civilians, and could be non-optimal or even dangerous. Indeed, civilians' behaviour is not prescribed by procedures, protocols and tactics defined in a manual, but based on their individual choices, and can therefore be more random, unexpected, inconsistent, or irrational.

As a result it is also harder to elicit information about their tactics. Citizens may have little idea about what they will do in a future situation. If they do, what they actually do in practice when faced with a real situation may be radically different to what they thought that would do. In addition, people sometimes have difficulty in verbalising their thoughts; this is a well known problem in knowledge elicitation. Therefore, instead of conducting interviews (as has been done with military experts), we extracted our knowledge about civilian tactics from the many surveys conduced after the 2009 bushfires in Victoria. This gives an accurate picture of what people actually did and since the event was still fresh in their minds, citizens are more likely to be able to recall their motivations and verbalise their thoughts. In addition, the surveys were conduced by emergency managers who are well aware of the specific local context and existing connections to the population, making them better able to draw out information.

5   Designing Our Model

In this section, we describe how we designed a preliminary model of tactical behaviour of the population in a bushfire, by doing a first superficial pass on the three phases of TDF. After validation, we will refine this model in an iterative way.

5.1   Scenario

The TDF methodology uses the notion of scenarios of how things could evolve in a certain situation. These scenarios are used in order to elicit the underlying **system specification**. Below we describe one such scenario for a bushfire. There could be an infinity of such scenarios, and the implemented simulator will help explore them.

- Fire risk warning
- Some residents already start to leave the area
- A fire starts in the area, fire alert is broadcast to residents
- More residents leave the area to avoid the fire
- Other residents get ready to fight the fire, gather helpers, check equipment
- Tourists or other people stay, continue their normal activities, or watch the fire
- Fire progresses towards the town
- Authorities send live updates about fire progression and weather forecast, plus information about shelters and escape routes
- The warnings and seeing everybody leaving pushes more people to leave to go to the advised shelters
- More civilians see their neighbours leave and decide to imitate them, roads become congested
- Fire progresses closer to the town, authorities issue an evacuation order (SMS and phone calls to residents, door to door if feasible)
- Some residents were waiting for that order and now evacuate
- Some residents want to defend their property and refuse to evacuate
- Fire fighters and residents fight the fire around the town
- After fighting the fire for a while, the remaining defenders and firefighters bring the fire under control
- The announcement is broadcast to the population, people return home

---

5.2   System Specification, Roles, Goals, Actions and Percepts

An important aspect in system specification is identifying **roles**. Roles describe the functional groupings and are associated with agents in the model. In addition to the firefighters and emergency managers, the scenario involves various civilian roles corresponding to the archetypes of behaviours identified above. Although agents may have a predisposition to a particular role, they can change role during the evolution of the scenario as the circumstances evolve. For instance farmers or hotel managers are more likely to be livelihood defenders, but might evolve to threat monitors or avoiders if the fire risk is too high. Tourists are more likely to be unaware reactors, while head of families are more likely to be threat avoiders, giving the highest priority to their family's safety. Someone might start out as a defender, then become in charge of a dependent neighbour or relative and turn into a threat avoider.

Each of these roles has their own goal-directed behaviour, that is, their own mission which might be to defend their life and/or their property. The goals can be decomposed to produce a hierarchical goal structure. TDF supports the specification of and/or goals, concurrent goals, conditional goals as well as asynchronous goals, etc. Figure 2 illustrates the goal hierarchy for the "prepare" goal of defenders roles, and for the "protect lives" goal of the threat avoider role.

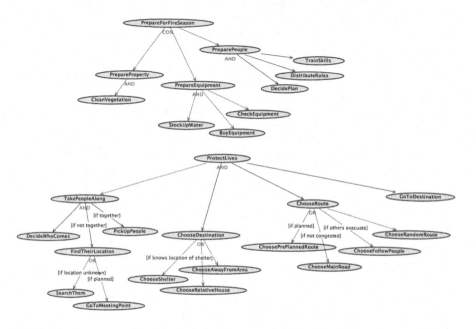

Fig. 2. Goal structures for "prepare for fire season" (defender role) and "protect lives" (avoider role) showing AND, OR, and CONcurrent goals.

Also associated with a role are the relevant percepts that role is more sensitive to, such as an awareness of the fire alert or the order for evaluation, their knowledge on the location of shelters, etc. It is interesting to mention at this point that not all of the agents in a particular role will perceive their environment in the same way. Using an agent based approach allows us to model individual characteristics of entities, even though several agents may share a common role. Roles also have associated actions that can be performed to achieve goals triggered by these perceptions. For instance threat avoiders will perceive fire alerts sent by the emergency managers, which will trigger their goal to avoid danger from the fire, that can be achieved via such actions as: taking shelter, choosing a route, etc. Livelihood defenders will react to directly perceiving the fire or receiving a

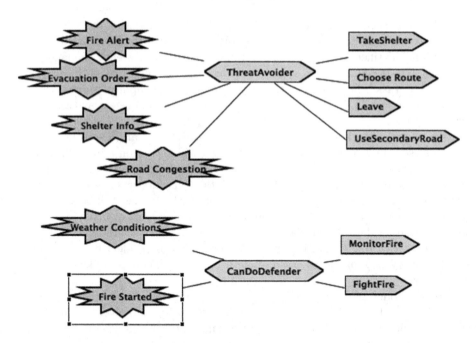

Fig. 3. Overview of percepts (pink star) and actions (green arrow) for two roles (blue box) (Color figure online).

fire alert, which triggers their goal to defend their house or property, therefore the evacuation advice is not relevant to them. Figure 3 shows the percepts and actions for "threat avoiders" and "can-do defenders".

5.3   Interactions

Agents may interact with their environment, for example as a result of an agent's action to leave, the road becomes further congested. This in turn will influence other agents (by their perception of the environment). Agents can also interact between themselves in the model, either locally by perceiving the presence of other agents and exchanging messages (*e.g.* talking), or distantly, by broadcasted information (for example alert warnings sent by the emergency managers, or information messages posted on social media). So far the TDF methodology (and Prometheus) uses Agent UML to represent agents interactions. This methodology will therefore need to be extended in future work to cover this important aspect of multi-agent systems.

6   Conclusion and Future Directions

This paper has described some first steps towards modelling realistic human behaviours in bush fire situations. The specific contributions and the future directions that we wish to take in this work are as follows.

Model of the Population. We have described a BDI model of the population behaviour by conceptualising and disambiguating the behaviour profiles that have been identified in surveys conducted by various emergency management agencies. The next step is to validate the model in terms of its faithfulness to reality. This task is facilitated by the easy to understand graphical representation generated by the TDF tool, allowing us to involve the managers and get their feedback at an early stage.

The model will then be implemented in GAMA [11], an open-source platform focused on a simple modeling language (usable by non expert programmers). GAMA not only allows us to develop large scale simulators, but it can also incorporate underlying geographical data, thus increasing the realism of the simulations. Once implemented, the model will be further validated by performing a sensitivity analysis and comparing its predictions to behaviour data, using a separate data set to that which was used to construct the model. It can then be used to run simulations over various scenarios to identify best strategies for emergency managers based on actual, rather than expected, population behaviour.

Such a model might also be applicable to other populations (different country) and other types of crisis (earthquakes, floods, etc.). However, so far we do not know the influence of the geographical and cultural context, or that of the type of event. Determining these influences could be subject to another survey and comparison. Implementing the model can also help in comparing its outputs with other simulators dedicated to other populations or other emergency events.

Methodological Contribution. We have ported a methodology, initially intended for modelling military tactics, to model civilian tactics in crisis situations. This proves the wider applicability of this methodology, and addresses the lack of supporting tools for BDI agents in ABMS. Such a methodology and tool should allow crisis managers and other stakeholders to design such models themselves, and to easily modify and maintain existing ones. The next step is to evaluate this methodology and tool via a user study, after identifying relevant evaluation criteria. The generated models should be evaluated in particular in terms of understandability (can managers answer questions about its content) and maintainability (how easily can they modify the model, see the propagation of changes, etc.).

Integrated Toolset. In the longer term, we plan to develop an integrated toolset for designing and implementing social simulators with complex decision making and behaviour of agents, which is essential for valid simulations. Future work towards that goal includes extending the code-generation capability of TDF to other BDI languages, and extending an existing framework for the integration of BDI agents into MATSIM simulations [6,15] so that GAMA simulations may also be handled. This framework will also allow us to design modular co-simulators, integrating various components such as MATSIM for the traffic model, and Phoenix for the fire model.

Future Societal Application. Apart from the technical advances described above, we anticipate that our research will also have a societal impact by further developing a serious game. The game will be targeted to stakeholders involved in bush fire management. These crisis managers would have the opportunity to test several preventive actions and to see the consequent outcomes such as the number of victims and evacuation efficiency. For example, they may test the effectiveness of global versus personal messaging, or the effectiveness of information campaigns targeted to different groups. In addition to the potential decrease in the number of fire-related victims in the future, there are two other benefits of the serious game. Firstly it can raise awareness amongst the different stakeholders on the management of a crisis; secondly it will allow different stakeholders to share their different perceptions of the event. These two benefits are highly important since a lack of awareness and a lack of shared understanding have been obstacles to successful crisis and emergency management.

Acknowledgements. The first author would like to thank Grenoble Informatics Laboratory for funding her mission to Melbourne, Australia between January–March 2015, and to RMIT University for hosting her during that time. She would like to particularly thank John Thangarajah and Rick Evertsz for their help with the TDF methodology and tool.

References

1. Adam, C., Gaudou, B., Hickmott, S., Scerri, D.: Agents BDI et simulations sociales. Revue d'Intelligence Artificielle (RIA) - Num. Spec. Simul. Multi-Agent. **25**(1), 11–42 (2011)
2. Adam, C., Herzig, A., Longin, D.: A logical formalization of the occ theory of emotions. Synthese **168**(2), 201–248 (2009)
3. Anderson, J.: The Architecture of Cognition. Harvard University Press, Cambridge (1983)
4. Balke, T., Gilbert, N.: How do agents make decisions? a survey. J. Artif. Soc. Soc. Simul. (JASSS) **17**(4), 13, 31 Oct 2014. http://jasss.soc.surrey.ac.uk/17/4/13.html
5. Beck, E., Dugdale, J., Van Truong, H., Adam, C., Colbeau-Justin, L.: Crisis mobility of pedestrians: from survey to modelling, lessons from Lebanon and Argentina. In: Hanachi, C., Bénaben, F., Charoy, F. (eds.) ISCRAM-med 2014. LNBIP, vol. 196, pp. 57–70. Springer, Heidelberg (2014)
6. Chen, Q., Wilsher, A., Singh, D., Padgham, L.: Adding bdi agents to matsim traffic simulator (demonstration). In: AAMAS, pp. 1637–1638 (2014)
7. F.S. Commissioner: Review of the community response in recent bushfires. Technical report, NOUS group, 12 Sept 2013. http://goo.gl/wJcGn3
8. Evertsz, R., Ritter, F.E., Busetta, P., Pedrotti, M., Bittner, J.L.: CoJACK achieving principled behaviour variation in a moderated cognitive architecture. In: BRIMS (2008)
9. Evertsz, R., Thangarajah, J., Yadav, N., Li, T.: Tactics development framework (demonstration). In: AAMAS, pp. 1639–1640 (2014)
10. Evertsz, R., Thangarajah, J., Yadav, N., Li, T.: Agent oriented modelling of tactical decision making. In: Bordini, R.H., Elkind, E., Weiss, G., Yolum, P. (eds.) AAMAS. IFAAMAS, Istanbul, Turkey, 4–8 May 2015

11. Grignard., A., Taillandier, P., Gaudou, B., Huynh, N., Vo, D.-A., Drogoul, A.: Gama v. 1.6: advancing the art of complex agent-based modeling and simulation. In: PRIMA (2013)
12. McNeill, I., Dunlop, P., Skinner, T., Morrison, D.: Information processing under stress: community reactions. Technical report, Bushfire CRC, Australia (2014). http://goo.gl/TkcC4d
13. Van Minh, L., Adam, C., Canal, R., Gaudou, B., Tuong Vinh, H., Taillandier, P.: Simulation of the emotion dynamics in a group of agents in an evacuation situation. In: Desai, N., Liu, A., Winikoff, M. (eds.) PRIMA 2010. LNCS, vol. 7057, pp. 604–619. Springer, Heidelberg (2012)
14. Padgham, L., Winikoff, M.M.: Developing Intelligent Agent Systems: A Practical Guide. Wiley, Chichester (2004)
15. Padgham, L., Nagel, K., Singh, D., Chen, Q.: Integrating bdi agents into a matsim simulation. In: ECAI, pp. 681–686 (2014)
16. Rao, A., Georgeff, M.: Bdi agents: from theory to practice. In: First ICMAS, pp. 312–319, San Francisco, USA (1995)
17. Rhodes, A.: Why dont they do what we think they should? understanding peoples response to natural hazards. Technical report, Emergency Management Victoria - AFAC, September 2014. Paper at http://goo.gl/D0R8YC, Slides at http://goo.gl/MUr7K9
18. Rosenbloom, P.S., Laird, J.E., Newell, A.: The SOAR Papers: Research on Integrated Intelligence. MIT Press, Cambridge (1993)
19. Scerri, D., Hickmott, S., Bosomworth, K., Padgham, L.: Using modular simulation and agent based modelling to explore emergency management scenarios. Aust. J. Emerg. Manag. **27**(3), 44–48 (2012)
20. Teague, B., McLeod, R., Pascoe, S.: Final report. Technical report, 2009 Victorian Bushfires Royal Commission (2009). http://goo.gl/dtXnHE
21. Truong, H.V., Beck, E., Dugdale, J., Adam, C.: Developing a model of evacuation after an earthquake in Lebanon. In: ISCRAM Vietnam (2013)
22. van Ruijven, T.: Serious games as experiments for emergency management research: a review. In: 8th International ISCRAM Conference, Lisbon, Portugal, May 2011
23. Wooldridge, M.: An Introduction to Multiagent Systems. Wiley, New York (2008)

Modelling PM10 Crisis Peaks Using Multi-agent Based Simulation: Application to Annaba City, North-East Algeria

Sabri Ghazi[1(✉)], Julie Dugdale[2,3], and Tarek Khadir[1]

[1] Laboratoire de Gestion Electronique de Documents, Department of Computer Science,
University Badji Mokhtar, PO-Box 12, 23000 Annaba, Algeria
{Ghazi,Khadir}@labged.net
[2] University Grenoble Alpes, LIG, Saint-Martin-d'Hères, France
Julie.Dugdale@imag.fr
[3] University of Agder, Kristiansand, Norway

Abstract. The paper describes a MAS (multi-agent system) simulation approach for controlling PM10 (Particulate Matter) crisis peaks. A dispersion model is used with an Artificial Neural Network (ANN) to predict the PM10 concentration level. The dispersion and ANN models are integrated into a MAS system. PM10 source controllers are modelled as software agents. The MAS is composed of agents that cooperate with each other for reducing their emissions and control the air pollution peaks. Different control strategies are simulated and compared using data from Annaba (North-East Algeria). The simulator helps to compare and assess the efficiency of policies to control peaks in PM10.

Keywords: Multi-agent system · Multi-agent based simulation · Agent-based modelling · Environmental modelling · Air pollution · Air quality · PM10

1 Introduction

PM10 (Particulate Matter with an aerodynamic diameter of 10 micrometers) is a complex mixture of polluted air, including organic and inorganic particles. The toxic build-up of PM10 may be considered as a slow onset crisis and is a major health threat in many cities throughout the world [1]. This may result in large social and economic costs. Many factors influence the concentration of PM10. Some are natural such as the local climatic and topographic conditions, while others are manmade, such as vehicle emissions and the result of industrial activities. A crisis peak occurs when the concentration of air pollutant exceeds pre-defined levels, thus concentration levels need to be accurately predicted and controlled. Simulation and decision support tools are valuable for decision-makers in order to assess the efficiency of their policies in the management of pollution during peaks periods.

Many air pollution modelling approaches have been proposed such as: mathematical emission models [2, 3], linear models, ANN (Artificial Neural Networks) models ([4]) and hybrid models [5]. Most of them only address the physical and

© Springer International Publishing Switzerland 2015
N. Bellamine Ben Saoud et al. (Eds.): ISCRAM-med 2015, LNBIP 233, pp. 65–72, 2015.
DOI: 10.1007/978-3-319-24399-3_6

chemical aspects of air pollution (concentration and dispersion) and do not consider human decision-making factors. Air pollution is, by nature, distributed and results from the complex interaction of many actors. Anthropogenic activities (road traffic, industrial and agricultural activities) are among the major sources of air pollution. Therefore, it is essential to include human decision-making factors in the modelling of air pollution. A multi-agent system (MAS) allows us to model the behaviours of human actors sharing the exploitation of environmental resources [6] and it is an appropriate method for simulating pollution related issues. [7] used a MAS approach to investigate the air pollution emission resulting from road activities by using a traffic flow MAS simulation linked to an emission calculation. A methodology for building an Environmental Information System (EIS) based on a MAS is presented in [8]. In that work an agent, which represents a human-being or a group of humans-beings, uses case based reasoning to make decisions. The methodology was used to develop a system for air quality reporting. [9] presents ECROUB, a MAS for managing the quality of an urban microclimate. Using physical models, the system was able to generate information about the climate in a very small geographic zone. The system shows that a hybrid approach (MAS and physical models) can be productively used for studying urban areas.

[10] describes a MAS system designed for monitoring air quality in Athens, Greece. It is composed of a set of software agents, controlling a network of sensors installed in different positions of an urban region. Agents verify the data measured by sensors. The system uses a prediction given by an ANN model. Real data about ozone concentration and meteorological data was used to feed the simulation system. In [11] a MAS is used to model air pollution in an urban area. The environment is represented by a two-dimensional grid. The purpose of the simulation is to find the dispersal of air pollution on the grid. Each cell of the grid has a value of pollutant concentration. Neighbours with a close pollution rate (according to an initially set threshold) form a cluster. The pollution sources are represented by homogeneous agents that emit pollution in their areas (polluters). Each agent pollutes according to its emission rate. As the simulation runs, clusters are formed with different values of pollution concentration. Although similar to our approach, this model does not include meteorological parameters, does not address a specific pollutant types, and does not use real data.

We aim to model and simulate the possible cooperation between pollution source controllers and investigate the impact of cooperation on PM10 concentration. The simulator focuses on PM10 crisis peaks and the regulations that should be adopted in order to manage and reduce its effect. To investigate these questions we present a MAS approach for simulating PM10 concentrations. The feasibility of our approach is demonstrated by a scenario using data from Annaba, a Mediterranean city in the northeast of Algeria.

The paper is organized as follows: Sect. (2) describes the architecture of the simulator and the representation of the environment. We also explain the dispersion and prediction models and their integration, and define the cooperation strategies. Section (3) presents a description of the simulation scenario using the data from Annaba city. The results of the simulation are presented and discussed in Sect. (4). We end the paper by a conclusion and possible future work.

2   Model Approach and Architecture

Our simulation approach models the agents' actions that affect the emission rate of the sources they control. The dispersion algorithm is then used to compute how PM10 spreads in the environment; the aggregated value of pollutant concentration is used together with climatic parameters to forecast the air pollution concentration k hours ahead. According to these forecasts, agents are rewarded or penalised using a regulation formula that takes into account how the agent has contributed to peak concentration. Agents then adapt their strategies to earn more reward and/or reduce penalties.

2.1   The Spatial and Temporal Scale of the Simulation Model

The simulator uses a discrete representation of time where each simulation step represents 2 h of real time. The environment is modelled as a set of *3D* boxes, each one represents one KM^3, every box is localised at *gp(x,y,z)* and has an attribute representing the concentration of PM10.

2.2   Dispersion and Prediction Models

The dispersion model describes how the pollutant will spread in the air. It is calculated according to the distance from the point source, the wind speed and the emission rate. We used a GPD (Gaussian Plum Dispersion) model (1), which is frequently used in atmospheric dispersion [12].

$$C(x,y,z,H) = \frac{er_{i,t}}{2\pi U_t \sigma_y \sigma_z} * e^{-\frac{y^2}{2*\sigma_y^2}} * \left[(e^{-(\frac{(z-H)^2}{2\sigma_z^2})}) + (e^{-(\frac{(z+H)^2}{2\sigma_z^2})}) \right] \qquad (1)$$

The concentration of PM10 is calculated according to: $er_{i,t}$: the emission rate in kilograms per hour of the source i at time step t, and U_i: the wind speed in metres per second at time step t, $\sigma_y \sigma_z$: the standard deviation of the concentration distributions in vertical direction crosswind.

The level of pollution resulting from each source is aggregated and the average per box is computed. Then the dispersal value of the PM10 is passed to an ANN prediction model. The ANN prediction model is designed to give a forecast of the air pollutant and also the overall air quality. This includes an uncertainty aspect caused by the weather conditions. The ANN predictor uses the aggregated air pollution concentration value from the dispersal model of each source and the four climatic parameters: wind speed, humidity, temperature and rainfall. These parameters greatly influence the pollutant concentration.

2.3   Decision-Making Mechanism

Based on its internal state (the value of its internal attributes) and the state of the environment (values of variables representing the environment), an agent has to choose which action to perform among all of its possible actions in order to reach its goals. This process is called decision-making. Our system supports two cooperation strategies (centralized and evolutionary game) each one defines a decision-making mechanism. The centralized strategy (CS) is based on defining a central agent that represents the air pollution control agency. The central agent makes decisions according to the current air pollution level. The second strategy is based on an evolutionary game, where agents are rewarded and penalized according to the pollution level; making decisions according to their rewards. In our system, the cooperation strategy is defined as part of the simulation parameters.

Centralized Strategy (CS): The task of maintaining the air quality is assigned to an agent, which represents the air pollution control agency. It uses the prediction about air quality and pollutant levels, and accordingly sends a reduce emission message to the emission agents. Then it will recheck the air quality. It will continue doing this until the end of the peak period. As in the real world situation, the central agent has sufficient authority to ensure that the emission source controllers execute its orders. Agents communicate their emission rate at each simulation step. We assume that agents are rational and are environmentally responsible, favouring air quality improvement over their own interests and communicating to the central agent their exact emission rate.

Evolutionary Game Cooperating Strategy: In the EG strategy, every agent has its own goals (earning more rewards and keeping its emission rate as high as possible) and shares a global goal of maintaining air quality with other agents. An agent participates with other agents in the game, its own goal is to maximise its reward earned from the game. We adopted the approach of [13], where agents keep traces of their K previous steps (actions, rewards and its neighbours' rewards). At each time step t the agent computes its weighted payoff according to (4) and updates its probability of increasing or decreasing its emission rate, respectively according to (5) and (6).

$$WP_t = \sum_{i=1}^{k} w_i * M_i \qquad (2)$$

Where: w_i is the weighting parameter where $\sum_{i=1}^{k-1} w_i = 1$ and $\forall i,j (i < j \rightarrow w_i > w_j)$, M_i is the i-th payoff, $i = 1$ means the payoff earned this step.

$$\begin{cases} Pc_i(t+1) = Pc_i(t) + 1 - Pc_i(t) * \alpha, \, if S_i = 0 \, and \, WP_t > 0 \\ Pc_i(t+1) = (1 - \alpha) * Pc_i(t), \, if S_i = 0 \, and \, WP_t \leq 0 \end{cases} \qquad (3)$$

$$\begin{cases} Q_i(t+1) = Q_i(t) + 1 - Q_i(t) * \alpha, \, if S_i = 1 \, and \, WP_t > 0 \\ Q_i(t+1) = (1 - \alpha) * Q(t), \, if S_i = 1 \, and \, WP_t \leq 0 \end{cases} \qquad (4)$$

Where: Pc_i and Q_i are respectively the probability to decrease ($S = 0$) and increase ($S = 1$) the emission for the agent i, α is the learning rate, S is the strategy played at time t. Agents are influenced by their neighbours at each time step; the average reward of the neighbours is calculated according to (9).

$$nP_{i,j}(t) = (\sum_{j=1}^{R} C_j)/R \tag{5}$$

Where C_j is the payoff of the neighbour j, and R is the number of neighbours for the i-th agent. The average of the K last nP is noted $avgNP$. The agent then uses the probabilities Pc, Pd and the average reward of its neighbours to choose an action according to the algorithm below: (Fig. 1).

```
Algorithm    Choose Action Emission Agent
   while t < MaxTemps do
      if (lastChoices[0] == 0) then
         if ((RPwt < pf_AVG)and(P < Q)and(Q > Ru)) then
            lastChoices[0] = 1;
            sourcesInfo.resumeEmission();
         else
            lastChoices[0] = 0;
            .sourcesInfo.reduceEmission();
         end if
      end if
      if (lastChoices[0] == 1) then
         if ((RPwt < pf_AVG)and(Q < P)and(P > Ru)) then
            lastChoices[0] = 0;
            sourcesInfo.reduceEmission();
         else
            lastChoices[0] = 1;
            sourcesInfo.resumeEmission();
         end if
      end if
   end while
```

Fig. 1. Algorithm for choosing an action using the EG strategy

When a crisis peak occurs, the system uses an agent's emission rate to calculate how much the agent has contributed to the current level of the pollution. The agent is penalised according to its level of participation.

3   Simulation Scenarios Using Data from the Annaba Region

The dataset used in this work covers the period 2003–2004 on a continuous basis of 24 h. Air pollutants, including PM10, are continuously monitored. The dataset also includes four meteorological parameters: Wind Speed (WS), Temperature (T), relative Humidity (H) and rainfall.

A simulation scenario for the region of Annaba was defined to include a 100 sources of PM10 with the maximum emission rate for each source being 2000 gram/hour. The goal level for pollutant concentration is fixed according to the air quality standards and must be bellow 70 microgram per cubic meter. The initial values (at $t = 0$) for the concentration of pollutant and the climatic parameters are fixed according to the dataset. For the case of EG strategies we fixed the initial proportion of cooperating agents (agents choosing to decrease emission) to 0.5, this means that $50\ \%$ of the agents decrease their emission at $t = 0$. This proportion will change during the simulation according to the game outcome. The prediction is 4 h in advance, the same as the simulation step. Each source emits pollutants according to its emission rate, which cannot be higher than the maximum level defined in the simulation scenario. The position of sources is randomly generated.

4 Results and Discussion

The scenario was run by choosing at each time a cooperation strategy: (with Penalties), (No Penalties), CS (Centralized Strategy) and NC (No-Cooperation). The last one is included for comparison purposes. Due to space limitations only the most significant results are presented. When executed 80 times the simulation showed that the CS gives similar results at each run, the same thing was also found for NC. Using the EG strategies, the simulations show slight differences between runs especially in the proportion of cooperating agents. These changes are due to the random values used in the initialisation of some variables (neighbours rewards, first chosen action, weights, k last actions and rewards).

Figure 2 shows the concentration of PM10 for each strategy during the simulation; each point is the peak level in 24 h. The CS strategy (PICPM10CS) performs the best, taking less time to bring the pollution level under control and keeping it below the goal level defined in the simulation scenario. The EG strategy (PICPM10CP) performs reasonably well, but it takes slightly longer than the CS strategy to bring the pollution level down. Nevertheless it manages to keep the pollution level near to the goal. The penalising regulations have a big effect on the PM10 level. As illustrated, the PICPM10CP (with penalties) controls the pollution and performs better than the non-penalising strategy (PICPM10NP). The NC strategy (No-Cooperation) is presented in order to show the impact of cooperation on the PM10 level. The CS gives the best performance since the pollution concentration rapidly decreases. When cooperation is not used (PICPM10NC), agents act selfishly and do not care about the pollution. As the agents reach their maximum emission rate, we can observe an oscillation that is caused by the climatic conditions. Consequently, the pollutant level reaches alarming values and many peaks periods occur.

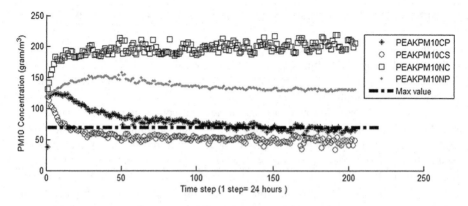

Fig. 2. Peak of 24 h of PM10 for the four tested controlling strategies compared with the no-cooperation strategy.

5   Conclusions

Computer simulations are a valuable tool for helping in the management of pollution related crisis. In our study we showed how a multi-agent based simulation approach could be successfully combined with classic modelling tools in order to model air pollution peaks. The simulation helps to investigate different controlling strategies by measuring how each strategy performs in managing the crisis peaks of PM10.

The regulation rules are computed according to how much the agent participates to the level of pollution; it is clear that this regulation has a big influence in controlling pollution. As shown in the simulation results, cooperation helps to reduce the pollution level and it also affects the evolution of the pollutant. This is especially noticeable during the peak periods where climatic conditions cause the pollutants to stagnate.

The current version of the system only models point emission sources of PM10. In future versions we aim to include continuous sources, such as roads, and to predict other pollutants. The simulator may also be enhanced by including a GIS interface. In addition, exploring other cooperation strategies are also among our future plans.

Acknowledgements. This work was funded by the Algerian Ministry of Higher Education and Scientific Research, PNE 2014/2015 Program.

References

1. WHO (World Health Organisation), Ecosystems and Human Well-being: Health Synthesis. WHO Library Cataloguing-in-Publication Data (2005)
2. Daly, A., Zannetti, P.: Air pollution modeling–An overview. Ambient air pollution (2007)
3. Lushi, E., Stockie, J.M.: An inverse Gaussian plume approach for estimating atmospheric pollutant emissions from multiple point sources. Atmos. Environ. **44**(8), 1097–1107 (2010)
4. Ghazi, S., Khadir, M.T.: Combination of artificial neural network models for air quality predictions for the region of Annaba, Algeria. Int. J. Environ. Stud. **69**(1), 79–89 (2012)
5. Russo, A., Soares, A.O.: Hybrid model for urban air pollution forecasting: a stochastic spatio-temporal approach. Math. Geosci. **46**(1), 75–93 (2014)
6. Ghazi, S., Khadir, T., Dugdale, J.: Multi-agent based simulation of environmental pollution issues: a review. In: Corchado, J.M., Bajo, J., Kozlak, J., Pawlewski, P., Molina, J.M., Gaudou, B., Julian, V., Unland, R., Lopes, F., Hallenborg, K., García Teodoro, P. (eds.) PAAMS 2014. CCIS, vol. 430, pp. 13–21. Springer, Heidelberg (2014)
7. Hülsmann, F., Gerike, R., Kickhöfer, B., Nagel, K., Luz, R.: Towards a multi-agent based modeling approach for air pollutants in urban regions. In: Proceedings of the Conference on Luftqualität an Straßen, pp. 144–166 (2011)
8. Athanasiadis, I.N., Mitkas, P.A.: A methodology for developing environmental information systems with software agents. In: Cortés, U., Poch, M. (eds.) Advanced Agent-Based Environmental Management Systems, Whitestein Series in Software Agent Technologies and Autonomic Computing, pp 119–137. Birkhäuser Basel (2009)
9. Borri, D., Camarda, D.: Planning for the environmental quality of urban microclimate: a multiagent-based approach. In: Luo, Y. (ed.) CDVE 2011. LNCS, vol. 6874, pp. 129–136. Springer, Heidelberg (2011)

10. Papaleonidas, A., Iliadis, L.: Hybrid and reinforcement multi agent technology for real time air pollution monitoring. In: Iliadis, L., Maglogiannis, I., Papadopoulos, H. (eds.) Artificial Intelligence Applications and Innovations. IFIP AICT, vol. 381, pp. 274–284. Springer, Heidelberg (2012)
11. Ahat, M., Amor, S.B., Bui, M., Lamure, M., Courel, M.-F.: Pollution modeling and simulation with multi-agent and pretopology. In: Zhou, J. (ed.) Complex 2009. LNICST, vol. 4, pp. 225–231. Springer, Heidelberg (2009)
12. Stockie, J.M.: The mathematics of atmospheric dispersion modeling. SIAM Rev. **53**(2), 349–372 (2011)
13. Power, C.: A spatial agent-based model of n-person prisoner's dilemma cooperation in a socio-geographic community, J. Artif. Soc. Soc. Simul. 12(18) (2009). http://jasss.soc.surrey.ac.uk/12/1/8.html

Multiple Regression and Artificial Neural Network for the Prediction of Crop Pest Risks

Yingwei Yan[1(✉)], Chen-Chieh Feng[1], Maffee Peng-Hui Wan[2],
and Klarissa Ting-Ting Chang[2]

[1] Department of Geography, National University of Singapore,
1 Arts Link, Singapore 117570, Singapore
yanyingwei@u.nus.edu, geofcc@nus.edu.sg
[2] Department of Information Systems, National University of Singapore,
13 Computing Drive, Singapore 117417, Singapore
diswp@nus.edu.sg, changtt@comp.nus.edu.sg

Abstract. The reduction of crop yield losses caused by pests is a major challenge to productive and sustainable food production for preventing food insecurity and emergencies, and for alleviating world food crisis. Multiple regression (MR) and artificial neural network (ANN) are two widely adopted modelling approaches for the prediction of crop pest risks, which are based on empirical statistics and artificial intelligence, respectively. Each of the two alternative approaches has its advantages and disadvantages. This study evaluates the two models from two aspects: their performances on pest risk prediction, and their methodological advantages and disadvantages. Two pest species are modelled using the two approaches as case studies, which are the melon thrip *Thrips palmi* Karny (*T. palmi*) and the diamondback moth *Plutella xylostella* (L.) (*P. xylostella*). Results show that ANN has higher prediction accuracy for both species. However, ANN has some methodological demerits compared to MR modelling.

Keywords: Pest risk prediction · Multiple regression · Artificial neural network · Melon thrip · Diamondback moth

1 Introduction

The world population is projected to increase by 30 % to 9.2 billion by 2050 [1]. This population increase will lead to notably increased demand for food production because dietary habits in developing countries will change towards higher quality food [2], for example, higher demand for meat and milk, which will also increase the need of food for feeding livestock. This effect can cause a slow onset crisis, namely food crisis in the world [3]. To tackle this problem, expanding cropland is a possible solution. However, expanding cropland is of limited availability and comes with huge costs. Highly productive and sustainable food production is therefore required.

Reduction of yield losses caused by crop pests is a major challenge to productive and sustainable food production [1]. Excessive pest population can lead to both short term emergencies like widespread crop failures and long term emergencies like nutritional

© Springer International Publishing Switzerland 2015
N. Bellamine Ben Saoud et al. (Eds.): ISCRAM-med 2015, LNBIP 233, pp. 73–84, 2015.
DOI: 10.1007/978-3-319-24399-3_7

emergencies. Managing pests and their damages to crops therefore has been one of the critical steps to prevent food insecurity and emergencies, and to alleviate world food crisis.

A wealth of pest risk management strategies for reducing pest infestations has been implemented, ranging from adopting resistance cultivars, pesticides, to integrated pest management. Mathematical modelling for early prediction of pest risks is one such strategy that has been widely adopted. Multiple regression (MR) [4] and artificial neural network (ANN) [5], based on empirical statistics and artificial intelligence, respectively, are two popular models for crop pest risk prediction. Each of the two alternative modelling approaches has its advantages and disadvantages. No one can always outperform the other in any situation. Therefore, their performance is dependent of the specific contexts and focuses of pest risk analysis. For example, whether we focus on more accurate prediction or on identifying key factors contributing to a pest outbreak.

The purpose of this paper is to evaluate these two approaches (i.e., MR and ANN) in terms of their performances on pest risk prediction and methodological advantages and disadvantages. It aims to provide insights to pest risk modelers regarding model selection for specific tasks of pest risk management.

The rest of this paper is organized as follows. The state of the art related to pest risk modelling is provided first, followed by a brief introduction of the basic principles of MR and ANN. An empirical application of MR and ANN in modelling two sets of pest development data is then presented, followed by comparison and discussion of their advantages and disadvantages in both quantitative and qualitative terms. The last section of this paper describes the conclusions and future works of this research.

2   Related Work

MR modelling has been widely adopted for evaluating crop pest risks. For example, [6] adopted MR for predicting the population fluctuations of bean leaf beetle in soybean; [4] used MR for predicting the population dynamics of paddy stem borer; [7] used MR to quantify the effect of cowpea field pests on grain yields. ANN is also a popular approach for assessing crop pest risks. For example, [8] used ANN for predicting the population dynamics of aphid; [9] built a prediction system about fruit tree insect pests based on ANN; [5] predicted the population occurrence of paddy stem borer based on ANN. These two approaches are popular because they are relatively easier to be understood and are currently available for use in many statistical software.

There are also other approaches that can be applied to crop pest risk modelling and prediction. A fairly popular one is bioclimatic model [10]. This model, however, focuses on predicting the occurrence probability of a pest species at a given location for a given period of time and then indirectly evaluating the occurrence risk of the pest. Bioclimatic model is suitable for long-term cropping planning (e.g., optimal selection of the crop variety to be planted at a given location to better avoid pest infestation problems over a relatively long period of time), but is not suitable for forecasting emergent or unexpected pest risks (e.g., pest outbreak). Compared to bioclimatic model, MR and ANN can directly predict pest population dynamics or their infestations with fine temporal resolutions [4–9]. In addition, degree-day model is also widely adopted for pest risk prediction [11]. Degree-day model is used to predict the timing of pest risks (e.g., the date of pest outbreak). However, this model is only temperature-based. This becomes the major disadvantage of degree-day model compared to the other models which can take multiple factors into consideration. Therefore, this study focuses on utilizing MR and ANN to predict crop pest risks.

To the best of our knowledge, despite that [12] compares regression model with a bioclimatic model in terms of *Helicoverpa* population prediction, study comparing MR with ANN in terms of pest risk prediction is currently lacking. In the following sections of this paper, a comparison between MR and ANN is thus presented.

3 Model Principles

3.1 Multiple Regression

MR is a commonly used linear regression method, which can be generally expressed as:

$$Y = \beta_0 + \beta_1 X_1 + \beta_2 X_2 + \ldots + \beta_n X_n + \varepsilon, \tag{1}$$

where Y is a dependent variable (i.e., model output), X_1, X_2, ..., X_n, $n \geq 1$, are a set of predictors or independent variables (i.e., model inputs) believed to be related to the dependent variable Y. β_0 is a constant called intercept, and β_1, β_2, ..., β_n are regression coefficients. Normally, β_0 and β_1, β_2, ..., β_n need to be derived by the procedure of ordinary least squares. $\varepsilon \sim N(0, \sigma^2)$ is the random error, which is the difference between desired outputs (i.e., observed values) and actual outputs (i.e., predicted values) not accounted for by the model. When the regression expression is applied to predictive mode, ε is omitted because its mathematical expectation is zero.

There might be multiple factors contributing as independent variables to a given dependent variable, which touches upon the problem of predictor selection. If a predictor significantly related to a given dependent variable is neglected, the regression equation loses its prediction power. However, it also loses parsimony if plethoric predictors are taken into account, some of which may be redundant or inter-correlated, leading to multicollinearity problem. Identifying appropriate predictor set thus is a crucial step in building an optimal regression equation in aspects of both prediction accuracy and model parsimony.

Additionally, mathematical transformation is usually desired when the assumptions of linear regression are violated (i.e., residuals should follow normal distribution, random pattern and homoscedasticity, and the phenomenon measured should follow linearity).

3.2 Artificial Neural Network

As a supervised learning technique, back-propagation artificial neural network (BP-ANN) is one of the most widely used structures of ANN [13]. A BP-ANN is typically composed of an input layer of source neurons (i.e., predictors), an output layer of computational neurons (i.e., dependent variables), and one or multiple hidden layers of computational neurons. The hidden layers are capable of detecting and learning the relationship between the predictors and dependent variables, including both linear and non-linear, and both simple and complex relationships. In a BP-ANN learning process, a training input pattern is first given to the input layer, and then the network propagates the input pattern from layer to layer until the output pattern is generated in the output layer. If this pattern is different from the desired output, an error is generated and propagated backwards through the network from the output layer to the input layer for retraining. The processing units (i.e., the neurons) in one layer are fully interconnected with every other neuron in its forward adjacent layer, which compose the network and are analogical to the biological neurons of human brain. The strength of connection between two neurons from adjacent layers is named 'weight'. The basic idea of BP-ANN is to minimize the error through iterative backward propagation of error signals, and adjusting the connection weights recurrently until the cost function is minimized (i.e., one consecutive step with no decrease in error). The cost function is defined as:

$$E = \frac{1}{2} \sum_{k=1}^{l} (y_{d,k} - y_k)^2, \tag{2}$$

where $y_{d,k}$ and y_k are the desired and actual output of neuron k in an output layer, respectively. l is the total number of neurons in the output layer. When the value of the cost function is sufficiently small, a network is considered to have converged.

4   Model Building

The MR and ANN modelling of this study were based on the datasets provided by the Agri-Food & Veterinary Authority (AVA) of Singapore. It includes historical pest surveillance data collected in AVA's farms at Northwest Singapore and a series of meteorological data recorded near the farms. The farms were geographically close to each other. Two pest species were chosen for modelling because of their high risks with worldwide presence and multiple host plants [14, 15]. The two species are the melon thrip *Thrips palmi* Karny (*T. palmi*) and the diamondback moth *Plutella xylostella* (L.) (*P. xylostella*), which have been continuously monitored during the last decade using pest traps. Pest traps were deployed in five different farms to monitor the *T. palmi*, and eight different farms to monitor the *P. xylostella*. For each species, the average catch per month was calculated from all the traps, representing monthly population of the pest. The surveillance over the *T. palmi* and the *P. xylostella* were conducted from January 2001 to December 2012 and from January 2003 to December 2012, respectively. Figure 1 shows the observed population variations of the two pest species over time.

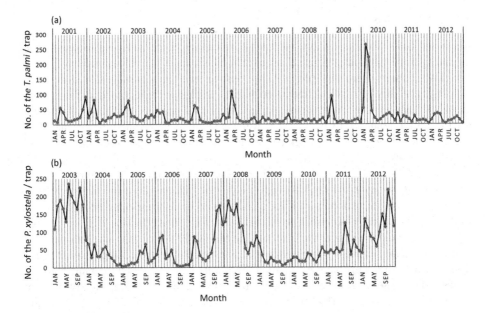

Fig. 1. Observed monthly population variation of (a) the *T. palmi* from 2001 to 2012, and of (b) the *P. xylostella* from 2003 to 2012.

4.1 MR Models

MR models were built to predict monthly *T. palmi* and monthly *P. xylostella* populations (dependent variables), which could be used to determine pest risk level and degree of emergency. According to prior studies, meteorological variables including monthly mean temperature, monthly mean maximum temperature, monthly mean minimum temperature, monthly mean relative humidity, monthly precipitation amount, and monthly mean wind speed, for both the prediction months and one month prior to the prediction months, are potential factors affecting development of the pests [16–19]. Temperature can be important factor that contributes to the growth of poikilothermic organisms such as insects. Humidity can adjust moisture needed by pest growth. Precipitation can also affect pest growth by adjusting ambient humidity or by creating floods that cause wash-off of eggs and larvae and drowning of young. Wind can be a factor that influences the dispersal of crop pests. There were therefore 12 variables being taken into consideration.

Data collected before 2012 were used as training dataset and data collected in 2012 were used as test dataset. Data outliers were removed appropriately and stepwise regression was performed for predictor selection. Base-10 logarithmic transformation was performed on the dependent variables to meet the assumptions of the regression, and the independent variables were Z-score standardized selectively to eliminate multicollinearity problems.

4.2 ANN Models

Individual BP-ANN models, one for each pest species, were built to also predict the monthly pest populations, using the same set of independent variables considered in the MR. Data outliers were also removed to improve training accuracy. Given the self-learning capability of ANN, all the independent variables were included in training the BP-ANN models without mathematical transformation. Data collected before 2012 were used as training dataset, of which 20 % were randomly selected and used as an independent set of data records for tracking the errors leading to over-fitting. Data collected in 2012 were used as test dataset.

Following the universal approximation theorem which states that a neural network with one hidden layer with a sufficient number of hidden neurons can in principle relate any given set of inputs to a set of outputs to an arbitrary degree of accuracy [20], three-layer back-propagation neural networks consisting of one input, one hidden, and one output layer were adopted in this study. More than one hidden layer is also adoptable, but meanwhile it may increase the computation complexity and thus decrease the training efficiency, i.e., more iterations may be needed to obtain training convergence. The number of hidden neurons was determined empirically using a trial-and-error method. Different numbers of hidden neurons, from 1 to 10, were tried for the network trainings, the optimal number of hidden neurons within this range was determined according to training accuracy. Numbers beyond ten were not tried because it was suggested that involving too many neurons in the hidden layer may cause over-fitting problem [21], which means that the network fits the training dataset too good to be generalizable if with prediction purpose. In addition, the optimal learning rates and the momentum constants were all parameters adjusted empirically based on the training efficiency and accuracy. Sigmoid activation function was used, which run within a domain between zero and one. In order to fit the sigmoid domain and to obtain convergence within an acceptable number of iterations, all the variables were linear normalized prior to the model training so that they fell in a range from zero to one.

5 Modelling Results

5.1 MR Models

The fitted MR models for the *T. palmi* and the *T. xylostella* are shown by the following equations, respectively. In each of the following equations, some of the 12 independent variables were excluded as they were not statistically significantly related to the given dependent variable according to the stepwise regression.

$$\text{Log}_{10}[Y_{T.palmi(r)}] = 1.249 + 0.212\text{ZMT}_{max(r)} - 0.157\text{ZMT}_{mean(r)}$$
$$-0.046\text{ZMPA}_{(r-1)}, \tag{3}$$

$$\text{Log}_{10}[Y_{P.\,xylostella(r)}] = 1.624 - 0.13\text{ZMT}_{max(r-1)}, \tag{4}$$

where ZMT$_{max}$ is the Z-score transformed monthly mean maximum temperature, ZMT$_{mean}$ is the Z-score transformed monthly mean temperature, ZMPA is the Z-score transformed monthly precipitation amount, r denotes the month for prediction, r-1 denotes one month before the prediction month r. All the regression assumptions were satisfied, and the constants and coefficients of the equations were significant at a 0.05 confidence interval. The overall fit of the regression models were significant ($F = 16.67$, $P < 0.00001$ for (3); $F = 10.24$, $P = 0.02$ for (4)).

The correlation of determination R^2 for (3) was 0.294 with ZMT$_{mean(r)}$ accounting for 48.3 %, ZMT$_{mean(r)}$ accounting for 43.5 %, and ZMPA$_{(r-1)}$ accounting for 8.2 % of the variation of the monthly T. Palmi population, according to the stepwise regression analysis. The R^2 for (4) was 0.117, which was low. Only ZMT$_{max(r-1)}$ was found being significantly related to the variation of the monthly P. xylostella population. Temperature was thus identified as a key factor contributing to the development of both species. Figure 2 plots the prediction results of the MR modelling for the test dataset of the T. palmi and of the P. xylostella, which were not that satisfactory, especially for that of the P. xylostella.

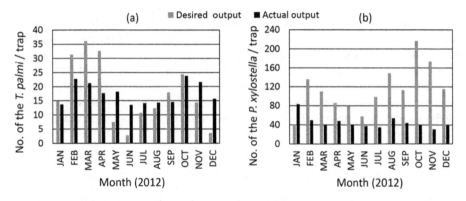

Fig. 2. Prediction results of the MR modelling for the test dataset of (a) the T. *palmi* and of (b) the P. *xylostella*.

5.2   ANN Models

The R^2 values for the T. *palmi* ANN data training and the P. *xylostella* ANN data training were 0.62 and 0.53, respectively. Both R^2 values were improved from those generated by the respective MR models, indicating that the ANN models fitted the training datasets better than the MR models did. Figure 3 shows the prediction results of the ANN modelling for the test dataset of the T. *palmi* and of the P. *xylostella*. It was found that the ANN prediction results were more satisfactory than the MR prediction results.

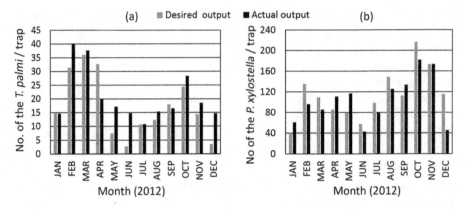

Fig. 3. Prediction result of the ANN modelling for the test dataset of (a) the *T. palmi* and of (b) the *P. xylostella*.

6   Comparisons and Discussion

In this section, the MR and ANN models are compared. The comparison will firstly adopt traditional evaluation approaches on their prediction performance, using root mean square error (RMSE), mean absolute error (MAE), and mean absolute percentage error (MAPE). These values for each model were calculated using the test datasets.

While the use of these indices allows us to evaluate prediction performances across different models, they do not account for their methodological differences. To address this issue, the comparison will secondly focus on the methodological advantages and disadvantages.

6.1   Comparison of Prediction Performance

The indices calculated for the test datasets were shown in Table 1. For both species, the ANN models produced lower index values while the MR models produced higher index values. The index values offer a global view that the ANN models generated higher agreement between the desired model outputs and the actual model outputs, meaning that the ANN models performed better than the MR models did.

Table 1.   Index values for the comparison of prediction performance.

	T. palmi			*P. xylostella*		
Model	RMSE	MAE	MAPE	RMSE	MAE	MAPE
MR	9.008	7.475	92.184	88.175	76.812	65.339
ANN	7.315	5.706	84.791	32.062	27.556	27.981

6.2 Comparison of Methodology

Although ANN is better than MR in its prediction performance, it cannot be readily concluded that ANN is always better than MR. Each of them might be suitable for different task requirements. In this section, the advantages of the two modeling approaches, or the lack thereof, are discussed. A summary of the advantages and disadvantages are provided in Table 2.

Table 2. The advantages and disadvantages of the two modelling approaches.

Issue	MR model	ANN model
Relationship modelled	Linear relationships, but suspected non-linear effect and polynomial relation can be mitigated by data transformation	Linear or non-linear, simple or complex, or even elusive relationships
Factor interpretation	Supported by test of statistical significance	Problematic (black box)
Assumed distribution	Normal distribution, can be mitigated by data transformation	Robust to deviation from a multivariate distribution
Possible overfitting	Less problematic	Problematic
Suspected Data noises/ Outliers	Problematic	Less problematic
Suspected multicollinearity	Mitigated by data transformation	Less problematic
Model parameter settings	Statistically derived (coefficients and constant)	Empirically derived (activation function, number of layers, learning rate, momentum factor)

As far as MR is concerned, it is the simplest and most widely used method for pest prediction. The advantage of regression is that all the considered variables can be statistically tested for significance based on given confidence interval. The statistical test makes the regression parameters more interpretable so that the variables which make no sense can be eliminated from the model. The variables which are statistically significant can be identified to be crucial to its dependent variable.

However, regression is established based on strict assumptions. The statistical power loses if the linearity of the measured phenomenon is not strong. Although suspected non-linear effect or polynomial relation can be mitigated by conducting mathematical transformation such as logarithmic and exponential transformation, it does not always solve the issue. In addition, MR requires the residuals to follow normal distribution, which is not always the case in real data.

As for ANN, its most remarkable advantage is that the modelling can be conducted without prior knowledge. Any relationship between given predictors and dependent variables can be learned by the neural networks, regardless of linearity or non-linearity. In our empirical application, the ANN performed better than the MR because the linearity of the phenomena measured was not strong, which in turns weakened the power of the regression. Non-normally distributed data, multicollinearity issue and data noise are also tolerable in the network training [22, 23]. It therefore offers greater flexibility in the modelling process.

However, the importance of predictors to a given dependent variable cannot be explicitly identified by ANN as it performs like a black box [24]. The subjectivity involved in building the networks and in determining the model parameters (e.g., number of hidden layers and number of hidden neurons, learning rate, and momentum factor) further worsen the problem. People can build completely different neural networks with inconsistent parameters. In addition, ANN is capable of fitting non-linear relationships, but it may encounter over-fitting problem in non-linear data training.

7   Conclusions and Future Works

With the goal of exploring more effective ways for predicting crop pest risks, in order to prevent food insecurity and emergencies, and to alleviate world food crisis, two mainstream modelling approaches were evaluated in terms of their model performances, and their methodological advantages and disadvantages. It was found that ANN model predicted the pest populations more accurately. But methodologically, ANN does not always outperform MR model. ANN has its disadvantages compared to MR.

In the future work, perhaps integrating these two models could offer a better way for pest prediction. For example, regression can be used to identify key variables contributing to pest development, by doing which regression can provide prior knowledge to ANN model building in order to reduce the model complexity and improve the training efficiency and/or accuracy. In addition, there are some other machine learning methods that can be applied to the prediction of crop pest risks such as support vector machine and Naive Bayes. This track can be explored in the future work. Finally, only meteorological factors were taken into account in our modelling, but there may be other factors that can affect the pest development, such as species competition, predation, phenological synchrony with host plants and parasitism. These factors can be explored to make more robust modelling and prediction.

Acknowledgments. This research is supported by Department of Geography, National University of Singapore and National Research Foundation, Prime Minister's Office, Singapore under its International Research Centres in Singapore Funding Initiative and administered by the Interactive Digital Media Programme Office.

References

1. Popp, J., Pető, K., Nagy, J.: Pesticide productivity and food security. A review. Agron. Sustain. Dev. **33**(1), 243–255 (2013)
2. FAQ: Feeding the world in 2050. In: World Agricultural Summit on Food Security. Food and Agriculture Organization of the United Nations, Rome (2009)
3. Holt-Giménez, E.: From food crisis to food sovereignty: the challenge of social movements. Mon. Rev. **61**(3), 142–156 (2009)
4. Yang, L.N., Peng, L., Zhong, F., Zhang, Y.S.: A study of paddystem borer (*Scirpophaga incertulas*) population dynamics and its influence factors base on stepwise regress analysis. In: Li, D., Zhao, C. (eds.) Computer and Computing Technologies in Agriculture II, vol. 2, pp. 1519–1526. Springer, US (2009)
5. Yang, L.N., Peng, L., Zhang, L.M., Zhang, L.L., Yang, S.S.: A prediction model for population occurrence of paddy stem borer (*Scirpophaga incertulas*), based on back propagation artificial neural network and principal components analysis. Comput. Electron. Agric. **68**(2), 200–206 (2009)
6. Lam, W.F., Pedigo, L.P., Hinz, P.N.: Population dynamics of bean leaf beetles (Coleoptera: chrysomelidae) in central Iowa. Environ. Entomol. **30**(3), 562–567 (2001)
7. Karungi, J., Adipala, E., Nampala, P., Ogenga-Latigo, M.W., Kyamanywa, S.: Pest management in cowpea. Part III. Quantifying the effect of cowpea field pests on grain yields in eastern Uganda. Crop Prot. **19**(5), 343–347 (2000)
8. Worner, S., Lankin, G., Samarasinghe, S., Teulon, D., Zydenbos, S.: Improving prediction of aphid flights by temporal analysis of input data for an artificial neural network. N. Z. Plant Prot. **55**, 312–316 (2002)
9. Liu, G., Shen, H.Y., Yang, X.H., Ge, Y.B.: Research on prediction about fruit tree diseases and insect pests based on neural network. Artif. Intell. Appl. Innov. **187**, 731–740 (2005)
10. Jeschke, J.M., Strayer, D.L.: Usefulness of bioclimatic models for studying climate change and invasive species. Ann. N.Y. Acad. Sci. **1134**, 1–24 (2008)
11. Herm, D.A.: Using degree-days and plant phenology to predict pest activity. In: Krischik, V., Davidson, J. (eds.) IPM (Integrated Pest Management) of Midwest Landscapes, pp. 49–59. University of Minnesota, Minnesota (2004)
12. Zalucki, M.P., Furlong, M.J.: Forecasting *Helicoverpa* populations in Australia: a comparison of regression based models and a bioclimatic based modelling approach. Insect Sci. **12**(1), 45–56 (2005)
13. Chiang, Y.M., Chang, L.C., Chang, F.J.: Comparison of static-feedforward and dynamic-feedback neural networks for rainfall–runoff modeling. J. Hydrol. **290**(3), 297–311 (2004)
14. Dentener, P., Whiting, D., Connolly, P.: *Thrips palmi* Karny (Thysanoptera: Thripidae): could it survive in New Zealand? N. Z. Plant Prot. **55**(18), 18–24 (2002)
15. Liu, S.S., Chen, F.Z., Zalucki, M.P.: Development and survival of the diamondback moth (Lepidoptera: Plutellidae) at constant and alternating temperatures. Environ. Entomol. **31**(2), 221–231 (2002)
16. Etienne, J., Guyot, J., Xavier, V.W.: Effect of insecticides, predation, and precipitation on populations of Thrips palmi on aubergine (eggplant) in Guadeloupe. Fla. Entomol. **73**(2), 339–342 (1990)
17. Castañé, C., Riudavets, J., Yano, E.: Biological control of thrips. In: Albajes, R., Gullino, M.L., Lenteren, J.C., Elad, Y. (eds.) Integrated Pest and Disease Management in Greenhouse Crops, vol. 14, pp. 244–253. Springer, Netherlands (2002)
18. Kobori, Y., Amano, H.: Effect of rainfall on a population of the diamondback moth, *Plutella xylostella* (Lepidoptera: Plutellidae). Appl. Entomol. Zool. **38**(2), 249–253 (2003)

19. Guo, S., Qin, Y.: Effects of temperature and humidity on emergence dynamics of *Plutella xylostella* (Lepidoptera: Plutellidae). J. Econ. Entomol. **103**(6), 2028–2033 (2010)
20. Haykin, S.: Neural Networks—A Comprehensive Foundation. McMillan College Publishing Company, New York (1994)
21. Wang, Y.M., Elhag, T.M.S.: A comparison of neural network, evidential reasoning and multiple regression analysis in modelling bridge risks. Expert Syst. Appl. **32**(2), 336–348 (2007)
22. Zhang, G.P.: Time series forecasting using a hybrid ARIMA and neural network model. Neurocomputing **50**, 159–175 (2003)
23. Chittineni, S., Bhogapathi, R.B.: A study on the behavior of a neural network for grouping the data. Int. J. Comput. Sci. Issues **9**(1), 228–234 (2012)
24. Setiono, R., Leow, W.L., Thong, J.Y.: Opening the neural network black box: an algorithm for extracting rules from function approximating artificial neural networks. In: Proceedings of the 21st International Conference on Information Systems, Brisbane, Australia, pp. 176–186 (2000)

Improving Players' Assessment in Crisis Management Serious Games: The SIMFOR Project

Ali Oulhaci, Erwan Tranvouez[(✉)], Sébastien Fournier, and Bernard Espinasse

Aix Marseille Université, CNRS, LSIS UMR 7296, 13397, Marseille, France
{ali.oulhaci,erwan.tranvouez,sebastien.fournier,
bernard.espinasse}@lsis.org

Abstract. Serious Games (SG) are more and more used for training in various domains, but notably in crisis management. In order to improve training results, learner assessment can provide insights on what went right or wrong during a training session. Such assessment is more complex when actors' individual actions must be considered, but also the results of their interactions (collective actions). Such interactions can either be engaged with real or simulated players, through adaptive dialogues immersing players in the different ways (actions, procedures, …) to manage a crisis. This paper presents a multi-agent simulation and assessment approach of SG players, targeting the management of distributed and heterogeneous information (in nature or source) based on the concept of Evaluation Space allowing the production of individual and collective assessments. This approach is developed and illustrated on the SIMFOR SG dedicated to crisis management.

Keywords: Serious game · Learner assessment · Multi-agent system · Agent based simulation · Crisis management

1 Introduction

The growing interest for Serious Games (SG), especially for training, has raised new needs in terms of learners' assessment [1] and behaviours simulation [2]. SG aims at immersing learners as players in a simulated environment improving thus their motivation and involvement by having players learning by doing [3]. SG can use simulation to reproduce a complex or expensive phenomena (physics, natural disaster, etc.) or when there is a high number of actors, to simulate the human actors' behaviors (called Non-Player Characters or NPC).

The goal of the SG is to teach one or more skills to one or more actors (players). Each SG answers in general to a particular training goal, in relation to a specific training context related to trades (crisis and risk management [3–5], firemen operations [6], …), or a specific body of knowledge (school or university courses), or even of social skills (conflict management, cooperation, etc.) [7]. The qualitative or quantitative measure of the success or failure of learning may at the same time implement *ad hoc* or generic

© Springer International Publishing Switzerland 2015
N. Bellamine Ben Saoud et al. (Eds.): ISCRAM-med 2015, LNBIP 233, pp. 85–99, 2015.
DOI: 10.1007/978-3-319-24399-3_8

solutions. This paper presents how automated assessment can improve the learning objective of a multi-player (and multi-skills) SG, as applied to Crisis Management based on a Multi-Agent Systems (MAS).

We first discuss this issue, before proposing a multi-agent approach to improve NPC adaptability and assessment especially in a collaborative context illustrated with the SIMFOR SG. We then detail the assessment conceptual framework and present briefly the implementation of the new SIMFOR SG as well as some preliminary experimental results. We conclude on the perspectives raised by our contribution.

2   Assessment in Serious Games

Serious Games (SG) are more and more used for training in various domains, but notably in crisis management [5, 8]. Learners' assessment in SG is a recognized as an important research issue [1, 9] and as in real field training exercise, Game-based crisis management assessment often relies on "human" post game debriefing either based on logs analysis, video or interviews [10]. Moreover, it is difficult to produce a collective assessment in this kind of SG, especially when some global goal is shared by all learners but learning outcomes differ from a learner to another. For example, the works presented in [11, 12], provide a framework for serious games and address the concept of learner's assessment and its importance. However, the learner's assessment is performed manually either by the learner itself (self-assessment) or by human monitors. In [7, 13], the authors show the potential of multi-learners in SG and were inspired by MMO RP Gales (*Massively Multi-player Online Role Playing Game*) for designing SG. Research in [7] points the lack of SG for collaborative learning and try to offer a response with *Escape from Wilson Island*, a SG for learning social skills of collaboration. This work falls within the field of Computer Supported Collaborative Learning, CSCL [14]. Nevertheless, the assessment of the collective performance is not addressed, and focuses on the experience of individual game players (with a survey). In [15], team score is computed as the sum of individual scores, and do not take into account players interactions.

It should be noted that these evaluations consider in most cases homogeneous skills as in a participatory teaching in a class of students: whether in a single learning system or group learning, the course of each participant may vary, but the goal of training is unique even when it incorporates the collective dimension. The issue of assessing both individually and collectively heterogeneous skills is not addressed.

The learner assessment can also be approached from the field of Intelligent Tutoring System (ITS) [16] were Learners' assessment is a major theoretical and experimental challenge. Combining the evaluation of an ITS with a serious gaming opportunities, we can thus improve learning outcomes in SG. Among works in ITS, we can cite HAL, Help Agent for Learning [17], an ITS for training TGV drivers and HERA, Help Agent for Learning [4], a training tools for security management in high risk industrial sites. The learner's monitoring and assessment is discussed but remains individual and the issue of collective assessment is not discussed.

Crisis management is a collaborative process that goes through the implementation of several different tasks (depending on the role of the actor and the context) [15], players have specific educational objectives but share the common goal of managing a crisis. We propose to combine ITS assessment methods to multi-player SG to improve players feedback and thus their learning of collective procedures.

3 How to Improve Assessment in a SG: Illustration with the Simfor SG

SIMFOR (Fig. 1) is a serious game developed by SII company (www.groupe-sii.com) in partnership with Pixxim company (www.pixxim.fr). SIMFOR is a multi-player game training for crisis management by allowing different people to learn skills (shared or specific). Managing a major crisis can mobilize several hundred stake-holders, from the regional Prefect in his office to the firefighter in the field. These stakeholders are required to communicate and work together in order to restore a normal situation. The project objective is to immerse users in a simulated real-time crisis management situation, realistic in terms of environment, self-evolving scenarios and actors (roles). Initially based on a human assessment of the players' skill and simplified NPC (Non-Played Characters), SIMFOR SG can benefit from Distributed Artificial Intelligence by: (i) improving the NPC simulation (complex behaviors and interaction); (ii) guiding the players assessment. Both objectives can be attained with a Multi-Agent Systems (MAS) approach.

Fig. 1. Different game user interfaces of the SIMFOR SG

NPCs are used to adapt the crisis management exercise perimeter to the available stakeholders as well as to specific training objectives. Therefore, SIMFOR is a hetero-geneous collaborative learning SG, where tasks are performed by different actors with a common purpose but each one with specific individual objectives. Thus, SIMFOR must deal with two types of learners' assessment: individual and collective. Solving the crisis requires the resolution of all procedures of the stakeholders, so individual evaluation can affect the collective evaluation, and conversely the collective evaluation can affect the individual evaluation too. For example if a learner has successfully executed his procedures, but the main purpose was not reached (material and human loss for example), the learners must be evaluated on their individual and collective performance to infer the reason of failure (lack of communication, missing procedure of another learner, …). The following sections explain how player's immersion and assessment can be improved.

3.1 Agent Oriented Simulation for Realistic Adaptive NPC

The use of MAS to develop software avatars simulating the behaviour of human players is not new [18]. The interest of the MAS for SG is well known (realistic and adaptive behaviour, modularity, behaviour models understandable by non computer science experts, organisational modelling …) [2], so this section will present briefly how NPC simulation capabilities of the SG has been dealt with. To design our agents, we have adopted a BDI architecture (Beliefs, Desires, Intentions), a classic approach to design agents using deliberative behaviours, giving them a certain ability to adapt through complex behaviours [19]. A design tool has also been developed to facilitate the design of game scenario in terms of behaviours and agent types. The NPC must also be able to interact with other players (human or NPC) and act during a game session, depending on the state of the physical environment (represented by the 3D environment in SIMFOR). We propose an *ad hoc* BDI model as a set of agents, actions and facts. The agent model is:

$$\text{Model}_{(\text{role})} = \{\text{Goal, Plans, Facts, Dialogues}\}. \tag{1}$$

A game agent (GA) seeks to achieve its goals (assets whose preconditions are verified) by activating the appropriate plans based on its knowledge (defined as a declarative list of facts). Each plan consists of actions directed towards the environment or towards other actors producing effects on this environment or sending messages. The concept of *effect* reflects the social actions and physical influence of agents in the environment. The reasoning of the agents includes (implicitly) decisions and actions. In the case of interactions between players (human or not), possible Dialogues are modelled as a tree where nodes are sentences, each having preconditions to be respected and a list of receiver (all roles, list of roles…). This interaction modelling choice is justified by the need to reference each interaction in relation to the behaviour expected in the crisis management procedure learned.

3.2 Multi-criteria and Distributed Assessment: The Evaluation Space Concept

Integrating evaluation in a serious game involves the use of knowledge, information or data produced or processed continuously until the end of the game. Each information requires a specific manipulation (or a reasoning about these knowledge) to extract evaluation. This section develops a modelling contribution which adds learners' assessment capabilities to the SIMFOR SG taking into account the various nature and origin of information elements required to produce these assessments. Each information element requires special handling (or reasoning on this knowledge) in order to produce an assessment. We define here the evaluation space concept, Sect. 4 will instantiate three evaluation spaces, each one constituting a point of view on the learner's assessment.

A natural way to deal with the complexity of this information management (in the broad sense) is to divide and organize this information into homogeneous groups which can have a dedicated primitive to produce an assessment. The evaluation space concept is part of this approach encompassing all the elements needed to produce assessments, considering the game scenario through different views, each corresponding to a particular assessment objective. An evaluation space is defined as:

$$\text{Evaluation Space} = \{\text{Kw, I, M, AM}\}. \tag{2}$$

- *Knowledge representation model* (**Kw**): There is different kind of knowledge (data, facts, procedures, learner model), each based on a specific modelling paradigm (data modelling, rule based, Bayesian networks …). To ensure homogeneity each space has a set of similar knowledge representation language.
- *Indicators* (**I**): An indicator is a quantitative data that characterizes an evolving situation (an action or consequences of an action) in order to evaluate their status. The use of indicators for the learners' assessment is recurrent in SG [9].
- *Metrics* (**M**): The metrics represents the methods and unit of measure used to exploit the knowledge. It can be used to compare expected results following actors' behavior/ decision to their actual doings or to analyze an interaction graph. Thus, the metric quantifies the indicator to compute an assessment.
- *Assessment model* (**AM**): There is different model of assessment, depending on the space and his knowledge representation. The assessment can relate to an action or a procedure or a global assessment. An indicator computation relies on a specific assessment model according to its associated metric.

Thus, an assessment model **AM** can be seen as a utility function (see formula 3) that produces an indicator **I** from a subset of knowledge **Kw** (expressed as a mode of representation) and its associated metric **M**.

$$\text{AM}: \text{Kw} \times \text{M} \rightarrow \text{I}. \tag{3}$$

In the particular case of crisis management, the variety of skills and related knowledge may make difficult the (re)design of a SG. By defining the components of a space evaluation, we seek to guide their characterization independently of the application domain, as well as the identification of skills to be assessed in a serious game. The concept of space and evaluation can facilitate the design process of SG.

4 Applying the Evaluation Spaces to a Crisis Management SG

Adding learners' assessment to SG raises issues in terms of representation, manipulation of knowledge and data acquisition, but also assessment methods (in a mathematical sense). The SIMFOR project presents interesting features by its multi-actors and collaborative nature. Therefore two different kind of assessments are needed, either computed in real time (to show the progress of the player) or at the end of the game:

- *Individual assessment* is a summative assessment that assesses and certifies the learning of the learner at the end of a game scenario.
- *Collective assessment* provides an assessment to the collective performance of the group. It is based on the various communications and interactions between actors (learners and NPC) and thus allows to infer a causal relationship between the missions of the various actors (actor A has failed in its mission because the actor B did not send the correct information to simulated actors).

The overall assessment, which can be determined at the end of a game session, will integrate both individual and collective assessment. Certification of competence or knowledge of the learner can be obtained by aggregation of such assessments. After analyzing the different characteristics of the learners' assessment for crisis management (interactions, behavior, environment) we have defined three different areas of assessment: consequences on the Physical environment, Behavioral and Social abilities. These different *Evaluation Spaces* are described below.

4.1   The Physical Evaluation Space

The *Physical Evaluation Space* represents the view of the SIMFOR virtual environment and allow to assess the learners' outcomes from the virtual environment. The knowledge **(Kw)** in this space is based on the information of the 3D models (avatars, transport means, disaster, vegetation, trees, etc.) as well as the meta data from the geographic information system (GIS) such as building type (commercial, residential, school, etc.), the number of people in a building, etc.

The indicators **(I)** used in this space will be used to produce an assessment of both individual and collective assessment. For example, an avatar moving from point A to point B (individual assessments) requires the starting position, the ending position, and the elapsed time. On the other hand the physical space can also provide indicators for collective evaluation: e.g. human and material losses. This indicator can give an idea about the overall performance of the group.

The metric **(M)** allow to quantify (unit, distance calculation function, etc.) the indicators previously defined. For example, the metric for material losses indicator may be the cost in Euros.

The assessment model specify how the learners' performance is computed (e.g. preferred travel time rather than travel cost). The assessment model is represented by an objective function that includes various indicators (human and material losses, means used, etc.) to compute the learners' performance (score).

4.2   Behavioral Evaluation Space

The *Behavioral Evaluation Space* represents the procedural view of SIMFOR and allows the SG to assess the learners' behaviors related to the crisis management.

The knowledge representation in the behavioral space includes the learners' actions and knowledge as well as the different information on the skills and procedures to learn (corresponding to the learner model and the domain model of an ITS [16]). The knowledge **(Kw)** involved in this space is modeled as a set of actions and missions. Each role (assigned to an actor) is assigned a set missions to perform for a given scenario. A mission is composed of a set of preconditions, a set of previous missions, and finally a set of actions to perform to reach the goal of the mission. Actions are declined in different forms depending on the actions that players can perform in SIMFOR such as *phone action, fax, radio, talk, move* (walking or with a vehicle), and *daybook* (simulate a web blog for disaster monitoring).

Given the heterogeneous nature of the actions, a specific indicator (**I**) is defined for each action, to compute the action efficiency. For assessing learners' missions, we have identified six general indicators (**I**) measuring if a player has acted accordingly to the situation: such as if he has respected the precondition of the mission and the actions sequence, how well and how fast each action has been executed, idle time etc. (see [20] for detail on the indicators computation).

The metrics used in this ES are mainly represented by the time or logical properties as precondition, or scheduling. To have an equal weight between all indicators, the maximum score for each indicator has been standardized as ranging from 0 to 1.

The assessment model **AM** allow to compute the mission score and it is the average of the scores produced by different indicators defined in Table 1. Each SIMFOR action is assigned a specific assessment model (given the heterogeneous aspect of the actions). For example, for the *phone* action, the indicators (I) are the communication time, the target actor and the information exchanged (in case of textual dialogue with a NPC). The action efficiency is the average of these indicators.

Table 1. Actions performed by the actor for the mission Inform the authorities.

Actions	Reference action	Indicator	Score
Phone(duration, target, msg) = (77, officer, {TMD})	Phone(45, officer, {TMD})	ActionPhoneIndicator(stime, target, msg) = (45/77, 1, 1)	0.86
Fax(duration, target, faxName) = (232, officer, information-Sheet)	Fax(120, officer, informationSheet)	ActionFaxIndicator(stime, tatget, faxName) = (120/132, 1, 1)	0.83
Fax(duration, target, faxName) = (13, mayor, information-Sheet)	Fax(120, mayor, informationSheet)	ActionFaxIndicator(stime, tatget, faxName) = (1, 1, 1)	1
...	...	...	...

In order to illustrate the learners' assessment in the behavioral space, we'll take a sequence of game play for an actor and try to analyze the influence of different indicators. Here, the CODIS actor (Departmental Center for Operational Fire and Rescue Services) has received information about the accident from a firefighter on the scene. The CODIS mission is to *inform the authorities* of the TDM accident.

Actions to achieve this mission are described in Table 2. The first column shows the action performed by the learner with the call duration, the target actor, and the messages exchanged. The second column shows the reference action (from the domain model). The third column represents the defined indicator to assess the action *phone*, the score will be an average between the time score (ratio between expected and real duration of the action), a score related to the target actor (0 or 1 if the right actor is contacted), and a score related to the messages exchanged (set of sentences exchanged during the dialogue). The execution time of the last action is low because the learner has sent the same fax to the officer, and only has to retransmit it.

Table 2. Mission assessment: inform the authorities (CODIS)

Indicators	Outcome	Score
Precondition	$Prec = \{TDM\}$	1
Order	$Actions = \{phone, fax, fax, fax, fax\}$	1
Actions count	$Nb\ action = 5,\ nb\ actions\ (expert) = 5$	1
Duration	$Time = 589,\ estimated\ time = 525$	0.7
Idle time	$Idle\ time = 246$	0.03
Actions efficiency	$Action\ efficiency = \{0.86, 0.83, 1, 1, 1\}$	0.93
Mission score		0.77

Table 2, describes how the indicators of the mission and the scores produce the mission assessment. The first indicator is the respect preconditions, the learner (CODIS role) triggered the mission after receiving information *(TDM)* from the firefighter on the scene and thus satisfies the precondition *TDM* and the score is equal to 1. The second and third indicator relates to the sequence of actions the learner has to perform (correct number) and in the correct order (both scores are 1). The execution time of the mission is the fourth indicator. The difference between the duration provided by the expert and the player actions are compared relatively to the duration itself (to differentiate small variations compared to short or long duration). The fifth indicator relates the idle time of the learner, calculated by accumulating the idle time between each action of the mission (inactivity score is 0.03). Idle time has a great influence on the score for crisis management, the learner must not lose time between the executions of each action of the same mission.

The last indicator relates to the actions efficiency, this indicator is calculated by the average of the actions efficiency scores presented in Table 3. The overall score of the mission is the average of six indicators and is equal to 0.77. After (or during) the game, the learner can have information on its performance, and can see that his idle score is low and he was not reactive enough for executing the mission actions.

Table 3. Exercises result from the TDM scenario.

Learners	Exercise 1 -				Exercise 2			
	Individual	*Social*	*Missions*	*Global*	*Individual*	*Social*	*Missions*	*Global*
CODIS	0.817268	0.804907	0.82963		0.85349	0.845879	0.861111	
Mayor	0.943310	0.882632	1		0.957254	0.914508	1	
Prefect	0.755899	0.865317	0.646481		0.763133	0.852076	0.675990	
Sub-Prefect	0.763071	0.88662	0.639522		0.783950	0.889330	0.678570	
Group		0.859869	0.778090	0,65		0.875448	0.803918	0,76
Global				0.762653				0.813122

4.3   The Social Evaluation Space

The *Social Evaluation Space* represents the interaction (simple communication, coordination/cooperation …) between different actors and including the collaborative dimension of learning. The social space is represented by a social graph that describe every interaction between actors and allows to compute an interaction strength between each actor as well as the global coupling of network. Assessment will be based on these measures. In [2], we find considerations on the representation and exploitation of interactions for the learners' assessment. The indicators presented in this space are the network coupling and the strength of interaction between actors and are calculated as in [21]. Short and frequent exchanges (between actors) produce a strong coupling, while long and rare exchanges reflect a weak coupling. This indicator will determine if the actor has interacted with the right actors.

The Knowledge (**Kw**) modeled in this space is represented by a set of interactions, wherein each interaction is characterized by:

- Actor at the origin of the interaction.
- Actor target of the interaction.
- Interaction type (phone, fax, radio, …).
- Interaction date.
- Interaction duration.

Indicators in the social space are based on the network coupling. The interactions between the actors enable us to compute the network coupling like the interaction network in [22], but taking into account specific considerations to the field of risk management and more particularly the study of interactions between firefighters in operation [23]. The metric used to compute the network coupling are based on the number of interactions and their duration, and the time between each interaction. From the coupling between actors, we compare the coupling of the exercise and the coupling provided by the domain expert (calculated on the domain model). If the coupling is weak between A and B whereas strong in the reference graph, it means that there was a lack of communication between A and B during the exercise.

Figure 2 shows an example of a network coupling of SIMFOR exercise. In graph (a), the maximum coupling is obtained by the relationship between the prefect and sub-prefect. In graph (c), the interaction between the prefect and the mayor is red (dashed line), showing thus a negative difference (the coupling during exercise between the two actors is lower than the reference coupling revealing a lack of communication). The interaction between CODIS and fireman is blue (dotted line), showing a positive difference (coupling during exercise between the two actors is greater than the reference coupling i.e. surplus of communication). Thus, by computing the network coupling, we can address the individual assessment of an actor in his relationship with others (comparing interactions between actors) and the collective assessment (through the global network coupling) by comparing the result of the exercise with the coupling provided by the expert (extracted from the domain model).

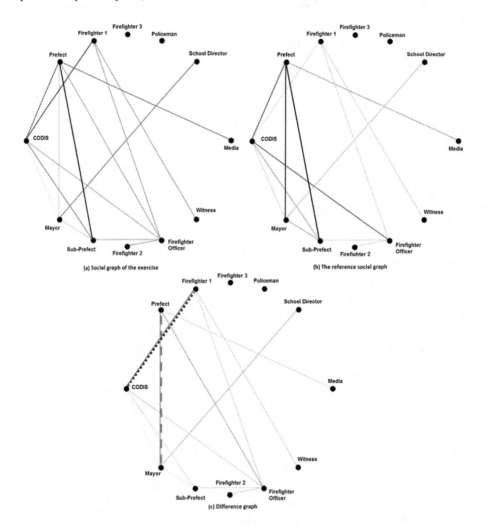

Fig. 2. An example of the network coupling for a SIMFOR exercise. The graph (a) shows the interaction force of the group during the exercise (a black color correspond to the maximum coupling). The graph (b) shows the reference graph computed from the domain model defined by the expert. The graph (c) shows the difference (b-a) between the graph (a) and the graph (b). Thicker lines indicate strong coupling and conversely thin lines low coupling (Color figure online).

5   Implementation and First Experiments

This section introduces the general architecture of our system and presents some preliminary experiments results.

5.1   General Architecture

The SIMFOR architecture combines elements from the Intelligent Tutoring System and Serious Game domains (Fig. 3). Our goal is to associate the playful learning of SG and the different modules of an ITS (domain model, learner model, pedagogical model) to get the optimal learning environment. The SIMFOR architecture is composed of the following components:

- **The SG module (SIMFOR):** this module includes the 3D models, user interface (as a communication channel between the learner and the system), simulation module (for natural phenomena such as fire propagation), and data models. This module constitutes the former "perimeter" of the SIMFOR SG to which behaviour simulation and user assessment capabilities are added.
- **The Behaviours Simulation module:** allows simulating humans' behaviours to replace absent players with "artificial" actors (Game Agent).
- **The Evaluation module:** the evaluation module provides skills assessment of players in real time to the pedagogical module.
- **The Pedagogical module:** which plays the role of a virtual tutor accompanying the learners by providing support and help during (and after) their training.
- **Knowledge representation module:** All knowledge used or produced by the previous modules of our proposed architecture are stored as an ontology in the domain model and the learner model. The ontology describe the general domain of crisis management (adapted to the SIMFOR context). The *Domain model* represents the general concepts of crisis management and is segmented into parts representing a role or a skill to learn. For each learner or agent, a *Learner Model* is associated, which represents its mental state at a time t.

The SIMFOR SG and its additional modules has been developed in C++ with QT interfaces. The evaluation module is based on agents Detail on the multi-agent architecture is described in [20]. Briefly, These agents collect learners' data, process and evaluate learners data and provide support to learners. They also simulate actors by acting in the 3D environment and exchanging messages with other actors.

5.2   Experimental Result

In this section we present an example of crisis management scenario, the case of a Transport of Dangerous Materials (TDM) scenario which is interesting as it involves several roles such as fire-fighters, police, mayor, prefect … Moreover, the TDM scenario may evolve into an environmental pollution scenario (chemicals leakage), or large fire disaster (flammable products), if badly handled.

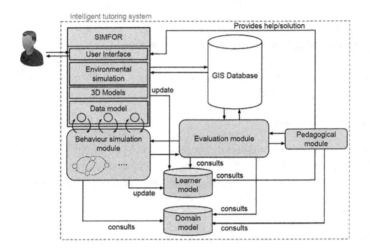

Fig. 3. The general architecture of SIMFOR

The TDM scenario was developed with the help of a crisis management expert and aims to sensitize the stakeholders to the different consequences that may result from a TDM accident. The scenario begins with a TDM truck overturned after a traffic accident on a roundabout in the outskirts of Arles (city in south of France), close to a school, the Rhone river and a railway. The tank is damaged and hydrocarbon spills on the road. A witness to the accident gave the alert. The domain expert defines beforehand (via the domain model editor) the missions related to each role as well as the exercise scripting (via scripts that can trigger events under certain conditions).

To start the exercise, we must first run a SIMFOR server with the selected scenario exercise. Once the server is launched, players connect to the server, either by internet or local network (for our tests, the exercise was a local network but learners were in different rooms). Once all learners are connected the exercise starts. In our first experiment, four learners and seven NPC are engaged in the TDM exercise.

The TDM scenario begins with the CODIS sending a fireman at the accident scene to interrogate the witness and gather information about the accident. Once the information confirms a TDM accident, the CODIS warns an officer (fireman) and drafts an information sheet on the incident and sends it by fax to the officer, the mayor, prefect and sub-prefect. The officer, for his part, must send a second fireman on the disaster scene with a Water-tender vehicles and gives first step instructions to the fireman in scene. Once the information sheet received, the prefect must discuss with the sub-prefect to agree on the location of the forward command post (FCP) and triggers ORSEC plan (filled and distributed via fax by the prefect). The civil security advise their actions through the daybook tool after each major action. The sub-prefect is responsible thereafter to inform the CODIS and the police of the FCP place before he goes, and discuss with the mayor to identify the potential risks around the disaster (school evacuation, area risk, etc.). The officer uses the FCP truck to go to the FCP place and engage in a debriefing with the fireman on the progress of the situation and reports it to the sub-prefect at FCP. Depending on the severity of the situation (pollution, hydrocarbon fire), the sub-prefect broadcasts a press communication to the media and requests an additional resources if needed. If the situation requires, the sub-prefect should contact the mayor to evacuate nearest building of the disaster such as the school. Once the disaster controlled, the prefect sends a prefectural order (decree), to call the end the ORSEC plan, to the CODIS, mayor and policeman.

All evaluation results and the learners' feedback are saved in a XML file containing for each learner:

- List of performed actions.
- Assessment result for each action performed.
- The history feedback of the learner.
- The assessment of each mission completed.
- The social and the final score of the learner.

In addition to individual assessments, the resulting file contains the history of all interactions between the different actors, which allows as to compute the interaction strength (network coupling), the difference graph and social score to produce a global and collective assessment (with the integration of other global indicators depending on the scenario exercise). Additionally, the result file provides also other indicators purely observable such as the global coupling history (we can deduce the key moments of the scenario exercise due to spikes in the coupling graph), or the actions sequence on the time scale.

This experiment aimed to (i) check the automatic assessment relevancy and (ii) to evaluate the learners' progress using the SIMFOR SG. To assess the first point, learners receive question forms related to the scenario exercise in order to compare these results to the automatic assessment provided by SIMOR. For the second point, we have performed two exercises and compared the learners' performance evolution between the exercises. The scores obtained are exposed in Table 3.

The exercise results in Table 3 show that all learners have improved their perform-ance between the two exercises. For each exercise, the first column contains the players' final individual score as the average of their individual behavioural scores (i.e. how well they have executed their mission) and social. The "group" row lists the collective (as a group) social score (average of all individual social scores), behavioural score (average individual behavioural/mission score), and physical score. The collective physical score is related to the area finally affected by the disaster which grows up until the disaster is controlled (fire propagation simulation). The last row gives the general performance of the group. All scores computed are normalized to the interval [0, 1] (actions, missions, social, physic, individual and collective).

Table 4 presents the players' score resulting from their answers to the question form (with specific questions related to their role). The forms' scores are coherent with the automatic assessment: all learners have improved their performance, and the consistency of the automatic assessment compared to the forms results is confirmed except for the prefect and the sub-prefect due to many and long procedures to do introducing some noise in the assessment (additional actions, delay, ...), but combining the missions score with the social score refines the automatic assessment.

Table 4. Forms results from the TDM scenario.

Learners	Exercise 1		Exercise 2	
	Forms responses	*Mission & Individual scores*	*Forms responses*	*Mission & Individual scores*
CODIS	60%	0.82963 - 0.817268	91%	0.861111 - 0.853495
Mayor	100%	1 - 0.943310	100%	1 - 0.957254
Prefect	81%	0.646481 - 0.755899	81%	0.675990 - 0.763133
Sub-prefect	75%	0.639522 - 0.763071	87%	0.678570 - 0.783950

6   Conclusion

With the growing interest of serious games for training, the issue of learners' assessment is increasingly crucial. This paper has presented how to improve NPC simulation and players assessment in a Crisis Management SG with an adapted BDI model and the Evaluation Space framework. Assessment is realized through a multi-criteria (evaluation of different trades and skills) and distributed (via dedicated evaluation spaces) assessment system supported by a multi-agent system. The new SIMFOR SG has been implemented and tested on a realistic TDM scenario, but more extensive on-field experimentation is required for complete validation.

Future work may consider adding emotional factors in the NCP behaviour (simulating panic) which can simulate time/stress constraints to the players facing such behaviours. Collective assessment is promising and deserves more investigation. The Evaluation Space concept allows quantitative evaluation of the interactions, but can be extended to qualitative interaction by analysing the content of the interaction (and not only who and when), but would not call into question the present framework as only new low level agents is required, confirming the relevancy of our approach.

References

1. Nieborg, D.: America's Army: More than a game. Transforming Knowledge into Action through Gaming and Simulation, SAGSAGA (2004)
2. Mathieu, P., Panzoli, D., Picault, S.: Virtual customers in a multiagent training application. In: Pan, Z., Cheok, A.D., Müller, W., Liarokapis, F. (eds.) Transactions on Edutainment IX. LNCS, vol. 7544, pp. 97–114. Springer, Heidelberg (2013)
3. Haferkamp, N., Kraemer, N.C., Linehan, C., Schembri, M.: Training disaster communication by means of serious games in virtual environments. Entertainment Comput. **2**, 81–88 (2011)
4. Amokrane, K., Lourdeaux, D., Burkhardt, J.M.: Hera: learner tracking in a virtual environment. IJVR **7**(3), 23–30 (2008)
5. Di Loreto, I., Divitini, M.: Games for learning cooperation at work: the case of crisis preparedness. In: ECTEL-meets-ECSCW, pp. 20–24 (2013)
6. Buche, C., Querrec, R., De Loor, P., Chevaillier, P.: Mascaret: pedagogical multi-agents systems for virtual environment for training. In: International Conference on Cyberworlds, pp. 423–430 (2003)
7. Wendel V., Gutjahr, M., Göbel S., Steinmetz, R.: Designing collaborative multiplayer serious games for collaborative learning. In: Proceedings of the CSEDU (2012)
8. GALA Consortium: Learning Analytics for SGs, Deliverable 2.4. Technical report (2014)

9. Thomas, P., Labat, J.-M., Muratet, M., Yessad, A.: How to evaluate competencies in game-based learning systems automatically? In: Cerri, S.A., Clancey, W.J., Papadourakis, G., Panourgia, K. (eds.) ITS 2012. LNCS, vol. 7315, pp. 168–173. Springer, Heidelberg (2012)
10. van Ruijven, T., Mayer, I., de Bruijne, M.: Multidisciplinary coordination of on scene command teams in virtual emergency exercises. IJCIP **9**, 13–23 (2015). Elsevier
11. De Freitas S., Jarvis S.: A framework for developing serious games to meet learner needs. In: The Interservice/Industry Training, Simulation & Education Conference. NTSA (2006)
12. Yusoff, A., Crowder, R., Gilbert, L., Wills, G.: A conceptual framework for serious games. In: 9th Conference on Advanced Learning Technologies, ICALT 2009. IEEE (2009)
13. Raybourn, E.-M.: Adaptive thinking and leadership training for cultural awareness and communication competence. Interact. Technol. Smart Educ. **2**(2), 131–134 (2005)
14. Stahl, G., Koschmann, T., Suthers, D.: Computer-supported collaborative learning: An historical perspective. In: Sawyer, R.K. (ed.) Cambridge Handbook of the Learning Sciences. Cambridge University Press, Cambridge (2006)
15. Oliveira, V., Coelhoa, A., Guimarães, R., Rebelo, C.: Serious game in security: a solution for security trainees. In: VS-GAMES 2012 (2012)
16. Burns, H., Capps, C.: Foundations of intelligent tutoring systems : an introduction. In: Polson, M.C., Richardson, J.J. (eds.) Foundations of intelligent tutoring systems, pp. 1–18. Lawrence Erlbaum Associates, Hillsdale (1989)
17. Lourdeaux, D., Burkhardt, J.M., Bernard, F., Fuchs, P.: Relevance of an intelligent agent for virtual reality training. Int. J. Continuous Eng. Life-long Learn. **12**(1/2/3/4), 131–143 (2002)
18. Chang, P.H.-M., Chen, K.-T., Chien, Y.-H., Kao, E.C.-C., Soo, V.-W.: From reality to mind: a cognitive middle layer of environment concepts for believable agents. In: Weyns, D., Van Dyke Parunak, H., Michel, F. (eds.) E4MAS 2004. LNCS (LNAI), vol. 3374, pp. 57–73. Springer, Heidelberg (2005)
19. Rao, A., Georgeff, M.-P.: BDI agents: from theory to practice. In: ICMAS 1995 (1995)
20. Oulhaci, A., Tranvouez, E., Fournier, S., Espinasse, B.: A multi-agent system for learner assessment in serious games: application to learning processes in crisis management. In: Seventh IEEE International Conference on Research Challenges in Information Science, Paris (2013)
21. Miller, J.-G.: Living Systems. Mcgraw-Hill, New York (1978)
22. Kay, J., Maisonneuve, N., Yacef, K., Reimann, P.: The big five and visualisations of team work activity. In: Ikeda, M., Ashley, K.D., Chan, T.-W. (eds.) ITS 2006. LNCS, vol. 4053, pp. 197–206. Springer, Heidelberg (2006)
23. Baumard, P., Vidal, R.: Fiabiliser la gestion des feux de très grande ampleur - enhancing reliability in large scale willand fire response organization. Ministère de l'écologie, de l'énergie, du développement durable et de la mer. Technical report (2009)

Information and Knowledge Management

Assessing Distributed Situation Awareness in Socio-Technical Systems with RiskSOAP

Maria Mikela Chatzimichailidou[(⊠)] and Ioannis M. Dokas

Department of Civil Engineering, Democritus University of Thrace,
Vassilissis Sofias 12, 67100 Xanthi, Greece
{mikechat, idokas}@civil.duth.gr

Abstract. This research work introduces the Risk Situation Awareness Provision (RiskSOAP) methodology. The concept of 'risk SA provision' reflects the inherent, according to the system design and development, capability of each system part to provide its agent with SA about the presence of system threats and vulnerabilities, possibly leading to accidents. The RiskSOAP methodology is accompanied by its corresponding indicator, which is used to measure the capability of a complex socio-technical system to provide its agents with Situation Awareness (SA) about the presence of its threats and vulnerabilities. The RiskSOAP indicator also enables analysts to assess Distributed SA (DSA). RiskSOAP is applied to the socio-technical system involved in the Überlingen mid-air collision accident as a demonstration of how to apply the methodology and calculate the corresponding indicator.

Keywords: Dissimilarity measures · Distributed situation awareness · EWaSAP · Safety · STPA · RiskSOAP

1 Introduction

In the literature there is a plethora of definitions for SA. One widely cited definition proposes SA as a state of working knowledge of an individual; it is how much and how accurately he/she is aware of the current situation and concerns (1) the perception of the elements within a system, (2) the comprehension of their meaning, and (3) the projection of their future state [1] The number of proposed definitions is analogous to the models which explain the different types of SA, including: the individual SA model [1], the team and shared SA models [2, 3], the meta [4], compatible [3], and collective [5] SA models, and the most complex one, the DSA model [6]. DSA implies that no one system agent, namely humans and automated controllers within a system has a complete picture of the situation in which the system finds itself, but just a facet of the corresponding situation at any point in time [4].

So far, the only reported DSA-focused method is the Event Analysis of Systemic Teamwork (EAST) [7]. It makes use of three networks, i.e. task, social, and information ones, that describe the relationships between tasks, their sequence and interdependencies, the organisation of the system and the communications between agents, along with the information that these agents use and communicate [7]. However, EAST is not a DSA measurement technique, but finally offers a depiction of information flow

© Springer International Publishing Switzerland 2015
N. Bellamine Ben Saoud et al. (Eds.): ISCRAM-med 2015, LNBIP 233, pp. 103–115, 2015.
DOI: 10.1007/978-3-319-24399-3_9

between the interacting human and nonhuman agents [8]. It is a stepwise description and guidance for studying and depicting agents and networks of agents involved in the acquisition and maintenance of DSA through information processing and assessment. The outcome of this method is qualitative and it mostly bears a resemblance to semantic networks [8].

The RiskSOAP methodology embraces a different perspective, compared to any other SA measurement technique that carries at least one of the *Seven Issues on DSA* [8], as recorded in the literature. According to those seven issues, complex socio-technical systems require more holistic reasoning and targeted approaches that the existing ones that focus either on individuals or on teams of individuals [8]. Overall, compared to RiskSOAP, no other, reported so far, SA measurement technique, gives a quantitative expression to the risk SA provision capability (for more see [8, 9]).

Turning to the subject of '*risk SA provision*', it reflects the inherent, according to the system design and development, capability of each system part to provide its agent with SA about the presence of system threats and vulnerabilities, possibly leading to accidents. In short, this capability stems from the number, type, and characteristics of each one of the system elements that together shape the different parts of it, laying thus the foundation for the emergence of risk DSA [9]. As a result, all or some parts of a socio-technical system can be designed and developed with more or less enhanced risk SA provision capabilities, integrating or leaving out elements, such as sensors capable of detecting more threats and vulnerabilities as well as agents whose mental or process models sufficiently represent possible accident scenarios etc.

The RiskSOAP methodology is applied to the Überlingen mid-air collision accident in order to demonstrate how to take the steps of the methodology and finally calculate the value of the corresponding indicator as an assessment of the system's DSA. Using the Überlingen accident, this paper also provides evidence that the risk SA provision capability is dynamic by nature in a manner that it varies according to the design specifications of each complex socio-technical system [9].

However, the main contribution of this paper is not the use case, but the RiskSOAP methodology for assessing DSA regarding safety issues. Given that systems consist of specifications and components possible to be mapped, RiskSOAP demonstrates the feasibility of measuring to what extent systems' elements contribute to the emergence of DSA.

2   The RiskSOAP Methodology

The methodology is grounded on two pivotal assumptions:

Assumption 1. The awareness of threats and vulnerabilities (i.e. the risk SA) enhances safety. This assumption accords to the works of [10, 11] supporting the positive correlation between safety and awareness.

Assumption 2. An 'ideal', in terms of the risk SA provision capability and risk DSA, system design could derive from hazard analyses, because they help designers gather essential system elements and characteristics that ideally should be included into the system design, serving to enhance its preparedness against accidents.

Grounded on these two assumptions, the methodology goes through three stages: (1) in terms of the system perceiving its threats and vulnerabilities, define the 'ideal'[1] or otherwise the 'to-be' image[2] of the system using a comprehensive hazard analysis and early warning sign identification techniques, (2) identify the real or otherwise the 'as-is' one, (3) employ a comparative strategy aiming to depict the distance between the two images of the system and interpret the distance value, obtained by the introduced indicator, on the basis of risk DSA. The phases of the RiskSOAP methodology are presented in Table 1.

Table 1. The RiskSOAP phases and steps.

Phase 1↓	Step 1.1. perform the STPA hazard analysis
	Step 1.2: carry out the EWaSAP approach
Phase 2↓	Step 2.1: create the ideal system vector
	Step 2.2: create the real system vector
Phase 3	Step 3: apply Rogers-Tanimoto dissimilarity measure

Existing approaches (from unrelated to each other research fields) are utilized to fulfill the objectives of the 1st and the 3rd Phase of the methodology. The methods used by RiskSOAP are: (1) the STAMP Based Process Analysis (STPA) [12] and (2) the Early Warning Sign Analysis based on the STPA (EWaSAP) approach [13], which both define the elements and the characteristics that should be included in the ideal image of the system, and (3) a binary dissimilarity measure to depict the distance between the ideal and the real system image.

Nevertheless, the researcher can use any other hazard analysis, early warning sign identification approach, or dissimilarity/similarity measure he/she prefers.

2.1 STPA and EWaSAP

Leveson's Systems-Theoretic Accident Model and Processes (STAMP) [12] advocates that accidents involve a complex, dynamic process, meaning that they are not simply chains of component failure events. Safety is treated as a dynamic control problem, rather than a component reliability problem. It is also an emergent property that arises when system components interact with each other within a larger environment. While encapsulating the STAMP principles, STPA is a top-down hazard analysis technique that generates high-level safety requirements and constraints. Compared to traditional hazard analysis techniques, e.g. fault and event tree analyses, STPA identifies not only detectable events, such as technical failures or human errors, but also inadequate control actions and scenarios or paths to accidents. It does not generate a probability

---

[1] No methodology can perfectly fit all purposes or cover all aspects of a complex socio-technical system. However, an approximation of its behaviour and components can be based on systems theoretic hazard analysis techniques and early warning sign identification approaches.

[2] The word 'image' was intentionally chosen, since the methodology is inspired by pattern matching; a comparison between a target image template and a query image.

number related to a hazard, since the only way to generate such a probability of an accident for complex systems is to omit important causal factors that are not stochastic or for which probabilistic information does not exist [12].

EWaSAP extents STPA by adding extra steps to guide analysts in identifying those perceivable signs, which indicate the presence of flaws and the violations of designing assumptions during the operations phase of a system [13]. EWaSAP introduces an additional type of control action, the awareness action. An awareness control action allows a controller to provide warning messages and alerts to other controllers inside or outside the system boundaries, whenever data indicating the presence of threats or vulnerabilities is perceived and comprehended. Table 2 shows the sequence of executing the STPA and the EWaSAP steps as one process.

2.2 Dissimilarity Measures

In the literature, there are plenty of distance/dissimilarity measures, which detect the mismatching bits of two binary data sets. The selection of the proper dissimilarity measure is customised to the assumptions made by the investigator during a specific problem statement. In this paper, Rogers-Tanimoto is chosen, on the basis that it is the only Boolean metric that gives weight to the dissimilarities between two compared vectors by multiplying them by two, i.e. '2*S10', '2*S01'. Its formula is [14]:

$$RTd(i, r) = \frac{2S10 + 2S01}{S11 + S00 + 2S10 + 2S01} \tag{1}$$

The terms: 'S00', 'S01', 'S10', 'S11' denote the total number of the corresponding (0,0), (0,1), (1,0), and (1,1) pairs of binary integers, of the two compared vectors. Figure 1 conveys that in order for vectors to be compared they have to have the same number of rows; the number of rows for both vectors on Fig. 1 is 5. There is therefore a one-by-one relationship between the binary integers that shape a specific pair.

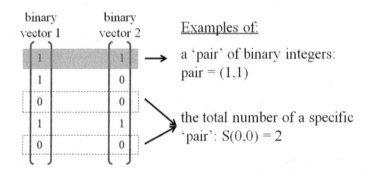

Fig. 1. A graphical explanation of the 'pairs' and 'totals' for the dissimilarity measures.

Table 2. The STPA and EWaSAP steps.

STPA steps and description	EWaSAP steps and description
STPA(1): Identify system hazards & translate them into top-level safety constraints	
	EW(1): Decide if there is anyone outside the system who needs to be informed about the perceived progress of the hazard or about its occurrence
STPA(2a): Create control structure	
STPA(2b): For each controller in the control structure identify its unsafe control actions	
STPA(2c): Restate the inadequate control actions as safety constraints/requirements	
	EW(2): Aim: Identify useful sensory services (i.e. video surveillance cameras pointing) installed in or possessed by systems outside of the system in focus and establish synergy
	EW(2a): For each top level safety constraint identify those signs which indicate its violation
	EW(2b): Find those systems in the surrounding environment with sensors capable of perceiving the signs defined in EW(2a) & request to establish synergy
STPA(3a): For each controller in the control structure create a model of the process it controls	
STPA(3b): Examine the parts of the control loops to determine if they can contribute to or cause system level hazards	
	EW(3): Aim: Enforce Internal Awareness Actions
	EW(3a): Describe what needs to be monitored & what type of features/capabilities the sensors must have so that to make the appropriate controllers capable of perceiving: - the signs indicating the occurrence of the flaw - the violation of the assumptions made during the design of the system
	EW(3b): After design trade-offs and selection of sensors, define which patterns of perceived data indicate the occurrence

(Continued)

Table 2. (*Continued*)

STPA steps and description	EWaSAP steps and description
	of the flaw and/or the violation of its designing assumptions
	EW(3c): Update the process models of the controllers with appropriate awareness and control actions, which should be enforced based on the perceived early warning signs, so that to warn about, adapt to, or eliminate the causal factor to the loss which is present in the system
	EW(3d): For each perceived warning sign, define its meta-data/attribute values to ensure that it will be perceived and ultimately understood by the appropriate controller/s
STPA(4): Restate any flaws identified as safety constraints & repeat STPA(3a) & STPA(3b)	

Some facts about dissimilarity measures are the following: (a) The minimum dissimilarity is '0'; when the dissimilarity of two binary vectors tends to '1', then the vectors are almost dissimilar. (b) All variables are brought into a common scale, between '0' and '1', i.e. they are normalised. (c) Distance can be defined as a dual of a similarity measure $d(i,r) = 1 - s(i,r)$; a similarity can be expressed as the complementary of the corresponding dissimilarity, and vice versa.

3   The Überlingen Mid-Air Collision Accident

In this accident two aircraft (i.e. Flight 2937 and Flight 611) controlled from Zurich were on a collision course. Normally, two ATCs handle the airspace, but because of low arrival traffic at the airport that night, the one of them was on a break and the other was monitoring simultaneously two display consoles, separated by over a meter. The main radar system was functioning in fallback mode overnight, without visual but with aural Short Term Conflict Alert (STCA) warning system, meaning that the ATC had to use a slower system. Additionally, on the night of the accident the main telephone system that enables ATCs to communicate with one another was out for maintenance and the back-up system had a software failure, which no one in the company had noticed. Under these circumstances, the only ATC on duty did not realise the problem in time, and thus failed to keep the two aircraft at a safe distance from each other [15]. Only less than a minute before the accident did the ATC realise the danger and contacted Flight 2937, instructing the pilots to descend in order to avoid the collision. The TCAS on Flight 2937 instructed the pilots to climb, and the TCAS on Flight 611 instructed the pilots to descend. Flight 611 initially followed the TCAS advisory and initiated a descent, but they could not immediately inform the ATC, due to the fact that he was dealing with Flight 2937. However, Flight 2937 disregarded the TCAS advisory to climb, and instead began to descend, as instructed by the ATC, thus both airplanes were now descending. Unaware of the TCAS-issued alerts, the ATC repeated his instruction to Flight 2937 to descend, giving the crews incorrect information as to their relative position.

As regards the causes of the accident, official accident reports [16, 17] involve both (a) technical and (b) organisational deficiencies. Referring to the technical ones, the German Federal Bureau of Aircraft Accident Investigation (BFU) [16] puts emphasis on the operation of the radar system in fallback mode. This degradation of the radar services induced more "system degradations" and "unusual situations" [16]: (1) no automatic correlation of the flight targets was possible and the optical STCA was not displayed, (b) the direct phone connections with the adjacent ATC units were not available to the ATC in Zurich, thus the calls from adjacent ATCs were registered but not answered. Besides, the written directives concerning the accomplishment of the work did not include explanations about the effects that the fallback mode would have on the availability of technical equipment [16]. With reference to the TCAS, BFU [16] argues that it normally contributes to the awareness of the crew, however, in the case of Überlingen it finally contributed to the accident because the regulations concerning TCAS were not standardised, but incomplete and partially contradictory. Finally, due to no automatic TCAS downlink in place, carrying information about the issued advisories to the ATCs, radio delays and loss of information were possible to occur [18]. Referring to organisational issues, in the BFU [16, p.84] accident investigation report is stated that: "at the conscious level humans have limited attention resources. When these limited resources are time-shared between multiple demanding tasks, as in the case of the controller, the continuous detailed analysis of all incoming external information is not possible". This practically means that the single man operation deteriorated the ATC's workload and reduced his ability to maintain an awareness of the situation in a timely manner. Under the same notion, Wong [18] regards information sharing among team members as a variable that positively affects controller's SA. Referring again to the ATC, Johnson [17, p.9] points out that "it is difficult to determine what might have made him aware of the potential conflict...it seems much more of a coincidence that the controller responded". This gives rise to the implication that there was no official mechanism for making the ATC aware of the situation in the airspace.

4   Applying RiskSOAP to the Überlingen Accident

As illustrated in Table 1, the RiskSOAP methodology consists of three phases. In Phase 1 and while considering that there are no limitations regarding the available resources, the STPA hazard analysis (Step 1.1) establishes safety constraints/requirements to define the ideal image of the system. Similarly, internal sensory services to capture early warning signs are determined by the EWaSAP approach in Step 1.2.

Based on the above findings, in Phase 2 one can create the ideal system vector (Step 2.1) consisting of qualitative values, i.e. safety requirements and sensory services.

Similarity, the real system vector is built (Step 2.2) by tabulating all elements that exist in the real system, as it is designed, and those that, according to Phase 1, should ideally be incorporated into the design, but they may be either present or absent. Then, all elements of both vectors have to be translated into quantitative ones, i.e. take binary values. These two vectors are the input to the dissimilarity measure.

In Phase 3, Step 3, Rogers-Tanimoto (Eq. 1) is chosen as a dissimilarity measure for comparing the two vectors. Thus, the 'S00', 'S01', 'S10', and 'S11' terms on Eq. 1 have to be substituted so as to calculate the value of the indicator. The obtained value express the inherent capability of the system to provide its agents with risk SA provision. Relying on the measurement of this capability, one can determine the degree to which system's risk DSA can be further enhanced.

4.1   Results

In this example, STPA was applied first, followed by EWaSAP. Beginning with the steps of the STPA hazard analysis, in STPA (1) the accident/losses, hazard(s), and system level safety constraints were defined:

Accident/losses definition: Loss of human life due to aircraft collision

Hazard: A pair of controlled aircraft violate minimum separation standards

System level safety constraint: The ATC must provide: (a) advisories that maintain safe separation between aircraft and (b) conflict alerts

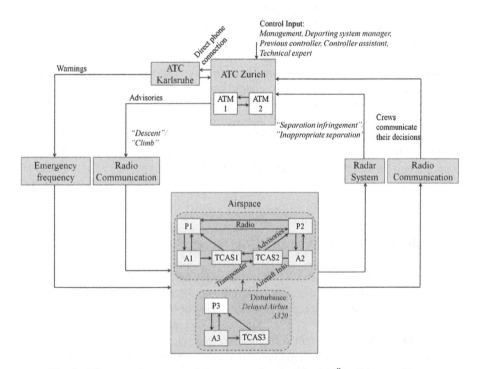

Fig. 2. The control structure of the systems involved in the Überlingen accident.

Table 3. Indicative results from the first phase of the RiskSOAP methodology.

System elements	STPA & EWaSAP	Original system
Safety requirements		
ATC Zurich		
1. When STCA is working in fallback mode the acoustical warning should be switched on at the beginning of the night shift	1	1
ATC Karlsruhe		
2. The Bypass System should be always available to the ATC, or in cases where it is out of service the ATC should be informed	1	0
Crews		
3. Time to comply with new safety policy requirements should be given to the officers	1	0
TCAS		
4. There should be a downlink in place to pass the TCAS advisories to the ATC	1	0
Sensor characteristics		
ATC Zurich		
5. Should be aware whether the radar system is working in fallback mode	1	1
ATC Karlsruhe		
6. Should be aware how long the Bypass System is out of order	1	0
Crews		
7. Should read the training hours of the pilots in unique situations	1	1
TCAS		
8. Should see the position of the TCAS/which modes are available	1	1
Mental models and Control algorithms		
ATC Zurich		
9. If "horizontal separation (from radar returns) $\leq$ 5 NM ($\approx$ 9 km)" OR "vertical separation $\leq$ 1000 ft ($\approx$ 300 metres)" Then "separate converging components: climb/descent to z FL (i.e. Flight Level)"	1	1
ATC Karlsruhe		
10. If "altered by his STCA of conflict situation" Then "warn the adjacent ATC by phone" If "warning not received by the adjacent ATC" Then "try again" Else "select international emergency frequency to contact crews"	1	0

In STPA(2a) the safety control structure of the Überlingen case was created, as depicted in Fig. 2.

ATC Zurich is the main controller of the two, directly involved in the accident, aircraft. He also communicates, and in case of emergency is aided by, with an adjacent but external controller; the ATC Karlsruhe. The former issues commands to the aircraft (here, three aircraft are controlled) via radio communications (see Fig. 2, left side). Again, in case of emergency, the latter can use international frequencies to reach the crews, although they are not under his control. Data from what is happening within the airspace controlled by the ATC Zurich is passed to him through the radio and radar system (see Fig. 2, right side).

The total number of safety requirements and sensor characteristics was 279; 119 safety requirements and 152 sensor characteristics were obtained by taking the STPA and EWaSAP steps respectively. Furthermore, 8 mental models and control algorithms were the output of the combination of the responsibilities and the safety constraints that each of the controllers of the system involved in the Überlingen accident should possess. Some indicative results are given in Table 3.

Every component of the 279-sized vector that came up from STPA and EWaSAP was equal to '1' because it reflected the ideal system design version. For the original design version, as it was involved in the accident, the elements detected by STPA and EWaSAP being absent from the systems were assigned the value '0', while the rest of them were given the value '1'.

Given the above binary values (along with those not included in the paper in hand due to space limitations), the Rogers-Tanimoto dissimilarity measure was calculated. The precise values are given in Table 4.

Table 4. Overall numerical results for the Überlingen accident.

System elements	STPA & EWaSAP (ideal)	Original system (real)
present:	279	74
Absent:	–	205
Vectors' length:	279	279
RiskSOAP indicator: $RTd(i,r)=$		$=2*205 + 2*0/74 + 0 + 2*205 +2*0$ $=0.8471$

As depicted in Table 4, from the 279 system elements identified by STPA and EWaSAP, the number of present system elements in the original system were 74; 205 were the absent ones. The number of 279 total system elements signify the length of the two combined vectors.

The RiskSOAP indicator value obtained after comparing the ideal system vector to the original one was 0.8471. This value is the measurement of the risk SA provision capability and constitutes an assessment of DSA for the Überlingen case. As an example, the value derived from the RiskSOAP indicator implies that the ATC Zurich may not to be able to perceive and prevent a hazard identified by STPA. If one recalls the conditions under which the Überlingen accident occurred, due to the STCA working in fallback mode, the ATC Zurich was not able to comprehend the two aircraft being in collision trajectory, at least not in time. This restricted operation of the STCA system (among others) is implied by the calculated RiskSOAP value. If the STCA working in fallback mode is to be remedied, then the betterment of that available information service will be depicted by the betterment of the indicator value.

5 Discussion and Conclusion

Aiming to provide a natural explanation of the value of the RiskSOAP indicator, if all 205 absent system element (see Table 3) are approved by the designers of the original system and finally implemented, then the value of the RiskSOAP indicator will turn to '0'. Zero distance corresponds to zero deficiencies and means that the system is fully self-aware of the threats and vulnerabilities that can be detected by STPA and EWa-SAP. It also implies that the system with the above modified composition has full possession of the risk SA provision capability and its risk DSA is expected to emerge in a greater extent, compared to the system composition as it was involved in the Überlingen accident.

In practice, since ideal system design versions are almost a utopia due to trade-offs, the designers of the system under investigation can set a threshold value for a satisfactory RiskSOAP indicator to determine the modifications that will best suit real-life conditions. Their decision will be probably based on the available resources, i.e. time, budget, available technology, and human operators. If, for example, the threshold is subjectively set at 0.5, the aim will be to obtain an indicator value lower than, or at least equal to, 0.5. Roughly meaning that the secondary aim is to decrease the distance by 0.3471. Simply put, because the value of 0.8471 exceeds the threshold set by the designers, this illustrates that no satisfactory level of risk SA provision capability has yet been reached. This entails an analogous assessment of risk DSA which, according to the original design composition and the designers of the system, can be further enhanced.

To conclude, this paper presented the RiskSOAP methodology accompanied by its corresponding indicator, aiming to facilitate the measurement of a system's risk SA provision capability and the assessment of its risk DSA. RiskSOAP is based on a verified hazard analysis leading to safety requirements and is also applicable in dynamic systems. Namely, it is easy to readjust the compared units, e.g. parts, subsystems, systems, by improving their design requirements and then recalculate their dissimilarity; just like it happened in the above case of setting a threshold value for the RiskSOAP indicator. All in all, RiskSOAP departs from the notion that a system has its fixed and predefined elements. It is harmonised, though, with the idea that it is feasible to reassess and amend the utility and influential role of system elements in the enhancement or degradation of the system's risk SA provision capability, even from the early design stages, before the system is booted.

It is worth mentioning that in order for one to take the steps required for STPA and EWaSAP methods, he has to be experienced, well qualified, and supported by a team of interdisciplinary, but with mutual and complementary understanding, researchers.

With a view to draw a conclusion about the risk SA provision capability and risk DSA, the subjective interpretation of the value of the indicator is inevitable. That is, setting a threshold value for this indicator, as discussed in the beginning of this section, may be considered as a limitation of the RiskSOAP methodology because it may differ from system to system and from designer to designer, affecting the degree of design modifications. Another limitation is the overabundance of dissimilarity measures that hinders the decision to select the suitable measure towards achieving the goals set by researchers.

Moreover, here it is neglected that the variables may have a truth value that ranges in degree between '0' and '1'. Acknowledging the limitation of using binary data used herein, future work is intended to involve fuzzy logic, to cope with crisp variables, and adopt continuous variables instead. Weights can also be assigned to the explanatory system elements since, in this paper, they are treated as equivalent to the risk SA provision capability enhancement or degradation.

RiskSOAP can be used a selection criterion between alternative designs of the same or different systems or as decision-making tool between alternative systems. As a further proof of its generality, additional engineering applications and studies are already under consideration.

References

1. Endsley, M.R.: Toward a theory of situation awareness in dynamic systems. Hum. Factors Ergon. Soc. **37**(1), 32–64 (1995)
2. Salmon, P.M., Stanton, N.A., Walker, G.H., Jenkins, D., Ladva, D., Rafferty, L., Young, M.: Measuring situation awareness in complex systems: comparison of measures study. Int. J. Ind. Ergon. **39**(3), 490–500 (2009)
3. Salmon, P.M., Stanton, N.A., Walker, G.H., Jenkins, D.P.: Distributed Situation Awareness: Theory, Measurement and Application to Teamwork. Ashgate, Aldershot (2009)
4. Salmon, P.M., Stanton, N.A., Walker, G.H., Baber, C., Jenkins, D.P., McMaster, R., Young, M.S.: What really is going on? review of situation awareness models for individuals and teams. Theor. Issues Ergon. Sci. **9**(4), 297–323 (2008)
5. Smart, P.R., Bahrami, A., Braines, D., McRae-Spencer, D., Yuan, J., Shadbolt, N.R.: Semantic Technologies and Enhanced Situation Awareness (2007). http://eprints.soton.ac.uk/264351/
6. Stanton, N.A., Stewart, R., Harris, D., Houghton, R.J., Baber, C., McMaster, R., Salmon, P. M., Hoyle, G., Walker, G.H., Young, M.S., Linsell, M., Dymott, R., Green, D.: Distributed situation awareness in dynamic systems: theoretical development and application of an ergonomics methodology. Ergonomics **49**(12–13), 1288–1311 (2006)
7. Stanton, N.A.: Representing distributed cognition in complex systems: how a submarine returns to periscope depth. Ergonomics **57**(3), 403–418 (2014)
8. Chatzimichailidou, M.M., Protopapas, A., Dokas, I.M.: Seven Issues on Distributed Situation Awareness Measurement in Complex Socio-technical Systems. In: 5th International Conference on Complex Systems Design & Management, pp. 105–117. Springer (2015)
9. Chatzimichailidou, M.M., Stanton, N., Dokas, I.M.: The concept of risk situation awareness provision: towards a new approach for assessing the DSA about the threats and vulnerabilities of complex socio-technical systems. Saf. Sci. **79**, 126–138 (2015)
10. Stanton, N.A., Chambers, P.R.G., Piggott, J.: Situational awareness and safety. Saf. Sci. **39** (3), 189–204 (2001)
11. Fioratou, E., Flin, R., Glavin, R., Patey, R.: Beyond monitoring: distributed situation awareness in anaesthesia. Br. J. Anaesth. **105**(1), 83–90 (2010)

12. Leveson, N.: Engineering a Safer World: Systems Thinking Applied to Safety. MIT Press, Cambridge (2011)
13. Dokas, I.M., Feehan, J., Imran, S.: EWaSAP: an early warning sign identification approach based on a systemic hazard analysis. Saf. Sci. **58**, 11–26 (2013)
14. Zhang, B., Srihari, S.N.: Binary vector dissimilarity measures for handwriting identification. In: Electronic Imaging, International Society for Optics and Photonics, pp. 28–38 (2003)
15. Nunes, A., Laursen, T.: Identifying the factors that contributed to the überlingen midair collision. In: 48th Human Factors and Ergonomics Society Annual Meeting, pp. 195–198. SAGE Publications (2004)
16. German Federal Bureau of Aircraft Accident Investigation (BFU). http://www.bfu-web.de/EN/Publications/Investigation%20Report/2002/Report_02_AX001-1-2_Ueberlingen_Report.pdf?__blob=publicationFile
17. Johnson, C.W.: Final Report: Review of the BFU Überlingen Accident Report. Contract C/1.369/HQ/SS/04 to Eurocontrol, http://www.dcs.gla.ac.uk/~johnson/Eurocontrol/Ueberlingen/Ueberlingen_Final_Report.PDF
18. Wong, B.: A STAMP Model of the Überlingen Aircraft Collision Accident. MIT Press, Cambridge (2004)

A SKOS Radiation Safety Thesaurus for People Living in Contaminated Territories

Antonin Segault[(✉)], Federico Tajariol, and Ioan Roxin

ELLIADD Laboratory, Franche-Comté University Numérica,
Cours Leprince-Ringuet, 25200 Montbéliard, France
antonin.segault@edu.univ-fcomte.fr,
{federico.tajariol,ioan.roxin}@univ-fcomte.fr,
http://elliadd.univ-fcomte.fr

Abstract. During the long-term period of a nuclear disaster, people living in contaminated territories need to gain knowledge in order to take protective actions. While existing representations of this knowledge are designed for experts, we propose a thesaurus of radiation safety built for the lay people. We present a methodology to extract such a thesaurus from a set of documents addressed to non-experts. Extension of the corpus and implementation of more automated processes are still required to improve the resulting thesaurus.

Keywords: Knowledge sharing · Crisis communication · Nuclear accident · Semantic web · Thesaurus

1 Introduction

After a nuclear disaster, people living in contaminated territories are strongly affected. The protective actions that they need to take in order to protect their health require an highly technical knowledge. Nowadays, the knowledge related to radiation safety is mostly locked in the experts' handbooks. Its highly technical vocabulary and its incompatibility with the needs of the non-experts generally hinders the spreading of this important knowledge amongst citizens.

In this paper, we posit that a formal representation of this knowledge, such as a thesaurus, could help its dissemination amongst the persons living in contaminated areas during the long term period of a nuclear disaster. We present a methodology to build such a thesaurus through the textual analysis of a set of documents addressed to lay people. We then show and discuss our results and, finally, propose some future improvements.

2 Ontologies for Crisis Management

The Semantic Web extends the original Web, by making it readable by both humans and machines [1]. While the original Web is linking documents, knowledge formatted to be read by humans, the Semantic Web is linking the knowledge

© Springer International Publishing Switzerland 2015
N. Bellamine Ben Saoud et al. (Eds.): ISCRAM-med 2015, LNBIP 233, pp. 116–123, 2015.
DOI: 10.1007/978-3-319-24399-3_10

itself, expressed formally. The RDF model defines the atom used to represent this knowledge, the {subject, predicate, object} triple. The expression of more complex data structures can be achieved trough the use of ontologies.

An ontology can be defined as the formal specification of a shared conceptualization [3]. It expresses, in an explicit and computable way, the concepts of a specific domain and the relations between these concepts. Ontologies allow different systems to use the same unified representation of the knowledge of a specific domain, thus supporting semantic interoperability [23].

Several ontologies have already been developed for crisis management, where interoperability is indeed a key factor to the success of a crisis response involving several actors [7]. A previous study [14] examined a set of 26 ontologies built for crisis management. These ontologies define concepts related to disasters, damages, victims, infrastructures, resources, geography, etc.

More simple structures, such as thesauri, can also be used to represent domain specific knowledge. Thesauri are concept schemes [15] or, more precisely, controlled vocabularies enriched with hierarchical and associative relations [17]. Thesauri have also been used to represent the knowledge required for crisis management and communication [13] even if they are far less expressive than ontologies. In this paper, we will use the term "ontology" in a broad acceptation that also includes thesauri.

Nowadays, citizens, volunteers, lay people, are becoming more and more involved in crisis management. In fact, the participation of citizens improves the efficacy of the risk management and the likelihood that they take self-protective actions [11]. During the last years, citizens facing a crisis widely used social media to share information contributing to the situational awareness [26], thus taking part in an highly parallel and distributed crisis management [16].

However, the existing ontologies only address information sharing amongst experts. The technical terminology used by experts is often an obstacle when communicating with citizens [19]. Furthermore, because of their different perceptions of the risk, experts and citizens may disagree on the importance of some informations [11], and thus on the concepts that need to be integrated in crisis management ontologies. Specific ontologies therefore need to be created to support the participation of non-experts in the management of crisis.

3   Ontologies for Nuclear Disasters Management

Nuclear disasters are situations in which semantic interoperability is particularly important. The management of such large scale and long term crisis indeed requires the coordination of particularly numerous organizations (e.g. civil protection, nuclear safety institutions, health professionals, meteorologists, etc.), especially in case of a cross-boundary accident [22]. Furthermore, the management of these disasters requires the use of highly technical concepts that need to be communicated without any ambiguity. International radiation safety organization thus started large efforts toward the creation of knowledge bases [12].

Some ontologies have already been developed to support communication on radiation safety. A first one [9] was created to ease the public access to the domain knowledge, and thus to facilitate communication and deliberation of the risk, in the context of prevention actions. This ontology was automatically generated using the tables of content of crisis management handbooks. More recently, a thesaurus was developed [13] to represent the concepts specific to the management of a nuclear accident. The concepts have been extracted from documents issued by international radiation safety organizations (such as IAEA), and will be used for the annotation and retrieval of nuclear safety documents by citizens. Despite the objectives of their authors, these ontologies are not really usable by lay people, as the vocabulary used is highly technical. Moreover, the concepts represented, extracted from documents written by and for experts, may not reflect the effective interests and concerns of the affected population.

However, the Fukushima Daiichi nuclear disaster has shown the importance of the actions of citizens to manage such a crisis. In reaction to the lack of official data regarding the radioactive contamination, the population used social media to share alternative measurement sources [8] and created collaborative radiation maps aggregating the readings of citizen-powered radiameters [18]. For this reason, ontologies should be developed to address the information needs of citizens in order to support crisis communication, amongst citizens and with the experts.

4   Thesauri for the Long-Term Period

Radiological accidents are generally divided in two successive temporal phases [5]: the emergency phase and the post-accidental phase. The first one comprises the accident itself, the leakage of radioactive substances, and the countermeasures implemented to stop it. During the second phase, the consequences of the accident need to be managed. This phase itself can be split into a transition period, when the contamination of the territories is not completely known, and a long term period, that may last for years or decades.

During this period, people living in contaminated territories face a chronic exposure to low doses of radiations. In order to reduce this exposure, and thus the risk of radiation induced diseases, they need to take protective actions (e.g. dietary regime, gardening practices, house cleaning, relocation, etc.). The assessment of the risk and, then, the selection and the application of the relevant protective actions, require an highly technical knowledge (e.g. radiation measurement, dose calculation, safety norms and comparison values) [20]. The affected population needs tools to access, integrate and share this knowledge.

We thus propose the creation of a thesaurus for the persons living in contaminated areas during the long-term period of a nuclear disaster. SKOS is an RDF vocabulary dedicated to the representation of thesauri and terminologies [15]. It allows the definition of concepts (skos:Concept) and the linking of these concepts through hierarchical (skos:broader, skos:narrower) and associative (skos:related) relations. It also offers a large range of textual data-properties such as labels (skos:prefLabel, skos:altLabel, skos:hiddenLabel) and annotations (skos:definition, skos:example, etc.).

These labels can be used to power semantic search engines [4]. In these systems, a textual query is semantically annotated using the concepts whose labels are included in the query. The search is then based on these concepts, and no longer on the terms of the query. It can thus match documents that are not annotated with the same terms, but with synonyms or alternative syntaxes of the same concepts. Moreover, the SKOS vocabulary natively supports the management of labels in different languages, facilitating the internationalization of these search engines.

To create this thesaurus, we firstly studied a set of glossaries already produced by three French expert radiation safety organizations: IRSN[1], ASN[2] and CIPR[3]. These glossaries define highly technical knowledge in engineering, physics, biology. However, they do not describe some of the most relevant concepts for people living in contaminated territories, such as food or children safety [20]. Accordingly, these glossaries do not seem to match the lay people's information needs. To fill this gap, in the same way the EMTerms terminology was extracted from a large corpus of tweets [24], we propose to extract the thesaurus from a set of documents written for lay people.

5 Methodology

5.1 Collected Documents

To extract the concepts and relations of the thesaurus, we gathered a set of documents, written in French or English, and addressed to non-experts:

- [20] is an handbook issued by the experts of the SAGE project, addressed to the population of contaminated territorie (in English)
- [5] is a document written by the experts of CODIRPA, addressed to local decision makers (in French, extract)
- [10] is the transcription of a TV documentary series, reporting the testimonies of Japanese after the Fukushima Daiichi nuclear disaster, broadcasted by the Arte TV channel in 2013 (in French)
- [25] is a short leaflet, created by both a doctor and a group of citizens, addressed to citizens (in English)
- we also transcribed the interview of an expert of the CEPN, talking to a researcher (non-expert in radiation safety) about his work during the long term period in Fukushima Daiichi nuclear disaster (in French, extract)

---

[1] http://www.irsn.fr/FR/connaissances/Glossaire/Pages/Glossaire.aspx.

[2] http://www.asn.fr/lexique/mot/%28lettre%29/95097.

[3] http://www.irsn.fr/FR/Larecherche/publications-documentation/
collection-ouvrages-IRSN/Documents/CIPR_103.pdf.

5.2   Concepts Extraction

We firstly collected the raw text of each document, stemmed the words (with the Porther algorithm for English texts, and the Snowball one for French) and removed the stopwords, using the NLTK library [2]. We calculated the frequency distributions of all words, 2-grams, 3-grams and 4-grams, and identified the most frequent ones, both for the individual documents and for the whole corpus. We then manually filtered these lists to keep only the terms relevant to the post-nuclear situation management. We obtained 77 words or groups of words.

To create concepts, we manually gathered the synonyms and the French-English equivalents (Fig. 1). This resulted in a list of 46 concepts, some having several labels in both French and English, while others ($N = 29$) only have one label in one language.

```
{
  "id" : "exposure",
  "en" : ["exposur", "expos", "radiat exposur"],
  "fr" : ["exposit", "irradi"]
}
```

Fig. 1. A concept with its stemmed labels

5.3   Relations Construction

We identified 25 hierarchical relations between these concepts, by manually linking hypernyms and hyponyms (such as "contamination" and "food contamination"), and other types of semantic hierarchies.

We then automatically extracted the associative relations. Using the previously extracted labels, we counted the co-occurrences of two concepts in the same paragraph. We then calculated a co-occurrence ratio, dividing the number of co-occurrences by the number of occurrences of the less frequent concept. When this ratio exceeded 50 % (i.e. more then 50 % of the occurrences of the less frequent concept appeared in paragraphs in which the other concept also occurred), an associative relation was declared. This threshold, defined after testing different values, allowed the identification of 57 associative relations (after removing the ones that were already declared as hierarchical relations).

We finally serialized all the resulting concepts and relations as a SKOS thesaurus[4], using the Turtle RDF syntax. We kept the stemmed labels as skos:hiddenLabels, so that they could directly be used for text search. We also manually added skos:prefLabels in both French and English (Fig. 2).

---

[4] Available online at http://purl.org/NET/scopanum.

```
scopanum-th:external_exposure a skos:Concept ;
   skos:prefLabel "external exposure"@en ;
   skos:prefLabel "exposition externe"@fr ;
   skos:hiddenLabel "extern irradi"@en ;
   skos:hiddenLabel "extern exposur"@en ;
   skos:hiddenLabel "extern radiat exposur"@en ;
   skos:related scopanum-th:glass_badge ;
   skos:broader scopanum-th:exposure .
```

Fig. 2. SKOS representation of a concept and its relations

6   Results and Discussions

Two main methodological limits hinder our methodology: the corpus size and
the manual processes.

The small size of the documents corpus cannot allow us to detect a large
number of concepts. Some expected concepts, such as the ones related to units
of measurements, didn't appeared in the resulting thesaurus. Moreover, only
a few labels have been associated to some concepts, which certainly affected
the automated detection of associative relations. We are still looking for more
documents addressed to lay people in order to increase the size of our corpus.

Furthermore, the selection of labels, their grouping as concepts, and the construction of hierarchical relations rely on manual processes. These processes,
based on the authors own knowledge of the radiation safety domain, have a limited reproducibility. They will also be less and less practicable as we scale up the
corpus. To solve this problem, we consider automatizing these processes by implementing knowledge-poor detection models (such as TF-IDF – Term Frequency-
Inverse Document Frequency – to identify the domain-relevant labels). However,
it seems difficult to completely eliminate manual intervention, particularly to
associate synonyms into concepts.

Since these issues highly limited both the size and quality of the produced
thesaurus, we did not conduct any evaluation of its usefulness yet.

7   Conclusions

Ontologies are valuable knowledge representations for crisis management and
communication. However, existing ontologies, in particular the ones focusing on
radiological disasters, fail to address lay people's information needs. We thus proposed the creation of a radiation safety thesaurus specifically designed to support
knowledge sharing amongst the lay people living in contaminated territories in
the long term period of a nuclear disaster.

We described a methodology to extract this thesaurus from a set of
documents addressed to non-experts. We combined manual and automated
approaches to generate concepts and relations from these texts. For now, the

small size of the corpus and the reliance on manual processes still limit the quality and the extent of our thesaurus. We have drawn some solutions to these problems.

This work is part of the broader SCOPANUM research project. This project aims to study the uses of ICT for crisis communication in the post-accidental phase of a nuclear disaster, and to develop tools to support the resilience process of people living in contaminated territories. The thesaurus we have presented will be used to power the semantic search engine of a web platform for knowledge sharing amongst citizens [6,21].

Acknowledgements. This work is supported by grants from the Conseil Supérieur de la Formation et de la Recherche Stratégiques and Pays de Montbéliard Agglomération.

References

1. Berners-Lee, T., Hendler, J., Lassila, O.: The semantic web. Sci. Am. **284**, 28–37 (2001)
2. Bird, S.: NLTK: the natural language toolkit. In: Proceedings of the COLING/ACL on Interactive Presentation Sessions, pp. 6–72. Association for Computational Linguistics, Stroudsburg, PA, USA (2006)
3. Borst, W.N.: Construction of Engineering Ontologies for Knowledge Sharing and Reuse. Universiteit Twente, Enschede (1997)
4. Celino, I., Della Valle, E., Cerizza, D., Turati, A.: Squiggle: a semantic search engine for indexing and retrieval of multimedia content. In: Proceedings of SAMT (2006)
5. CODIRPA: éléments de doctrine pour la gestion post-accidentelle d'un accident nuclaire. In: ASN (2012)
6. Cotfas, L.-A., Segault, A., Tajariol, F., Roxin, I.: A semantic mobile web application for radiation safety in contaminated areas. In: Proceedings of the IE 2015 International Conference, Bucarest, Romania (2015)
7. Di Maio, P.: An Open Ontology for Open Source Emergency Response System. Open Source Research Community (2007)
8. Friedman, S.M.: Three Mile Island, Chernobyl, and Fukushima: an analysis of traditional and new media coverage of nuclear accidents and radiation. Bull. At. Sci. **67**, 55–65 (2011)
9. Furuta, K., Ogure, T., Ujita, H.: Nuclear safety ontology-basis for sharing relevant knowledge among society. In: Systems and Human Science for Safety, Security and Dependability, pp. 397–408 (2005)
10. De Halleux, A.: Récits de Fukushima. ARTE France (2013)
11. Heath, R.L., Palenchar, M.J., OHair, H.D.: Community building through risk communication infrastructures. In: Heath, R.L., OHair, H.D. (eds.) Handbook of Risk and Crisis Communication, pp. 471–487. Routledge, New York (2009)
12. IAEA: Nuclear Knowledge Management (NKM). https://www.iaea.org/nuclearenergy/nuclearknowledge/about-nkm.html
13. Konstantopoulos, S., Ikonomopoulos, A.: A conceptualization of a nuclear or radiological emergency. Nucl. Eng. Des. **284**, 192–206 (2015)

14. Liu, S., Shaw, D., Brewster, C.: Ontologies for crisis management: a review of state of the art in ontology design and usability. In: ISCRAM 2013 Proceedings of the 10th International Conference on Information Systems for Crisis Response and Management (2013)
15. Miles, A., Matthews, B., Wilson, M., Brickley, D.: SKOS core: simple knowledge organisation for the web. In: International Conference on Dublin Core and Metadata Applications, pp. 3–10 (2005)
16. Palen, L., Anderson, K.M., Mark, G., Martin, J., Sicker, D., Palmer, M., Grunwald, D.: A vision for technology-mediated support for public participation & assistance in mass emergencies & disasters. In: Proceedings of the 2010 ACM-BCS Visions of Computer Science Conference, pp. 8:1–8:12. British Computer Society (2010)
17. Pidcock, W.: What are the differences between a vocabulary, a taxonomy, a thesaurus, an ontology, and a meta-model? http://www.citeulike.org/group/258/article/166888 (2003)
18. Plantin, J.-C.: The map is the debate: radiation webmapping and public involvement during the Fukushima issue. In: A Decade in Internet Time: OII Symposium onthe Dynamics of the Internet and Society (2011)
19. Reuter, C., Pipek, V., Wiedenhoefer, T., Ley, B.: Dealing with terminologies in collaborative systems for crisis management. ISCRAM 2012 Proceedings of the 9th International Conference on Information Systems for Crisis Response and Management (2012)
20. SAGE Project: Guidance on Practical Radiation Protection for People Living in Long-Term Contaminated Territories (2005)
21. Segault, A., Cotfas, L.-A., Tajariol, F.: A semantic system for knowledge sharing in post-nuclear-accident situations. Presented at the Workshop on Semantics and Analytics for Emergency Response (SAFE 2015), Kristiansand, Norway (2015)
22. Segerståhl, B. (ed.): Chernobyl. A Policy Response Study. Springer, Heidelberg (1991)
23. Sheth, A.P.: Changing focus on interoperability in information systems: from system, syntax, structure to semantics. In: Goodchild, M., Egenhofer, M., Fegeas, R., Kottman, C. (eds.) Interoperating Geographic Information Systems, pp. 5–29. Springer, Heidelberg (1999)
24. Temnikova, I., Castillo, C., Vieweg, S.: EMTerms 1.0: a terminological resource for crisis tweets. In: ISCRAM 2015 Proceedings of the 12th International Conference on Information Systems for Crisis Response and Management (2015)
25. Tsubokura, M.: Radiation and Health Seminar. Veteran Mothers Society (2014)
26. Vieweg, S., Hughes, A.L., Starbird, K., Palen, L.: Microblogging during two natural hazards events: what twitter may contribute to situational awareness. In: Proceedings of the SIGCHI Conference on Human Factors in Computing Systems, pp. 1079–1088. ACM (2010)

Towards a Generic Semantic Model for the Representation of Accident Scenarios in the Field of Transport

Ahmed Maalel[1,2(✉)], Lassad Mejri[2], and Henda Ben Ghézala[2]

[1] Higher Institute of Applied Science and Technology of Sousse, ISSATSO, University of Sousse,
Sousse, Tunisia
ahmed.maalel@ensi.rnu.tn
[2] RIADI Laboratory, National School of Computer Sciences, ENSI, University of Manouba,
Manouba, Tunisia
mejrilassad@yahoo.fr, henda.benghezala@ensi.rnu.tn

Abstract. In order to streamline and strengthen the knowledge acquisition process from experience feedback (accident scenarios in transport), it is necessary to harmonize and standardize the terminology used by experts and actors in the security domain. Despite all the efforts to propose approaches and techniques to manage experience feedback, most of the approaches suggested in the literature suffer from the lack of acceptable definitions and from ambiguity due to the lack or even the absence of formalism to express or model the accident scenarios. In order to build an accessible and usable knowledge model and thus provide assistance to domain experts in their crucial task of analyzing and improving security, this paper presents a generic semantic model for the representation of accident scenarios in the field of transport, based on ontologies.

Keywords: Experience feedback · Accident scenario · Knowledge representation · Ontologies · Security analysis

1 Introduction

The terrible cost of accidents, the fatal consequences and the occurrence of serious failures and disasters in spite of the new advances in technology are the basis for establishing a feedback experience process (often called Rex) as one of the key methods to improve security analysis in the high-risk domains. The risk analysis in transport is a fairly significant, complex and interdisciplinary step. It is largely based on a thorough analysis of the risks resulting from accident scenarios. An accident scenario is a succession of events that can cause a potential risk.

Indeed, despite the undeniable interest of existing approaches and methods of security analysis, the completeness of the analysis remains limited, and this is due mainly to the lack or absence of a proper knowledge representation. To better understand this gap and in order to build an accessible and usable knowledge model and so provide assistance to domain experts in their crucial task of analyzing and improving security, we have used ontologies. In fact, ontologies are used to establish a common vocabulary and a structure to formalize an important knowledge to the security and risk analysis.

© Springer International Publishing Switzerland 2015
N. Bellamine Ben Saoud et al. (Eds.): ISCRAM-med 2015, LNBIP 233, pp. 124–131, 2015.
DOI: 10.1007/978-3-319-24399-3_11

The interest in ontologies also comes from their ability to structure the explicit knowledge of the studied field and to derive another valuable knowledge.

The paper plan revolves around four parts. The second part presents the proposed works of the literature in the security knowledge modeling. The next part is devoted to our suggested approach, through the generic conceptual model and the development steps of the domain ontology. Finally, the last section presents an example of integration of ontology into a decision support system.

2   Related Works

Several studies have been proposed to security analysis. We describe in this paragraph some recent works in this area (see Table 1). We can mention the works of [1–3] who put forward the model feasibility, called "ACASYA", for the help of certifying automated railroad transport systems. Also, [4] suggested the SAUTREL system dedicated to the software errors' analysis in the field of railroad security analysis. Mazouni [5] proposed the SIGAR system with an abstract model of a railroad accident representation. We can mention also the approach of Yanping [6] which was applied in the railroad sector through the prediction of railroad accidents/incidents.

Table 1. Related works

Reference	Proposed system	Case study (transport)	Knowledge representation	
			Conventional practices (Data base, etc.)	Semantic practices (Ontologies, etc.)
[1–3]	ACASYA	Railroad	×	
[5]	SIGAR	Railroad	×	
[6]	–	Railroad	×	
[7]	ROSAC	Road	×	
[4]	SAUTREL	Railroad	×	
[9]	–	Air	×	
[8]	TERMINATE	Road		×
[10]	SAGEO	Maritime		×

Furthermore, concerning the suggested works in the field of transport safety; we can mention those of Capus L. and Tourigny N. [7] who put forward the ROSAC system (Road Safety Analysis with Cases) which provided aid to the analysis road safety. Després S. and Ceausu V. [8] devoted their system to associate a profile scenario of accidents where each accident occurred in a particular geographic location group. Whereas, the approach of Zubair, M. and Khan, M.J [9] was for predicting air incidents.

Finally, Arnaud and Napoli Arnaud V. and Napoli A. [10] proposed the SAGEO system for the analysis of behaviors of vessels at risk.

Despite the numerous efforts made so to put forward approaches to the security analysis, and although those works have made significant contributions (e.g., the work of [8, 10]) which are very useful in developing our approach), some limitations can be detected. In spite of the diversity of proposed architectures, it turns out that their knowledge representations are based on conventional aspects and practices (database, text files, etc.). It is a question of proposing in this article a generic semantic model for the representation of security knowledge. This is going to have resorts to ontologies.

3   Towards a Generic Semantic Model for the Representation of Accident Scenarios

The structuring work of accident scenarios related to the knowledge from experience feedback has allowed raising issues related to a large project in a high-risk industrial environment. Several sources of security knowledge (experts, researchers, articles, etc.) are used for this purpose. Most knowledge about the field of safety of transport systems derive mainly from the analysis of conflicting security situations represented in the form of potential accident scenarios. In this article, we have agreed on proposing, at first, a conceptual model (core model and domain model) and reaching the development of the domain ontology (see Fig. 1).

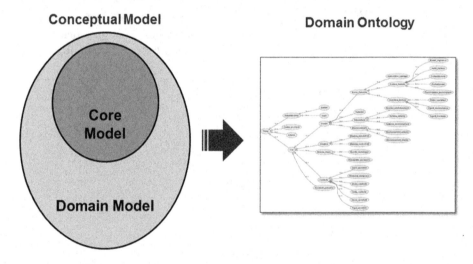

Fig. 1.   Implementation steps of the semantic model of representation of accident scenarios

3.1   Conceptual Model

To establish the conceptual model, it seems wise to choose a conceptual notation that allows identifying all the concepts, relationships and constraints forming the ontology.

To do this, we have used a Unified Modeling Language (UML) which is a standard notation in the object-oriented modeling. According to [11] and [12], the UML could be undoubtedly considered an appropriate language for modeling ontologies. The UML, in particular the UML class diagram, provides a rich notation to define classes, concepts and relationships between classes. Therefore, the conceptual model we propose will be well expressed as class diagrams. An accident scenario describes a combination of circumstances which can lead to a dangerous situation. It is characterized by a context and a set of parameters. In our context, this step has initially resulted in developing a core model for the representation of accident scenarios (see Fig. 2).

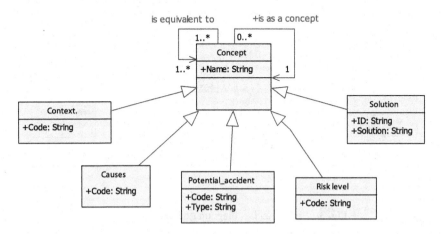

Fig. 2. The main classes of the core model

This model is based on the identification of five general parameters describing an accident scenario: the context of the accident, the possible causes, the risk level (characterized by the probability of occurrence and severity of damage of the accident), the potential accident, and the adopted solutions (preventive and corrective measures). Figure 3 shows the class digraph that will serve as the access point for the domain ontology. The classes in the core ontology will be extended in subclasses with corresponding cardinalities. We also opted for integrating human error in the conceptual model. According to [13, 14], human error due to a decrease in alertness has become a critical component in the reliability of a man-machine system. Human operators in the field of transportation are subjected to psychological, behavioral and physical constraints. Human error is a symptom of a poor work organization, poor or inadequate training, etc.

3.2   Ontology Development

The literature offers several ontology building methodologies. Some authors have proposed methodologies inspired by their experience of building ontologies [15–17]. To share our work, we have used an approach used in [18] that is largely based on Methontology [19]. The development cycle involves four consecutive steps. First, the

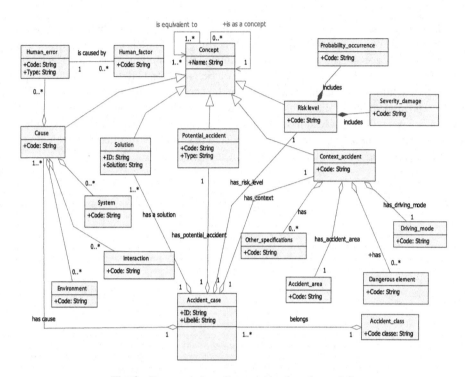

Fig. 3. Proposed class diagram (the domain model)

specification, which is the objective of this phase, gives a general description of the ontology. Then, the conceptualization consists in producing the conceptual model of the ontology that contains the domain concepts and their properties (see Sect. 3.1). Next, the implementation consists in moving from the conceptual model to a model implemented in one of ontology languages such as OWL, RDF etc. The ontology editor "Protégé" is then used to implement our ontology. Finally, the maintenance refers to the change in the ontology after its implementation to correct errors and improve efficiency. During the implementation of ontology, this maintenance aspect has been asked several times which has finally helped to reach an exploitable ontology. Figure 4 presents the class hierarchy of the ontology based on our domain model.

4   Integration of the Ontology in a Decision Support System

At this stage, it is appropriate to conduct an exploitation of the developed ontology. Several alternatives are present and allow inferring much knowledge within the ontology. To better exploit the developed ontology, in our work, we have integrated it in a feasibility model based on Adast System [20] (see Fig. 5).

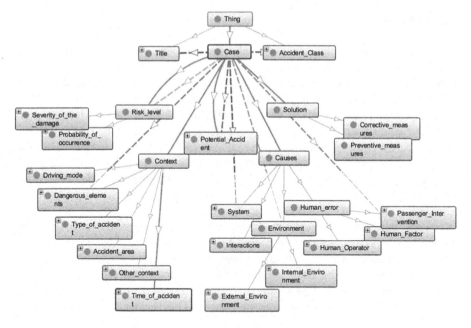

Fig. 4. Class hierarchy of the domain ontology [20]

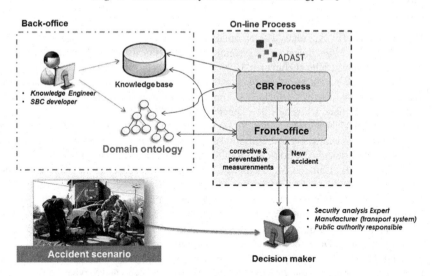

Fig. 5. Integration of the ontology in the aid decision process

It is used to use the knowledge from historical railroad accidents so as to help security experts take a better advantage by providing solutions to new insecurity situations.

5   Conclusion

The treatment of an accident scenario requires passing through several major phases: acquisition, modeling, capitalization and exploitation. Now, the research is generally limited, particularly in the context of the transport field, to a purely statistical phase; it turns out that the knowledge representations are based on conventional practices' aspects (database, text files, etc.). This can harm the downstream phases for knowledge exploitation. Our goal is to propose a generic semantic model for the representation of any kind of accident in the transport field. The efforts in our work could extend and standardize all terms used for a richer representation of the accident scenario, taking into account also the human component as well as the technical component. Then as a second step, the domain ontology of the security analysis, validated by security experts, is suggested.

To consolidate and validate our work, it is necessary to integrate the ontology in our decision support system, called Adast, so that we can proceed an effective exploitation of the represented knowledge with the proposed model. We set the scale in the context of this article on a crucial phase related to the security knowledge representation. Our future works are addressing the inclusion of dynamic modeling of accident scenarios to better illustrate the event successions in the genesis of the accident.

References

1. Hadj-Mabrouk, H.: Apprentissage automatique et acquisition des connaissances : deux approches complémentaires pour les systèmes à base de connaissances. Thèse de doctorat en Automatique Industrielle et Humaine, Université de Valenciennes (1992)
2. Mejri, L.: Une démarche basée sur l'apprentissage automatique pour l'aide à l'évaluation et à la génération de scenarios d'accidents. Application à l'analyse de sécurité des systèmes de transport automatises. Université de valenciennes, p. 210 (1995)
3. Mejri, L., Hadj-Mabrouk, H. Caulier, P.: Un modèle générique unifié de représentation et de résolution de problèmes pour la réutilisation des connaissances de sécurité. Revue Recherche Transports Sécurité, n°103, Éditions LAVOISIER, 2009, pp.131–148 (2009)
4. Hadj-Mabrouk, H., Darricau, M.: SAUTREL: Outil d'aide aux analyses des effets des erreurs de logiciels de sécurité dans les transports guidés. LM 10, 10ième Colloque national de fiabilité et maintenabilité, France, Saint-Malo, tome 2, pp.790–797 (1996)
5. Mazouni, M.H.: Pour une Meilleure Approche du Management des risques: de la Modélisation Ontologique du Processus Accidentel Au système Interactif d'Aide à la Décision. Thèse de Doctorat à l'Institut National Polytechnique de Lorraine (2008)
6. Yanping, C., Zhenmin, T., Haibing D.: Case-based reasoning and rule-based reasoning for railway incidents prevention. In: Proceedings of Services Systems and Services Management (2005)
7. Zubair, M., Khan, M.J.: Prediction and Analysis of Air Incidents and Accidents Using Case-Based Reasoning. (GCIS), Third Global Congress on Intelligent Systems, pp. 315–318 (2012)
8. Capsus, L., Tourigny, N.: Le raisonnement à partir de cas : une aide à la formation en analyse de sécurité routière. Technologies de l'information et de la communication dans les enseignements d'ingénieurs et dans l'industrie. Colloque International No. 2, Troyes, France, pp. 227–235 (2000)

9. Després, S., Ceausu, V.: Raisonnement à partir de cas pour contribuer à améliorer l'aménagement du réseau urbain en prenant en compte la sécurité, (2004). http://old-lipn.univ-paris13.fr/seminaires/AtelierRaPC/Articles/despres.pdf
10. Arnaud, V., Napoli, A.: Modélisation ontologique pour l'analyse de comportements de navires à risques. Colloque SAGEO 2013 - Spatial Analysis and GEOmatics, Brest, France (2013)
11. Cranefield, S., Purvis, M.: UML as an Ontology Modelling Language. Department of Information Science, University of Otago, New Zealand (1999)
12. Bergenti, F., Poggi, A.: Exploiting UML in the Design of Multi-agent Systems. In: Omicini, A., Tolksdorf, R., Zambonelli, F. (eds.) ESAW 2000. LNCS (LNAI), vol. 1972, pp. 106–113. Springer, Heidelberg (2000)
13. Amalberti R.: L'erreur humaine en perspective, Risques erreurs et défaillances : approche interdisciplinaire. Publications de la MSH-ALPES, mai 2001, pp. 71–106 (2001)
14. Hadj-Mabrouk, A., Hadj-Mabrouk, H.: Approche d'intégration de l'erreur humaine dans le retour d'expérience, Application au domaine de la sécurité des transports ferroviaires. Synthèse n° 43, INRETS-IFSTTAR (2003)
15. Noy, N.F., McGuinness, D.L.: Dveloppement d'une ontologie 101: Guide pour la création de votre première ontologie. Université de Stanford, CA, 94305 (2008)
16. Fernandez, M., Gomez-Perez, A., Juristo, N.: Methontology: From Ontological Art Towards Ontological Engineering. In: Proceedings of the AAAI97, Spring Symposium Series on Ontological Engineering, pp. 33–40 (1997)
17. Uschold, M., Grüninger, M.: Ontologies: principles, methods, and applications. Knowl. Eng. Rev. **11**(2), 93–155 (1996)
18. Abou-Assali, A., Lenne, D., Debray, B.: Ontology development for industrial risk analysis. In: IEEE International Conference on Information & Communication Technologies: from Theory to Applications (ICTTA 2008), Damascus, Syria April 2008
19. Fernandez, M.: Overview of methodologies for building ontologies. In: Workshop on Ontologies and Problem-Solving Methods: Lessons Learned and Future Trends, (IJCAI 1999) August 1999
20. Maalel, A., Mejri, L., Hadj-Mabrouk, H., Ben Ghézala, H.: Towards a decision support system for security analysis. In: Hanachi, C., Bénaben, F., Charoy, F. (eds.) ISCRAM-med 2014. LNBIP, vol. 196, pp. 46–56. Springer, Heidelberg (2014)

Dynamic and Context Aware Reporting of Observations from the Field for Situation Assessment in Crisis Situation: An Integrated System for Information-Gathering and Sense-Making

Andreas Horndahl[(✉)] and Linus Gisslén

FOI, Swedish Defence Research Agency,
Gullfossgatan 6, 164 90 Stockholm, Sweden
{andreas.horndahl,linus.gisslen}@foi.se

Abstract. An efficient process for gathering data from the field is crucial in managing crisis scenarios. In this paper we present a concept system for crisis management with focus on how observations from the field are reported using hand held devices and integrated into a common operational picture. The application used for reporting situation from the field adapts to the current situation in real time by adding and hiding input field based on what the user is reporting. Moreover, the user interface will also adapt to external information request. This is realized by utilizing risk event models for real time risk assessment and identification of areas where information is lacking which can generate new requests for information.

Keywords: Crisis management · Semantic techniques · Dynamic forms · Risk alert · Information management · Situation assessment · Continuous and real-time risk assessment

1   Introduction

In big scale disasters such as tsunami and earthquakes the sheer information to process to achieve an overview of the situation is a daunting, and sometimes an overwhelming task. An efficient information management process is crucial in a crisis situation in order to understand and assess the situation in terms of damages and needs, both present and future. Situation awareness is achieved by collecting data from sources in the field and combining this information with background data. Many systems exist today that focus on the geospatial aspect which is realized by plotting data on a map. In order to speed up the process of gathering data from the field, responders have started to use hand held devices such as tablets which has many benefits. The data reported is in digital format which makes it easier to process and if the telecommunication infrastructure is intact, the information can also be transmitted to stakeholders immediately. Unfortunately, most solutions do not deal with the problem of filtering data and information very well: the operator gets an unfiltered view which contains both the relevant and the irrelevant information to the operational picture. Furthermore, information gaps might not be easy to spot

© Springer International Publishing Switzerland 2015
N. Bellamine Ben Saoud et al. (Eds.): ISCRAM-med 2015, LNBIP 233, pp. 132–139, 2015.
DOI: 10.1007/978-3-319-24399-3_12

because the amount of data might be overwhelming, especially in a larger operation. This flood of data partly comes from that the information gathered from the field. The data is often in the format of free text or predefined forms covering different event types. Structured data can be analyzed with a lesser amount of processing which makes it usable with lesser delay. Therefore it is common to use pre-defined static forms, tailor-made for different reporting situations, in order to make sure that no information piece is forgotten also ensures that data is structured. However, this approach is not always the best way to gather information. In this paper a concept is presented which deals with the filtering of data and how dynamic forms can be generated to help with the data gathering.

2   Related Work

There are several tools available for gathering data by the use of mobile devices available today. Many of these support basic features such as creating forms and questionnaires that can be answered using a mobile device. Other commonly supported features are data analysis, data aggregation and plotting the collected data on a map. Some systems support a two way communication where data can be requested from the mobile device or pushed to it.

In systems like KoBo Toolbox [1] and EPIcollect [2] the questionnaires allows for logic that makes the form more dynamic in terms of hiding and adding questions based what has been entered so far. In GDACSMobile [3], categories are used to specify the context of a situation report. The categories are linked to templates that contains specific assessment question. When the user selects a category for the situation report, he/she will be asked to answer additional question based on the template. The templates are flexible and can be re-configured to match the specific needs as the situation evolves.

3   Concept Model

In the following sections the concept model is introduces. In Sect. 3.1 the main objectives are defined. Section 3.2 contains the overview of the concept, Sect. 3.3 contains the risk model logic, Sect. 3.4 the reporting system and Sect. 3.5 the operational picture. Finally Sect. 3.6 describes how the individual parts are connected.

3.1   Main Objectives

Efficient information management is important in crisis situation and situation assessment includes numerous factors which will affect the final picture [4]. One of the most important challenges is how to collect relevant information and make sense of it in a timely manner so that response actions can be initiated in time. The key to making good decision is situation awareness which is achieved by analyzing available data collected from the field in combination with context and background data. Situation assessment includes assessing what the damage and needs are as well identifying potential cascading effects that needs to be taken into account. Improving the crisis response team ability to understand the situation, by providing efficient tools for structuring and analyzing the available information, can decrease the time taken from getting data to taking the necessary actions. To achieve this a system should support:

- Dynamic information gathering: Information that the personnel are asked to collect and details asked for in incident reports should be based on actual information needs active at the moment instead of relying on a fixed set of question. The information needs are based on the current situation type (e.g. geography, demographics, disaster, etc.) and other factors such as risk event (e.g. epidemics, starvation, injured people, etc.). In this way it is ensured that the questions asked to the personnel in the field is relevant to the current situation.
- Information need analysis: To support above point, the system should be able to assist the crisis management team in the task of identifying what information that needs to be collected.
- Automation and sense making: Algorithms and techniques for automatic deductions that reduce the time spent on structuring information and simple aggregation should be available which reduce the time to decision. To some extent, the system should also provide sense-making capabilities such as calculating risk probabilities.

3.2   Concept Overview

In order to meet the above described objectives, a concept with three main components is proposed:

(1) *Models* describing risk events: Models are used to assess the current likelihood of a specific risk event. The inputs to a model are information objects like flooding, power outage, crowds, etc. Each information object have attributes like coordinates, time, scale, etc. The models can then be used to automatically access information gaps, especially where the data flow is too large and too fast for a human operator to manage. See Sect. 3.3 for details.

(2) A *reporting system* used by personnel on the field in the form of a hand held device or similar. With the use of models these system can work on dynamic forms instead of static. Either the operator chooses the questions or the system adapts the questions depending on the situation. See Sect. 3.4 for details.

(3) A *situation awareness operational picture* (in a form of a GUI) that gives a filtered overview of the crisis area. See Sect. 3.5 for details.

The data collected from the fields via the reporting system (2) are feed into the operational picture (3). The personnel on the field are guided, in terms of what kind of data to collect, by the operators that has the overview of the situation (3) or by RFIs generated by the models (1). RFIs can both be manually or algorithmically managed. The interaction between the three main components are depicted in Fig. 1 and discussed in Sect. 3.6. A proof-of-concept implementation of this concept has been developed and described in Sect. 4.

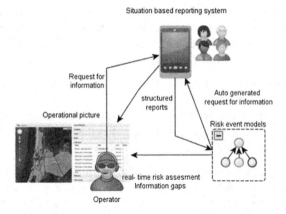

Fig. 1. Schematic overview of the information management system presented.

3.3 Risk Event Models and Information Gap Management

The concept described in this paper proposes models for aggregating, fusing and structuring information relating to a risk can be used to enhance the crisis management team ability to understand crisis situations. Moreover, the models can speed up the decision process. The top node of a model is the risk even itself (e.g. epidemic risk) and the branching nodes are indicators of the risk (e.g. sanitary problems). Each node represents events and indicators that contributes to the probability of the top node (e.g. Epidemic risk) to be true/happening (See Fig. 1). The model is created using a model development tool described in [5].

The idea is that relevant information (gathered on the field by the operators or sensors) are connected to, and can be access via, the leaves in the model which makes it easy to navigate through the information available. The models can also be used to manually, semi-automatically, or automatically calculate the probability of the risk based on the observed indicators. Besides providing structure to the information and giving estimate of the current risk, models can also be used for two additional reasons:

- For each observable node in the model an *information need* is associated. Therefore, the risk models can help the operator and the system to identify information gaps.
- To assess if the current assessment of a risk has too high level of uncertainty. For example, if weak indication is obtained from one source it can be necessary to confirm it.

After the identification of information gap the question is how to use the information acquisitions resources available to close these gaps. The information need can for example be filled by asking a questions to the personnel on the field that has access to the hand held device. This is where the RFI functionality can be used. The information needs are transformed into RFIs that can be distributed to the information acquisitions resources available. When collecting the RFIs one central aspect to take into consideration is the relevance of a certain question with the respect to the field personnel current situation (role, capabilities and task). Neglecting this aspect and broadcasting all questions to all personnel would overwhelm them with irrelevant and annoying questions. Therefore there is a need to carefully select the receivers to send the RFIs. There is a match between the question at hand and the personnel if either:

- The question is related to a location or objects that's close to the personnel on the field
- The question is related to any of the entities the personnel has previously answered
- There is a custom made rule/pattern that specifies that a certain question is relevant to specific situation

Depending on the resources available and their capabilities, situations where the crisis management team must prioritize which information gap to focus on can occur. This can be a non-trivial task in complex large scale crisis situation. Computer algorithms can be used to generate optimal resource allocation suggestion. The idea to calculate optimal resource allocations based on a models similar to the ones presented in this paper has explored in [6] in a military intelligence scenario, which is analogous to a crisis scenario in terms of constraints.

In the next section it is discussed how the RFIs are received and managed in the field by the reporting system.

3.4 Reporting System

The reporting system is designed to be run on a hand held device in the field. The idea is that a personnel in the crisis area can use it to create observation reports or to gather data explicitly requested by and then later upload/report in to the COP system (Sect. 3.5) located in a HQ. The reporting system user interface is dynamic in the sense that which input form fields that are displayed depends upon the RFIs that exists at the moment. The RFIs may be generated automatically based on an information gap (Sect. 3.3) or created manually. This follows the idea of generating a user interface based on information needs discussed in [7]. Each RFI has a priority that is used to determine displayed order and the user is to answer them in this order to ensure that the highest priorities are handled first. The priority can be set either manually or by an algorithm. A typical reporting workflow can look like this:

1. A field personnel creates a report by either receiving a RFI or selecting a form for the situation that the user want to report about.
2. The user answers questions related to the type situation that the user selected in step 1.
3. Optionally the user enters additional information if needed.
4. The user interface is updated (via the models) with questions that are related to the information provided based on the RFI currently active.
5. If the user has more information to report, steps 3 to 5 are repeated, otherwise the report is considered complete and the user submits it.
6. If the report matches an indicator in a risk model, the report will be connected to the indicator. The process of connecting reports to indicators can be manual, semi-automatic or automatic.

The heavy use of ontologies and semantic technologies is beneficial for making use of background data. If a user of the systems mentions a building that the system has some background data about, this data will be immediately associated to building mentioned and accessible in the app. The output (report) of the reporting system is represented as a set of RDF (Resource Description Framework) statements.

3.5 Operational Picture

The persons in charge of coordinating response actions have access to an interface where the location of each personnel on the field is visible. Other information can be displayed including objects like:

- Events/reports: Reports of event that has relevance to the situation assessment.
- Facilities: Hospitals, bridges, roads, etc. with information about their current status.
- Areas: Pre-defined areas the divided into administrative units or similar.
- Risks: An icon will represent if a risk occurs at the location. In the GUI information about the risk probability and impact can be found.
- Indicators: An icon will represent an observable factor at the location. In the GUI information about the indicators priority, status, location, etc. can be found.

3.6 Integration

The section describes how the risk event models, the reporting system and the operational picture benefits from each other and forms an integrated system for situation awareness in crisis situations.

The key technology used to implement the concept is ontologies. An *ontology*, in information science, defines a hierarchy of concepts within a domain using a shared vocabulary. Furthermore, it defines properties for each concept and the relationships between the concepts. An ontology can be used for several purposes in the context of the proposed concept: shared formal vocabulary, matching RFIs with the current reporting situation, enable automatic binding of incoming reports, and to speed up the input process by making suggestions based on the situation.

In essence, three categories of data are exchanged between the modules: RFIs, risk information and reports generated by the Reporting system. The reports created by the personnel on the field are fed into the operational picture as well as the risk models. Since the reports are represented as RDF statements which have a formal specification and precise meaning, it can be matched with the RFIs connected to the indicators in the risk models. Once the reported is connected to the model, a new risk index can be calculated. As soon as a risk index is updated, the operational picture is updated to reflect the changes. The risk event models feeds the operational picture with up-to-date estimates risk values. From this risk map overlays can be automatically drawn. This allows the operator to quickly get an aggregated view of the situation in contrast to only looking at individual observations.

A key feature of the proposed concept is the support for dynamic forms that take RFIs into account. RFIs can be manually created by the operator or as the result of an algorithm analyzing what the current information gaps are as based on the risk event models described in Sect. 3.3. The fact that ontologies are used to represent the RFIs and the fact that the reporting app use the same ontology (or mapping between) to represent the reporting situation makes it possible to apply standard graph matching techniques to find out if a RFI is relevant to an reporting situation. If the RFI is relevant to the situation, a new question will be added to the reporting GUI.

4 Implementation and Validation

The proposed concept has been implemented as a proof-of-concept prototype by integrating and extending research prototypes and open source software. The reporting module has been implemented as a native Android App. The support for risk event models has been implemented by extending the concept (Impactorium) described in [5] with new capabilities (see Fig. 1). The COP has been implemented as a web app using the Typesafe Play framework. Bootstrap and angular-js has been used to implement the COP GUI. The map service used is Google maps. The support for ontologies and semantic data has been implemented by supporting RDF and RDFS. SPARQL has been used to represent RFIs. The individual components have been integrated using RESTful webservices. All components are exchangeable and the system is not relying on a specific software.

The concept has yet to be validated in the field. The tool has however been demonstrated to crisis management personnel where mock-up scenarios (including a tsunami scenario in a Mediterranean country) were used to show the functionalities and the concept. Larger experiments will be performed in the near future. The idea to use models in the way that is described in this paper has not been validated in crisis management context. The method of using similar models in a military context has however proven to be useful [8].

5 Future Work and Conclusions

This proof-of-concept implementation uses SPARQL to represent RFI. At current date, these questions need to be formulated manually. Manual construction of these queries are only feasible if the user is very experienced with the SPARQL syntax and have basic understanding of how RDF work which is not reasonable to expect.

The concept presented is the product of fusion from many different research areas such as information fusion, information management, threat modeling and ontology based graphical user interfaces. The concept described in this paper has addressed generic challenges related to information management in a crisis situation with focus on reducing the time to decision by proposing an integrated solution for how information is gathered from the field and used for decision making purposes. The implemented concept use risk models, dynamic forms (for field personnel) and ontologies in order to understand a crisis situation faster.

The risk models are a preamble for the dynamic forms and information gap assessment. The ontologies gives structure to the information and can be used to describe information needs. Ontologies are also the core technique used to create dynamic context aware forms. The filtered COP map will further contribute to give a better overview of the situation as the components shown on the map is aggregation of information of the current situation via the risk models. The system can better support the crisis management team in doing correct decisions on actions to be taken and on which information need that is the most important. This is partly done by handling the information gaps problem and alerting when new crisis have, or might, arise. This combined allows for handling larger amounts of data at a higher rate than previous solutions.

Acknowledgement. The research leading to these results has received funding from the European Community's Seventh Framework Programme (FP7/2007-2013) under Grant Agreement n 607798

References

1. KoBO toolbox. http://www.kobotoolbox.org
2. EpiCollect.net. http://www.epicollect.net
3. Link, D., Hellingrath, B., De Groeve, T.: Twitter integration and content moderation in GDACSmobile. In: ISCRAM Conference 2013, pp. 67–71 (2013a)
4. Endsley, M.R.: Toward a theory of situation awareness in dynamic systems. Hum. Factor. J. Hum. Factor. Ergon. Soc. **37**(1), 32–64 (1995)
5. Fensel, A., Gustavi, T., Horndahl, A., Mårtenson, C., Rogger, M.: Semantic data management: sensor-based port security use case. In: Intelligence and Security Informatics Conference (EISIC), 2013 European, IEEE (2013)
6. Johansson, R., Martenson, C.: Information acquisition strategies for Bayesian network-based decision support. In: 2010 13th Conference on Information Fusion (FUSION), pp. 1–8, IEEE, July 2010
7. Cohen, M., Horndahl, A., Mårtenson, C.: First steps towards a context aware ontology-driven reporting system. In: Proceedings of the 8th International Conference on Semantic Systems, pp. 103–108, ACM, Quarterly, **24**(4), 665–694, September 2012
8. Svenson, P., Forsgren, R., Kylesten, B., Berggren, P., Fah, W.R., Choo, M.S., Hann, J.K.Y.: Swedish-Singapore studies of Bayesian modelling techniques for tactical intelligence analysis. In: FUSION, pp. 1–8, July 2010

Engineering of Emergency Management Systems

Extending AUML for Interaction Protocols Specifying in the Context of Adaptive Coordination of Crisis Management Processes

Wassim Chtourou[✉] and Lotfi Bouzguenda

MIRACL Laboratory, University of Sfax, Route de Tunis, km 10, BP 242 3021
Sakeit Ezzit, Sfax, Tunisia
chtourouwassim@gmail.com, lotfi.bouzguenda@isimsf.rnu.tn

Abstract. This work deals with Interaction Protocol (IP) adaptation at build time for coordination in the context of Crisis Management Processes (CMP). CMP refer to the coordination of several partners in a dynamic and unstable context. One possible way to deal with this coordination is the use of IP. In order to guarantee an efficient use of IP, we need to adapt them. In previous work, we proposed an MDA (Model Driven Architecture) framework for IP adaptation based on version and context notions. In this paper, we focus on the PIM (Platform-Independent Model) level of the proposed MDA framework. More precisely, we propose an extension of AUML (Agent UML) sequence diagram meta-model in order to specify graphically the contextualized versioned IP. We also give two examples of contextualized versioned IP specified with extended AUML. Finally, we illustrate the IP adaptation based coordination through a well-known case study « Air Crash Management Process ».

Keywords: Interaction protocols · Crisis management processes · Adaptation · Version · Context · AUML · Extension

1 Introduction

Nowadays, we are witnessing the proliferation of crises in all areas such as political, socioeconomic and climatic. In this context, the Crisis Management Processes (CMP for short) take a considerable importance by the communities engaged in crisis response and management.

The CMP refer to the coordination of several tasks running in different organizations (governmental organizations, humanitarian organizations, hospitals, civil protection, etc.) and in an open, dynamic and unstable context [1].

A fundamental problem for CMP is the semantic coordination of the different partners. By semantic coordination, we mean all the rules ensuring the semantic coherence of interactions between organizations involved in crisis management. However, the coordination in CMP is still a challenge and current crisis management systems [2–4] are too rigid to deal with the variety of contexts due to the presence of heterogeneity at different levels: processes, policies, objectives, authorities, local and

© Springer International Publishing Switzerland 2015
N. Bellamine Ben Saoud et al. (Eds.): ISCRAM-med 2015, LNBIP 233, pp. 143–154, 2015.
DOI: 10.1007/978-3-319-24399-3_13

global commitments and security. Regarding the analysis and synthesis of pre-existing processes how to coordinate them in an efficient way and within a coherent framework?

One possible way to deal with this coordination is the use of interaction protocols (namely contact nets, negotiation or vote as defended in multi agent system area) ruling and structuring the communication between partners [5]. In effect, the interaction protocols (IP) based coordination is widely recognized as an efficient mechanism to share resources and coordinate the activities of agents [5]. Several works have been proposed in the literature for instance in [5–7]. These research works consider protocols as entities of first class and address the engineering issue such as specification, validation and implementation of protocols for specifying and developing a Multi-Agent System (MAS) in stable context.

In our work, we also consider IP as first class entities but to deal with coordination in CMP viewed as open MAS and within an engineering perspective. Thus, the interaction protocols adaptation is needed in order to support the coherent interaction between organizations involved in open, dynamic and unstable context. Roughly speaking, IP adaptation can be investigated in the context of the two following distinctive approaches. The first one concerns the management of problems (called exceptions) which can occur under the execution of protocols while the second approach aims at the re-use and the modification out (i.e., at build time) and in progress of execution of the IP modeled. This approach is based on meta-modeling aspect. In this paper, we concentrate on the IP adaptation according to the second approach. One possible way to deal with this adaptation is the use of versioning technique [8] which captures all the predicable changes of the considered interaction protocol and permits to keep trace of the previous versions of an entity, which supports the re-use of these versions if the same situation arises.

In our previous work, we have proposed an MDA framework for IP adaptation based on version and context notions. We have also presented a meta-model, at CIM level, for supporting the modeling of contextualized versioned IP. In this paper, we focus on the PIM level of the proposed MDA framework to specify graphically the contextualized versioned IP.

Obviously, the design of different IP versions can be represented without specific information regarding the version. However, it is more interesting to propose an appropriate notion or language allowing in the design step to represent the IP version concepts to the designer.

Various notions, languages and formalisms have been proposed to design the IP. The majority have been focused on the representation of IP behavior such as AUML [9, 10], RDP [11], EVENT B [12], COMMITMENT [13] and ALGEBRA PROCESS [14]…

AUML language is the result of collaboration between the OMG [14] and FIPA [15] organization which allow the design of IP behavior. In our work, we use the AUML language for three reasons. First, its ability to represent the behavior of IP using AUML sequence diagram. Second, it apprehended by user due its graphical interface. Finally, it provides extensions mechanisms thanks to the stereotype and constraint OCL. These latter will be used to extend the sequence diagram meta-model with protocol profile, version and context [17] concepts.

The main contribution of this paper is to extend the AUML sequence diagram meta-model to specify graphically the contextualized versioned IP.

The remainder of this paper is organized as follows. Section 2 recalls our MDA framework that we proposed for interaction protocols adaptation based on the version and context notions. Section 3 proposes our extended AUML sequence diagram meta-model. More precisely, it first exposes the key requirements that must be supported by a formalism or language to specify graphically a contextualized versioned IP. Then, it gives a comparative study of existing languages/formalisms in order to underline their limitations. Finally, it shows how we extend the AUML sequence diagram meta-model to deal with contextualized versioned IP specifying. We also present two examples of contextualized versioned IP specified with the extended AUML. Section 4 exposes a crisis scenario to illustrate the IP adaptation based coordination in CMP. Finally, we conclude the paper and underline the main perspectives.

2   An MDA Framework for Interaction Protocols Adaptation

The purpose of this section is to recall our MDA (Model Driven Architecture) frame-work, proposed in our previous work [21], for interaction protocol adaptation. More precisely, this framework supports the design of IP versions and their contexts, valida-tion and implementation. We have chosen to use MDA because it promotes the devel-opment of abstract models and it is a standard recommended by the OMG [14] since it supports the engineering perspective. The three abstraction levels proposed by MDA are the following:

- CIM Model: Such model should be independent of any computer system [15]. In our context, the proposed CIM model is the Contextualized Versioned Interaction Protocol Meta-Model (CVIP2 M for short). By instantiating this meta-model, the designer creates an IP with its versions. It is noted that our proposition is inspired from [18]. This work [18] aims at supporting the flexibility of business processes by using the versioning technique. We believe that the IP can be viewed as a set of coordinated actions and consequently, it can benefits from this technique.
- PIM Model: Such model should be independent of any technology platform [15]. It represents an enriched and less abstract view of CIM. In our context, the PIM level is divided in two sublevels: PIM1 and PIM2. The first one provides a graphical repre-sentation of contextualized versioned interaction protocols with graphic languages such as BPMN, AUML and so on. Regarding, the second sublevel, it provides a formal specification to validate the IP versions by using formal languages (Petri nets, Z, Event-B, etc.).
- PSM Model: The consideration of the execution platforms has for objective the management of the dependence between the applications and their platforms of execution [15]. In our context, we propose to migrate to the XML specification for instance in order to execute the IP by extracting the roles and implement them within software agents.

It is noted that the CIM and PIM models support the IP adaptation at build time. Regarding the latest model (PSM), it supports the IP adaptation at run time.

In this paper, we only focus on the first row of the second level of abstraction (PIM model: PIM1) by extending the meta-model of the AUML sequence diagram with the version and context notions in order to specify graphically the IP modeled according to the proposed CVIP2 M meta-model. For more information about the IP2 M (Interaction Protocol Meta-Model) and VIP2 M (Versioned Interaction Protocol meta-Model), the reader can refer to [17].

3   Extending AUML Sequence Diagram for Contextualized Versioned IP Specifying

3.1   Key Requirements of Contextualized Versioned IP Specifying Language

The general requirements that one awaits from a Contextualized Versioned Interaction Protocols Specifying Language (CVIPSL) are mainly the expressive power and the adaptability management at design time.

- An appropriate expressive power: a CVIPSL must make it possible to describe all the basic concepts: behavior and profile of IP. For the behavior concept, the language must express the protocol spectrum, role, conversation and action concepts. Regarding the profile it must describe the protocol properties and categories.
- Adaptability management at design time. A CVIPSL must make it possible to model the adaptability of IP by using the version and context notions. It must specify for each component (i.e., role, profile, behavior) the details of its version (i.e. the version number, the version creator, the creation date of the version, the state of the version, the statute of the version). Regarding the context of versioned IP, it can be specified through comments.

Besides to these two requirements, described above, other requirements must be taken into account: Those related to the quality of a language in general such as usability and extensibility. The usability of the language corresponds to its facility of use while extensibility corresponds to its capacity to extend to support a specific application domain (i.e., agents for instance).

3.2   A Comparative Study of Some Existing Notations and Languages

In this section, we summarize the result of our comparative study between some existing notations and languages compared to the requirements defined previously. The studied languages are: AUML [9], Petri-Net [11], EVENT B [12], COMMITMENT [13] and Process algebra [14].

The signs +, − and ± used in the comparison table are interpreters as follows:

+ means that the language answers the criterion,
− means that the language does not answer the criterion,
± means that the language answers partially the criterion.

The Table 1 summarizes the features of each studied language.

Table 1. A comparative study between existing notations and languages

			AUML	Petri-Net	CONSTRAINT & PROCESS ALGEBR	EVENT-B	COMMITMENT
expressive			Protocol Behavior				
	Protocol spectrum	Sequence	+	+	+	+	+
		Choice	+	+	+	+	+
		Iteration	+	+	+	+	+
appropriate		Parallelism	+	+	+	+	+
	Role		+	+	-	+	+
	Abstract Action		+	+/-	+	+	+
An	Conversation- act		+	+	-	+	+
power			Protocol Profile				
	Categories		-	-	-	-	-
	Properties		-	-	-	-	-
Adaptability management at build time			-	-	-	-	-
Usability			+	+	-	-	+/-
Extensibility			+	+/-	-	-	+/-

According to this table, we can deduce the four following remarks:

- All the existing languages/notations support the design of protocol spectrum,
- All the existing languages/notions support the design of role expect Process Algebra,
- No languages/notations support the design of protocol profile.
- No language supports the adaptability management at build time using versioning technique.

At the conclusion of this comparative study, we chose the use of AUML language for the following reasons:

- AUML offers a graphic notation whose syntax is at the same time simple, intuitive and expressive,
- Its notation is extensible. It is equipped with an extension mechanism based on stereotypes, constraints and labelled values. This mechanism makes it possible to personalize the AUML meta-model in order to take into account the needs for specific modelling. The result of this personalization is a profile AUML.
- Lastly, AUML allows the description of basic coordination patterns thanks to its appropriate expressive power.

However, UML does not support all specificities of the IP and those inherent in their adaptability. To compensate these limitations, we propose to extend AUML and in particular the diagram of sequence in order to model the contextualized versioned IP.

3.3   Extending AUML Sequence Diagram Meta-Model

To model a contextualized versioned interaction protocol by using the AUML sequence diagram, we propose the following extensions:

- For the *Interaction class* which present units of behavior we have added the following attributes. The attributes devoted to the IP version are: Pro_Nam: protocol name; Ide_Ver_Pro: interaction version identity; Nam_Cre_Ver: name of version creator; Dat_Ver_Cre: date of version creation; Sta_Ver: status of version which can be created or derived. While the attributes devoted to the IP context are: Goa: goal of interaction protocol; Off_par: the offer part in protocol which can be the initiator or participant; Cho_Cri: define the choice criteria to accept a proposal which can be single or multiple; Ini_Pri: initial price used in auction protocol to initiate the object price; Pri_Stra: price strategy of offer in auction protocol which can be increased or decreased. Then we use OCL language to apply constraint to some attributes values: {context Interaction inv: self.Sta_Ver = created or derived from self.Ide_Ver_pro= "xxx", self.Cho_Cri = single or multi-dimensional, slef. Off_Par = initiator or destinator, slef. Pri_Str = Increased or decreased}.
- For the *LifeLine* class we kept the AgentRole and AgentIdentifier attributes proposed in [19] which present an extension of object class and we added the following attributes. The attributes devoted to the IP version are: Ide_Lfl_Ver: version of lifeline; Nam_Cre_Ver: Name of version creator; Dat_Cre_Ver: date of version creation, Sta_ver: version status which can be created or derived; Ide_Ver_Int: used to specify the identifier of the version of the belonged interaction. While the attributes devoted to the IP context are Ind_Rat: IndividualRationality and Rol_Beh: Role Behavior. Then we use OCL language to apply constraint to some attributes values: {context LifeLine inv: self.Sta_Ver = created or derived from self.Id_Lfl_Ver = "xxx", self.Ind_Rat = rational or Irrational, self.Rol_Beh = cooperative or competitive}
- We added two stereotyped sub classes Initiator and Participant and we provide to the participant stereotyped class two attributes devoted the context notion: Par_Num: participant number and Con_Num: Contracting Number. Then we use OCL language to apply constraint to some attributes values: {context Participant inv: self.Par_Num = limited or unlimited, self.Cont_Num = 1 or < self.par_Num}.
- In the UML sequence diagram meta-model the message class is an abstract class. To deal with semantic aspect of message we added ConversationAct class in association with message class having enumerative attribute performatif (Fig. 1).
- An enumerative attribute eventthread is added to the EventOccurrence class describing the parallelism and decision (AND, OR and XOR) to deal with concurrent thread of interaction.
- We added two classes Category and Proprieties to describe the protocol profile as defined in [18]. The first one contains Cat_desc attribute defining the category of protocol.

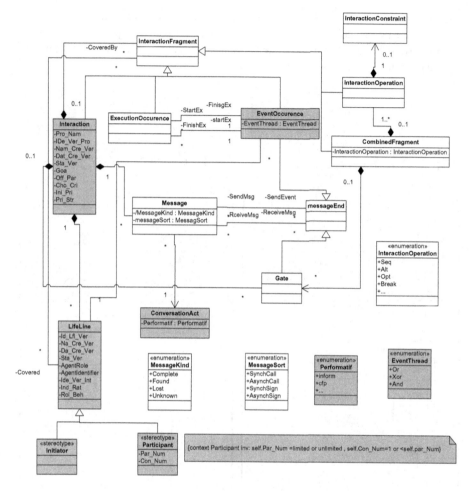

Fig. 1. A extended meta-model of AUML sequence diagram.

While the second class, it contains Context_Ontology, Multiplicity, participant_Inclusivity, Souscription_required, Conversation_Visibility, participant_Visibility attributes.

3.4 An Illustrative Example

To better illustrate our solution we expose in this section the design of two version of auction interaction protocol (see Fig. 2). In the first one (see Fig. 2a) we present an English auction interaction protocol version. In this case, the price is growing and the iteration continues until participants respond by emitting at least a proposal equal to the call for proposal. So we have an increasing strategy price, an initial price is lower than market price and the participant as conversation part. Regarding the second part (see Fig. 2b) we present a Dutch interaction protocol version. In the Dutch auction, the price is higher than the market price, and then it is decreasing in each iteration. At first no participant responds and the auction ends as soon as one or more participants propose to iterate. So we have a decreasing strategy price, an initial price is higher than the market price and the initiator as conversation part.

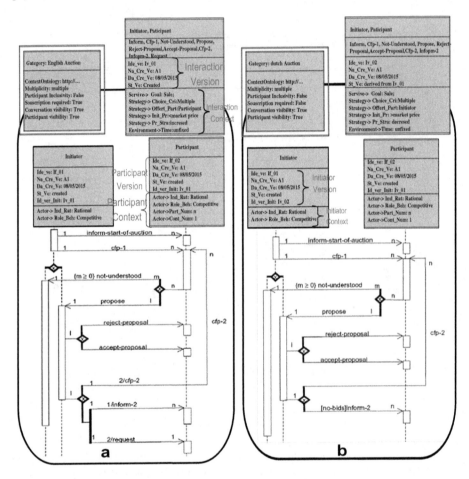

Fig. 2. Examples of two contextualized versioned IP specified with extended AUML

4   An Illustrative Case Study

4.1   Description

To better illustrate the IP adaptation based solution for crisis management processes, we give a well known crisis scenario called "air crash resolution process". Firstly, the controller agent should declare the disappearance of an airplane from the radar screen. Further to this statement, the transport ministry designates a main investigator belonging to the BEA (Bureau of Survey and Analysis) to lead this technical investigation. Furthermore, the prefect establishes a crisis unit formed by a SDIS (Departmental Service of Fire and Rescue Firemen), SAMU, Police, Investigator, Direction of civil aviation and health professionals. We suppose the occurrence of an air crash after its takeoff. The policemen deal to locate the air crash place. Meanwhile, the principal investigator takes care of building 7 groups of investigation to determine and collect the necessary information for the investigation in the following areas: site and wreckage; aircraft systems and engines; preparation and conduct of the flight; information about the crew; recorders; aircraft performance; testimonies and review of past events.

As soon as the policemen locate the place of crash, a security perimeter will be released to allow others actors to intervene. The SDIS sends seven teams of Firefighters (T1...T7): the former five deals to put out the burned, while other deal to evacuate injured and informs the crisis unit of 6 burn victims and 113 died persons. Immediately the crisis unit makes a call to the regional and neighbor hospitals to requisition that having available beds, specialists of serious burned victims and empty places in the mortuary. Then, it selects adequate hospitals and sends the SAMU to transport injured persons. When the fire is put out, the police collect the plane debris in order to help investigator teams to collect and examine necessary information. Further to collected information, a preliminary report is established. Finally, the BEA sends its final report to the Civil Aviation Directorate containing the final report and the safety recommendation that will be published in a press conference.

For more detail concerning the activities of this case study, the interested redears can refer to our previous work [21].

4.2   IP Adaptation Based Coordination for Crisis Management Processes

After being specified using our extended AUML sequence diagram, we propose in this part to use an IP in a CMP. This technique consists to insert an activity to choose a version of IP. It aims at using the appropriate Interaction Protocol Version during the execution of process in accordance with the execution context. This solution is inspired by [20] which integrate the IP for the coordination of activity to compose a flexible process. Moreover we used our ontology proposed in [21] to select the appropriate IP version. In our case, we have chosen a version of interaction protocol to affect the adequate person for the execution of "training of working group" (see Fig. 3(a)) and "choose hospital" (see Fig. 3(b)) activities. In the first activity, the principal investigator looks to form 7 groups of investigator. To better choose, he decides to use the matchmaker protocol which consists to find the adequate agents and have the following context (find agent as goal, direct conversation type and the contracting agent as offer part). In the latest activity, the choice of hospital is done through a call for tenders lunched by the Crisis unit to hospitals using contract net protocol. As context used to choose this protocol we have an offer as goal, multi-dimensional criteria of choice, direct conversation type, participant offer part, limited interaction type, unlimited participant number, several contracting, a cooperative role behavior and a rational individuality.

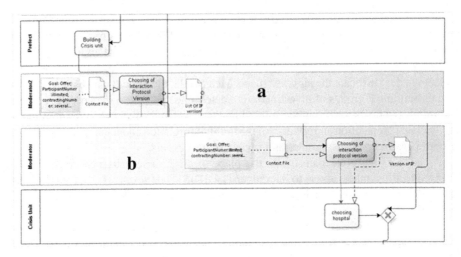

Fig. 3. Extract of air crash process model with BPMN

5   Discussion and Conclusion

Existing propositions in the literature for the specification of IP are depicted to describe the behavior using various languages and notions. To the best of our knowledge the description of protocol profile and the adaptation aspect are not studied. For instance [9, 10] proposed an extension of UML sequence diagram to describe the sequence of conversation act. In [11] they presented a framework combines a FIPA Protocols approach to specify interaction protocols of agents with coordination. This model is meant to compete with existing FIPA protocols for it applies to mediated interaction scenario rather than direct. For [13], they proposed 2CL language based commitment describing the behavior of protocol which accounts both for the constitutive and the regulative specifications and that explicitly foresee a representation of the latter based on constraints among commitments. Regarding [14], they proposed a language for specification of agent interaction protocols as first-class entities, which, in addition to specifying the order of messages using process algebra, also allows designers to specify the rules and consequences of protocols using constraints.

In this paper we called our MDA framework proposed in [21] to deal with interaction protocol adaptation at build time (CIM and PIM models) and at run time (PSM model). More precisely, we focused on the first level of the PIM model and we proposed an extension of the AUML sequence diagram meta-model with version, context notion and basic concepts of IP. Using our specified IP, we have proposed a concrete crisis scenario called "air crash management process" in order to illustrate how we exploit the IP adaptation based solution for coordination of this crisis using our ontology proposed in [21].

As future work, we plan, to study the second part of PIM level of the proposed MDA framework. More precisely, we plan to cheek these specifications through a formal language... Then we plan to propose an interaction protocol management and adaptation system supporting the adaptation at run time.

References

1. Pearson, C.M., Clair, J.A.: Reframing crisis management. Acad. Manag. Rev. **23**(1), 59–76 (1998)
2. Kienzle, J., Guelfi, N., Mustafiz, S.: Crisis management systems: a case study for aspect-oriented modeling. In: Katz, S., Mezini, M., Kienzle, J. (eds.) Transactions on Aspect-Oriented Software Development VII. LNCS, vol. 6210, pp. 1–22. Springer, Heidelberg (2010)
3. Hölzl, M., Knapp, A., Zhang, G.: Modeling the car crash crisis management system using HiLA. In: Katz, S., Mezini, M., Kienzle, J. (eds.) Transactions on Aspect-Oriented Software Development VII. LNCS, vol. 6210, pp. 234–271. Springer, Heidelberg (2010)
4. Smari, W., Clemente, P., Lalande, J.F.: An extended attribute based access control model with trust and privacy: application to a collaborative crisis management system. Futur. Gener. Comput. Syst. J. **31**, 147–168 (2014)
5. Hanachi, C., Sibertin-Blanc, C.: Protocol moderators as active middle-agents in multi-agent systems. JAAMAS **8**(2), 131–164 (2004). Springer
6. Mazouzi, H., Seghrouchni, A.E.F., Haddad, S.: Open protocol design for complex interactions in multi-agent systems. In: AAMAS, Part 2, Bologna, Italy, pp. 517–526, ACM (2002)
7. Stephen, C., Martin, P.: Ontologies for interaction protocols. In: Proceedings of the Workshop on Ontologies in Agent Systems, AAMAS, Bologna, Italy (2002)
8. Chtourou, W., Bouzguenda, L., Gargouri, F., Laouar, R.: Using versioning technique for interaction protocol adaptation in opened multi-agent systems. In: The second International Conference on Software Engineering and New Technologies, Hammamet, Tunisia (2013)
9. AUML. http://www.auml.org 2
10. Bauer, B., Müller, J.P., Odell, J.: An extension of UML by protocols for multiagent interaction. In: Proceeding, Fourth International Conference on Multi Agent Systems, ICMAS 2000, Boston, IEEE Computer Society (2000)
11. Marzougui, B., Barkaoui, K.: Interaction protocols in multi-agent systems based on agent petri nets model. IJACSA **4**(7), 166–173 (2013)
12. Jemni Ben Ayed, L., Siala, F.: From AUML protocol diagrams to event B for the specification and the verification of interaction protocols in multi-agent systems. In: Proceedings of the 3rd IEEE International Workshop on Engineering Semantic Agent Systems (ESAS 2008), International Computer Software and Applications Conference (COMPSAC 2008), pp. 581–584, Finland, Juillet 2008
13. Baldoni, M., Baroglio, C., Marengo, E.: Behavior oriented commitment-based protocols. ECAI **215**, 137–142 (2010)
14. Miller, T., McBurney, P.: Using constraints and process algebra for specification of first-class agent interaction protocols. In: O'Hare, G.M., Ricci, A., O'Grady, M.J., Dikenelli, O. (eds.) ESAW 2006. LNCS (LNAI), vol. 4457, pp. 245–264. Springer, Heidelberg (2007)
15. Belaunde, M., Burt, C., Casanave, C., et al.: MDA guide version 1.0.1. http://www.omg.org/docs/omg/03-06-01.pdf
16. http://www.fipa.org/
17. Chtourou, W., Bouzguenda, L.: Interaction protocols adaptation for negotiation in opened multi-agent systems. In: Zaraté, P., Kersten, G.E., Hernández, J.E. (eds.) GDN 2014. LNBIP, vol. 180, pp. 160–167. Springer, Heidelberg (2014)
18. Chaâbane, M.A.: De la modelisation à la specification des processus fleibles: Une approche basée sur les versions. Defended thesis at UT-1, Mai 2012
19. Song, J., Zhou, Z., Guan, Y.: Agent UML sequence diagram and meta-model. Am. J. Eng. Technol. Res. **15**(1) (2015)

20. Faure, C., Andonoff, E., Hanachi, C., Sibertin-Blanc, C., Salatge, N.: Flexibilité de processus de gestion de crise par intégration de protocoles d'interaction. In: Actes du XXVII° congrès INFORSID, Toulouse (2009)

21. Chtourou, W., Abdelkafi, M., Bouzguenda, L.: Interaction protocols adaptation based coordination for business processes. In: Tenth International Conference on Signal-Image Technology & Internet-Based Systems: SITIS, pp. 201–208, Marrakech, 23–27 Nov 2014

A Tool for Assessing Quality of Rescue Plans by Combining Visualizations of Different Business Process Perspectives

Alvaro Jose Peralta[1], Nguyen Tuan Thanh Le[2,3], Serge Stinckwich[5,6,7(✉)],
Chihab Hanachi[4], Alexandre Bergel[1], and Tuong Vinh Ho[5,6,8]

[1] Pleiad Lab, Department of Computer Science (DCC), University of Chile,
Santiago, Chile
ajperalt@gmail.com, alexandre.bergel@me.com
[2] University Paul Sabatier Toulouse III, IRIT Laboratory, Toulouse, France
nguyen.le@irit.fr
[3] University of Science and Technology of Hanoi, Hanoi, Vietnam
[4] University of Toulouse I, IRIT Laboratory, Toulouse, France
hanachi@univ-tlse1.fr
[5] IRD, UMI 209, UMMISCO, IRD France Nord, 93143 Bondy, France
serge.stinckwich@ird.fr, ho.tuong.vinh@ifi.edu.vn
[6] Sorbonne Universités, University of Paris 06, UMI 209, UMMISCO,
75005 Paris, France
[7] Université de Caen Basse-Normandie, Caen, France
[8] Institute Francophone International, Vietnam National University, Hanoi, Vietnam

Abstract. Rescue plans for crisis situations such as natural or made disasters are mostly presented in a textual format to the relevant authority. Assessing the quality of a rescue plan requires analyzing different perspectives, such as plan complexity, resources costs, service time, allocation strategy and organization efficiency. Unfortunately, textual rescue plans lack a formal structure to ease the reading and navigation through the document. To address this problem we are composing tailored visualizations, each visualization representing a particular perspective. We provide a domain specific language to describe domain specific visualizations of processes. We validate our approach using static and dynamic analysis of the Ho Chi Minh city rescue plan in case of a tsunami. Our approach provides recommendations that are useful for the authority to improve the original rescue plan.

Keywords: Rescue plans assessments · Business process modeling · Visualization · BPMN

1 Introduction

Disaster situations including natural disasters, man-made disasters or combined natural and man-made disaster with environmental consequences, require the efficient coordination of various stakeholders (public sectors, private sectors, as

© Springer International Publishing Switzerland 2015
N. Bellamine Ben Saoud et al. (Eds.): ISCRAM-med 2015, LNBIP 233, pp. 155–166, 2015.
DOI: 10.1007/978-3-319-24399-3_14

well as citizens) in order to minimize damages. When the Hurricane Katrina stroke the United States in 2005, it has been estimated that the lack of efficient coordination caused the death of more than 1200 people in Louisiana, Mississippi and Alabama, left hundreds of thousands homeless and caused tens of billions of dollars in damage [1]. In the context of crisis resolution, rescue plans unfortunately are mostly expressed in textual guidelines. It has been shown that textual guidelines suffer drawbacks [2–4]. Ambiguities make the coordination among stakeholders difficult and error prone. Moreover, textual guidelines are not easy to analyze and simulate.

An alternative to textual plans is to use Business Process Modeling (BPM) as we did in our previous work [2–4] with a BPMN (Business Process Model and Notation) diagram. This diagram, built by examining an official textual plan, supports subsequent formal analysis: process complexity, end-to-end process time, resources costs, allocation strategy, process simulation, transformation to multi-agent simulation, etc.

Rescue plans cost resources and lives. Even expressed as a business process, the quality of rescue plans is still difficult to be accurately assessed. A rescue plan is generally validated during the recovery phase, after a disaster occurred. Moreover, the process has to be assessed from multiple points of view that could induce an information overload for the rescue plan expert.

This papers has two contributions. First, it presents a new modeling of rescue plan based on Business Processes. This modeling reproduces the results we have previously obtained [4]. Second, we explore multiple perspectives on processes using interactive, expressive, and domain specific visualizations. We build a tool named A4BP (Assessment for Business Processes) that will allow rescue experts to evaluate the quality of these processes. The originality of our approach is summarized as follows:

- We use a model-based approach: BPMN models may be imported and represented as a set of objects; queries and metrics may be formulated on BPMN models to specify visualizations.
- Rescue plans can be visually assessed with specific visualizations.
- Visualizations are interactive and explorable in order to reduce the feedback loop when the end-users adapt the initial rescue plan.

The paper is organized as follows. First we model a rescue plan as business processes using BPMN diagrams (Sect. 2). We use the rescue plan of Ho Chi Minh City (HCMC) tsunami as the running example along this paper. Second, our approach is detailed using two visualizations of the HCMC tsunami rescue plan (Sect. 3). After briefly presenting the related work (Sect. 4) the paper concludes (Sect. 5).

2   Model Rescue Plans as Business Processes

Today, BPMN 2.0 is the standard notation for modeling business processes. Developers, business analysts, enterprise architects could effectively use this graphic notation to express business rules. A great deal of existing open-source and commercial Business Process tools are available (*e.g.,* jBPM[1], BonitaSoft, Camunda[2], Activiti Modeler[3], Bizagi Modeler[4]).

In our previous work, we presented a BPMN modeling of the Ho Chi Minh City Tsunami rescue plan from textual plans. These plans were provided by the Vietnamese authorities [2] (Fig. 1).

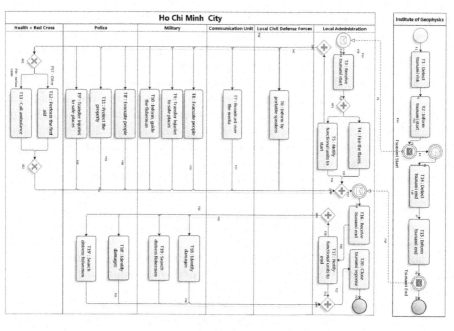

(a) BPMN Model

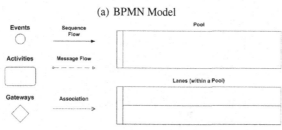

(b) BPMN Elements

Fig. 1. BPMN representation for Tsunami response plan

[1] https://www.jboss.org/products/bpmsuite/overview.
[2] https://camunda.com.
[3] http://activiti.org/components.html.
[4] http://www.bizagi.com.

In the BPMN process model, eight actors are represented by rectangular boxes, called swimlanes. These actors are two pools (Ho Chi Minh City and Institue of Geophysics) and six lanes (Health + Red Cross, ..., Local Administration). Besides, in order to visualize the task, we use the activity notation (like T1: Detect tsunami risk), depicted by a rounded-corner rectangle. These activities are connected by the Connectors (Sequence Flow and Message Flow), and the Flow Objects like Start Event, Intermediate Event, End Event. Furthermore, the control structures help to coordinate the different activities using parallelism (diamond including "+") or alternatives (diamond with "X").

Quality of rescue plans is assessed in a number of different ways. For example, in our previous work [4], we show the benefice of combining two different levels of analysis of rescue plans: a BPMN diagram that provides a graphical view easily understandable by end-users and a multi-agent perspective that provides an aggregate representation of the behavior of the actors involved in the plan. The first level allows one to analyze the rescue plan from the complexity of the workflow and may be used in a simulation, while the second level focus on dependencies between roles and enable the analysis of the robustness, flexibility and efficiency of the organization.

In order to analyze rescue plans, different perspectives have be taken into account at the various phases of the disaster (Fig. 2). The analysis during the preparedness, when pre-disaster strategic planning is done and when all the resources are not completely known, is not the same that we will be done during the response phase just after the disaster.

Another specificity of a rescue plan is to be modified at run time depending of the crisis current situation to be adapted to new actors appearing in the scene, excess or lack or resources, etc.

Our proposition in this paper is to use visualizations to provide a convenient and practical means for the end-users to analyze complex rescue plans with

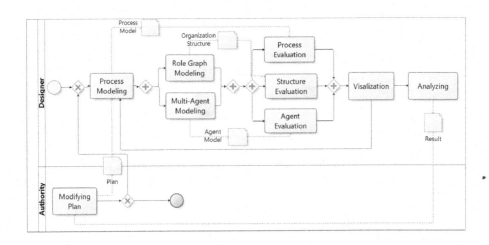

Fig. 2. Lifecycle of rescue plan assessments

different perspectives. Visualizations also allow us to combine different perspectives in a compact graphical and contextually pertinent presentation. For example, we can reuse the common blueprint of a BPMN diagram and add on top of each BPMN elements some information related to the simulation (time or resources needed for this element).

Another useful feature of visualization is to be able to view flaws or defaults using graphical patterns. This feature has already been used in the context of software process modeling by Alegria et al. [6].

Visualizations allow us to have a very short feedback when the rescue plan is modified in order to see the consequences. Visualizations further allow us to have an explorable way to test different rescue plans among all the possible scenarios.

3   Assessing Rescue Plans with Visualizations

We first describes the A4BP tool that allow us to model, analyze and visualize multiple perspective on Business Processes (Sect. 3.1). Subsequently, two examples of assessments done on the HCMC tsunami plan are shown and we give the code of the domain-specific language use to do the visualizations (Sect. 3.2).

3.1   A4BP Tool Description

A4BP (Assessment for Business Processes)[5] is a platform based on the Pharo[6] programming environment. Its purpose is to craft custom analysis of Business Process models (like BPMN 2.0). A4BP allows developers, engineers, process managers and end-users to import, transform and navigate Business Process meta-models descriptions.

The main idea of A4BP is to provide a tool to navigate the entire business process definition including relation between process and technological services related to process execution. It provides multiple perspectives to measure and visualize business process code to identify quality and design problems.

The top architectural level (e.g., Fig. 3) is composed by (1) a meta-model process engine to parse the process definition, build an object model of BPMN instances and calculate quality metrics; (2) a simulation engine based on BPSim[7], a standard to configure simulations, defines scenarios and captures results according to five dynamic perspectives: Time, Control, Resources, Cost and Task priority; (3) a front end environment using Roassal[8] [15], an agile visualization engine to produce dynamic visualization using elements of the Business Processes.

---

[5] http://www.a4bp.com.

[6] A Smalltalk-inspired live programming environment to edit, manipulate and execute objects interactively: http://pharo.org.

[7] http://www.bpsim.org.

[8] http://objectprofile.com/Roassal.html.

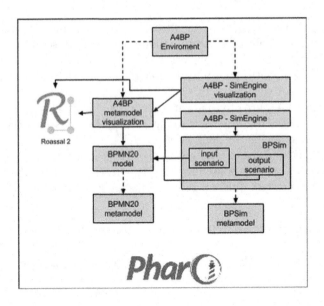

Fig. 3. A4BP layered architecture

A4BP includes the following metrics:

Metric	Description
Numbers of elements	Counting the number of element defined in the formal meta-model description
Control Flow Complexity (CFC) [9]	Using Cardoso proposal for control flow complexity in business process
Control Flow Complexity Absolute (CFCAbs)	A variant of CFC used to find the complexity when the elements have more related split elements. The basic idea is to sum all CFC in oder to have the absolute value
Process Length [8]	$N = n_1 \times log_2(n_1) + n_2 \times log_2(n_2)$
Process Volume [8]	$V = (N_1 + N_2) \times log_2(n_1 + n_2)$
Process Difficulty [8]	$D = (n_1/2) \times (N_2/n_2)$

where: n_1 is the number of unique activities, splits &joins, and control-flow elements of business process; n_2 is the number of unique data variables manipulated by the process and its activities; N_1 and N_2 are respectively the total number of elements and data occurrences.

3.2 *A4BP Assessments Scenarios*

A4BP may be used by a rescue plan analyst in two different ways:

1. Using the default predefined visualizations provided by the tool,

2. Building their own visualization with the scripting engine provided by A4BP, based on the ROASSAL agile visualization engine. We will focus only on this way in the rest of the section.

The usual workflow for process modeler is to load a process model in A4BP, explore the interface navigator, and decide which element has relevant information to make a custom visualization (See Fig. 4 for the navigation interface used in the modeler).

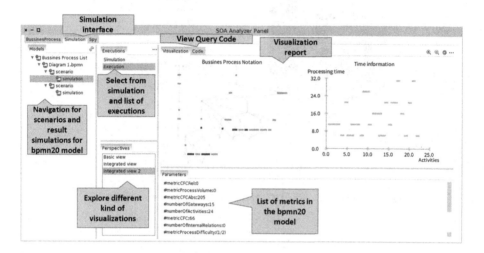

Fig. 4. A4BP model navigation interface

In order to illustrate the workflow that end-users could follow to assess a rescue plan, we show first how to build a static visualization from the HCMC tsunami rescue plan (Fig. 5) with all flow elements and their relations. We evaluate each element with the flow complexity and flow absolute complexity using rectangle width (CFC metric) and height (CFCAbs metric) to identify which element has more complexity in the model.

We obtain a visualization that is roughly similar to Fig. 1(a) with more information regarding each element. This information is more valuable for end-users than just plain BPMN diagrams.

The visualization given in Fig. 5 is obtained by executing the following script. The main part of the script is to select the nodes from the BPMN model that will be displayed and given to these nodes. The suitable shapes and colors depend on the metrics that business analysts want to examine.

This script may be built interactively and incrementally by the user during the exploration of the model.

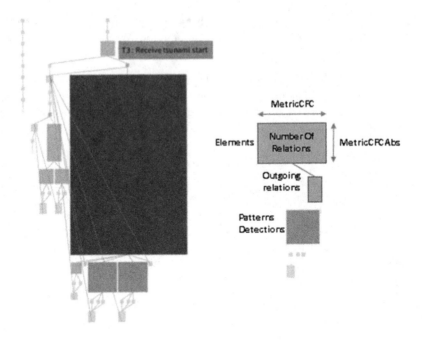

Fig. 5. Visualization of HCMC rescue plan process complexity

```
"Start Scripting visualization, using flowElements as main imput"
 values := model flowElements.
"Configure each node in the view with the metrics, using visual properties"
view shape rectangle
    "Add control flow complexity metric"
    width: [: nn | (nn metricCFC + 1) * 10 ];
    "Add control flow complexity absolute metric"
    height: [: nn | ( nn metricCFCAbs + 1 ) * 10 ].
view nodes: values.
"Add number of relations metric to normalize the color"
view normalizer
    normalizeColor: #numberOfRelations
    using: (ColorPalette sequential colors: 9 scheme: 'YlOrRd') using: #value.
"Connect the elements depending on the outFlows relationship"
eb := view edges.
eb shape line color: (Color lightGray alpha: 0.2).
eb connectFrom: #yourself toAll: [:n | n outFlows ].
"Generate a tree layout to organize using outFlows references"
view layout tree.
"Execute the visualization"
 view build.
```

Thanks to this visualization, the end-user might gain insights from the process. For example, it is apparent that one element (a parallel gateway element) has a very high complexity (width) and a high number of relations with other elements (color). This element corresponds probably to a critical task in the rescue plan. Another fact that we discover is that there are some recurrent patterns not only in terms of structure but also in terms of complexity.

From the output of first assessment, the rescue plan analyst might decide to enrich this first visualization with some information provided by another perspectives, like the simulation one.

The visualization is an output result after executing BPSim engine with time and resource as input parameters used to simulate real execution process. The visualization uses static meta-model to paint elements and dynamic BPSim meta-model to capture time processing, then set width and height values for each rectangle (Fig. 6).

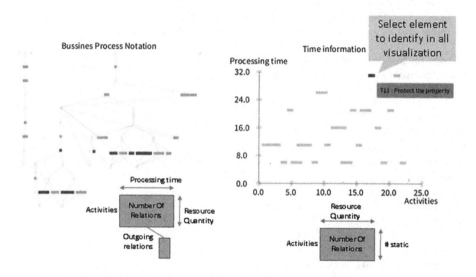

Fig. 6. Visualization of HCMC process time information

The standard BPMN view combines static BPMN diagram on the left with dynamic visualization of the BPMN simulation (time chronograph) on the right.

In the following script, the end-user adapts the shape size of BPMN elements according to some metrics (like processing time) coming from the simulation model:

```
"Script on the left side"
"Using color builder to find color for each element"
cv := A4BPUIBVFactory color.
values := model flowElements
"Find the result scenario to explore"
out := bpSimExecution fullOutputScenario.
view shape rectangle color:[: n | (n accept: cv)].
"Configure each node in the view with the metrics, using visual properties"
view shape rectangle
    "Add processing time value result"
    width: [:n | (out getParameterAt: n) processing vv ];
    "Add control flow complexity metric"
    height: [:n | ( n metricCFC + 1 ) ].
view nodes: values.
"Add quantity of resource necessary to do the activity using normalize the color"
view normalizer
    normalizeColor: [:n | (out getParameterAt: n ) quantity vv]
    using: (ColorPalette sequential colors: 9 scheme: 'YlOrRd')
    using: #value.


"Script on the right side"
"each simulation is a scenario to display"
b := RTGrapher new.

cv := Dictionary new.
cvv := A4BPUIBVFactory color.
"Find the result scenario to explore"
scenario := bpSimExecution fullOutputScenario.
"Prepare the datasource to put in the graph"
ds := RTStackedDataSet new.
"Configure the element inside the graph"
ds dotShape rectangle
    width:[ :el | ( scenario getParameterAt: el ) quantity vv )];
    height: 5.
"Insert the elements in the dataset"
ds points: bpSimExecution processModel allActivities.
"capture the processing time from scenario results"
ds y: [ :el | (scenario getParameterAt: el) processing vv ].
"Add the dataset in the graph"
b add: ds.
"Configure details"
b axisX title: 'Activities'; axisY title: 'Processing time'.
b build.
```

By combining these two perspectives together, the rescue plan analysis, could understand the relationships between the complexity of each activities of the Business Process according to the time needed to process each element. Selecting an element in one these views highlights the corresponding element in the other one.

4   Related Works

In the context of software process modeling [6] proposed model blueprints for visualizing and analyzing different perspectives of a software process model. These blueprints are used to identify process anomalies like exceptional entities and recurrent errors [14]. Error patterns are identified with process elements that are graphically "abnormally different" from the remaining elements. We are doing something similar by decorating elements like tasks with information from others perspectives.

This is also possible to assess a business process from the organizational point of view. Grossi *et al.* [7] proposed a set of metrics in order to evaluate organizational structure based on the role graph with three dimensions: power, coordination and control. We already implement these metrics in a previous paper [3]. Cardoso *et al.* [8] presented a set of metrics such as *Process Length, Process Volume, Process Difficulty* in order to assess the complexity of process model. A4PB offers these metrics making them easy to be combined in exploratory visualizations.

Cardoso *et al.* [9] presented a metric to measure control-flow complexity of a work-flow or a process. He also suggested other metrics such as: *Activity Complexity, Data-Flow Complexity, Resource Complexity*. These metrics, combined with the equations of Role Graph [7], can help us determine the quality of a coordination plan according to two points of view: process and organization.

5   Conclusion

Modeling rescue plans with business processes eases their engineering, including formalization, simulation, analysis, quality assessment activities. To be accepted by end-users and authorities in charge of disaster management, quality assessment has to be based on understandable graphical artifacts. To this end, our paper has presented different graphical perspectives of a plan on top of which static and dynamic analysis are possible. For that purpose the A4BP visualization tool has been implemented and experimentations on a Ho Chi Minh City rescue plan have been conducted. However, our tool remains general enough to deal with any other type of application domain including complex processes. The only constraint is that processes should be expressed in the BPMN standard notation. Regarding our case study, our tool should now be evaluated by users to have real feedback on its usability and the understandability of graphics produced. A process includes three dimensions: control structure, organization, and information. This paper focussed on the process control structure dimension but does not take into account the two others. As future work, we plan to provide additional visualizations and metrics to measure the quality of the organization (structure and communication). Analyzing actor interactions is likely to be the base of our future analyses.

Acknowledgment. We gratefully acknowledge the financial support of the European Smalltalk User Group (http://www.esug.org). This work has been partially founded by Lam Research and FONDECYT project 224857 (Chile).

References

1. Prizzia, R.: The role of coordination in disaster management. In: Public Administration and Public Policy-New York, vol. 138, pp. 75 (2008)
2. Le, N.T.T., Hanachi, C., Stinckwich, S., Ho, T.V.: Representing, simulating and analysing Ho Chi Minh City Tsunami plan by means of process models. In: ISCRAM Vietnam 2013 (Information Systems for Crisis Response and Management) (2013)
3. Le, N.T.T., Hanachi, C., Stinckwich, S., Ho, T.V.: Combining process simulation and agent organizational structure evaluation in order to analyze disaster response plans. In: Gordan Jezic, G., Howlett, R.J., Jain, L.C. (eds.) Agent and Multi-Agent Systems: Technologies and Applications, Part II. Smart Innovation, Systems and Technologies, vol. 38, pp. 55–68. Springer, Switzerland (2015)
4. Le, N.T.T., Hanachi, C., Stinckwich, S., Ho, T.V.: Mapping BPMN processes to organization centered multi-agent systems to help assess crisis models. In: 7th International Conference on Computational Collective Intelligence Technologies and Applications (2015)
5. Saoud, N.B.B., Mena, T.B., Dugdale, J., Pavard, B., Ahmed, M.B.: Assessing large scale emergency rescue plans: an agent based approach. Int. J. Intell. Control. Syst. **11**(4), 260–271 (2006)
6. Alegría, J.A.H., Bastarrica, M.C., Bergel, A.: AVISPA: a tool for analyzing software process models. J. Softw. Evol. Process. **26**(4), 434–450 (2013)
7. Grossi, D., Dignum, F.P.M., Dignum, V., Dastani, M., Royakkers, L.M.M.: Structural aspects of the evaluation of agent organizations. In: Noriega, P., Vázquez-Salceda, J., Boella, G., Boissier, O., Dignum, V., Fornara, N., Matson, E. (eds.) COIN 2006. LNCS (LNAI), vol. 4386, pp. 3–18. Springer, Heidelberg (2007)
8. Cardoso, J., Mendling, J., Neuman, J., Reijers, H.A.: A discourse on complexity of process models. In: Eder, J., Dustdar, S., et al. (eds.) BPM 2006 Workshops. Lecture Notes in Computer Science, vol. 4103, pp. 115–126. Springer, Berlin (2006)
9. Cardoso, J.: Business process control-flow complexity: metric, evaluation, and validation. Int. J. Web Serv. Res. (IJWSR) **5**(2), 49–76 (2008). IGI Global
10. van der Aalst, W.M.P., Nakatumba, J., Rozinat, A., Russell, N.: Business process simulation. In: Brocke, J., Rosemann, M. (eds.) Handbook on Business Process Management 1. International Handbooks on Information Systems, pp. 313–338. Springer, Heidelberg (2010)
11. Makni, L., Khlif, W., Haddar, N.Z., Ben-Abdallah, H.: A tool for evaluating the quality of business process models. In: ISSS/BPSC, pp. 230–242 (2010)
12. Curtis, B., Kellner, M., Over, J.: Process modeling. Commun. ACM **35**(9), 75–90 (1992)
13. Lanza, M., Ducasse, S.: Polymetric views - a lightweight visual approach to reverse engineering. Trans. Softw. Eng. **29**(9), 782–795 (2003)
14. Demeyer, S., Ducasse, S., Nierstrasz, O.: Object-Oriented Reengineering Patterns. Square Bracket Associates, Kehrsatz (2008)
15. Bergel, A., Cassou, D., Ducasse, S., Laval, J.: Deep Into Pharo. Square Bracket Associates, Kehrsatz (2013)

Ethical Framework for a Disaster Management Decision Support System Which Harvests Social Media Data on a Large Scale

Damian Jackson[✉], Carlo Aldrovandi, and Paul Hayes

Irish School of Ecumenics, Trinity College Dublin, Dublin, Ireland
{Damian.Jackson,aldrovac,hayesp4}@tcd.ie

Abstract. This paper presents preliminary results of ongoing research on the ethics of using social media on a large scale in disaster management.

To date social media use by disaster response agencies has been relatively ad-hoc. The Slándáil project aims to build a system for harvesting publicly available data from social media and using it in an ethically responsible and appropriate way to enhance the response of emergency services to natural disaster.

The ethical framework draws on the traditions of Isaiah Berlin's value pluralism and Giorgio Agamben's State of Exception in its approach. Value pluralism relates to an understanding that every pluralist society is organized around several and different sets of values and traditions. State of Exception theory is concerned with ethical consequences that arise when governments or state agencies arrogate to themselves extra powers in response to extraordinary circumstances, such as a natural disaster.

The implications of these ethical approaches for the Slándáil system are examined and discussed according to their impact on the various stakeholders: the system end-users, the public at large, the state and the emergency responders themselves. Implications for the technical design and governance of the system are also deduced and evaluated.

Keywords: Ethics · Value pluralism · State of exception · Disaster management · Social media

1 Introduction

The advent of social media provides an opportunity to better inform disaster response by collecting and using this publicly-contributed information to develop better technology systems. However the ethical implications of using social media data in this way demand consideration. Slándáil (EU FP7 Security sponsored project #6076921) is a project that aims to build a platform that will ethically use social media data to better inform emergency managers during a natural disaster. It is a collaboration between 9 beneficiaries in Italy, Ireland, Germany and the UK including academics, emergency operatives, civil protection organisations and four SMEs with expertise in software and communications.

© Springer International Publishing Switzerland 2015
N. Bellamine Ben Saoud et al. (Eds.): ISCRAM-med 2015, LNBIP 233, pp. 167–180, 2015.
DOI: 10.1007/978-3-319-24399-3_15

The need for an ethical framework to inform the design of and use of the Slándáil system was recognised and integrated into the project from the outset. This need arises for two reasons: Firstly, the world of social media and information technology is continuously evolving at a pace which far outstrips the legislative process. This entails a growing role for ethics. [25]

Technologies such as Slándáil which are being developed with the intention of benefitting society therefore need to go further than mere legal considerations in order to fulfil those intentions.

The second reason is related: the legislative context is also continuously evolving and changing, even during the course of the project. In considering potential ethical concerns, future legal measures may also be anticipated.

The project participants have drawn on two fields of ethical theory in the development of the ethical framework: value pluralism and state of exception theory.

2   The Slándáil System

The Slándáil System will be comprised of both hardware and software that will be installed and used as a decision support tool by emergency managers, such as police or fire departments.[1] The platform will harvest social media data, including textual, image and video data, during a natural disaster (data which will include sensitive data such as individuals' names) and will aggregate this data and provide outputs to emergency managers that identify vulnerable areas. While other systems have been developed which analyse textual information with the aim of providing actionable outputs, [1, 10, 11, 14, 26] the multimodal scope of Slándáil represents a new development.

These outputs will be in the form of actionable information that has been derived from aggregated social media data and identifies key places to target that are under particular threat of damage or loss of life from a natural disaster. The system is designed to increase efficiency in emergency response, but it cannot be understated that the level of data collection may be intrusive or may cause some level of distress to the general public.

The system, due to launch fully in 2017, is in its early prototyping phase at time of writing. The ethical framework has been written to coincide with the early prototype launches to ensure that ethical guidelines are in place prior to the harvesting od social media data.

3   Value Pluralism

Value pluralism is a strand of ethical theory that flows from the claim that there are a plurality of genuine moral values. It was initially developed by the philosopher Isaiah Berlin in the essay "Two Concepts of Liberty" [2].

---

[1] For the purposes of clarity, this paper uses the phrase 'end users' to refer to the users of the Slándáil system (i.e. emergency managers), not to the end users of social media technologies.

It differs from much mainstream ethical theory is that it does not primarily concern itself with demonstrating a way to make decisions ethically.[2] Rather, it recognises that the many ethical perspectives and culturally varied value systems in a society have intrinsic merit and that they can't be reduced to one over-arching system that can be used to determine the best course of action in a given circumstance.

Where value pluralism gets its teeth is in the further assertion that this diversity of systems of value, which reflect the cultural, ethnic and social diversity of the community, need to be protected and fostered. Berlin recognised that great harm has been done when one particular value system dominates in a specific period of human history. He therefore concluded that the valuing of pluralism itself needs to be explicit.

It represents a kind of value-system equivalent to the oft-cited expression of the principle of free speech: "I wholly disapprove of what you say - and will defend to the death your right to say it." [3] Berlin argues that we have an ethical obligation to defend others' right to live according to their ethical value systems and cultures, even if we wholly disapprove of them, because the alternative is hegemony and domination.

In addition to its implications for protection of pluralism at a societal level, value pluralism can be applied at the personal level of an individual's decision-making. As individuals, we subscribe to a plurality of values. These genuine values contend with one another in influencing our decisions and actions and will sometimes come into conflict.

In such circumstances not only may it be impossible to determine which value is more important in the circumstances than the other, but it may be impossible to compare them at all as they are incommensurable.[4]

Such decisions are very much a part of lived human experience: we find certain decisions difficult because no matter what we decide, some harm will result to our principles or values. This is experienced as "the agony of choice" [16].

3.1 Implications of Value Pluralism

Societal Level: William Galston recognises that, although value pluralism is not relativism, it does nevertheless allow for a "[f]ragmentation of value" [5]. He therefore asks how (an ethically fragmented) society is to be held together and a decently ordered public life sustained?

He adopts the notion of legal presumption (or precedent) to provide a model for a system of *ethical* presumption, where "practical [ethical] principles function as powerful but rebuttable presumptions" [5]. The objective should be to provide for the fulfilment, to the greatest extent possible, of each of the values in question, rather than a winner-takes all situation, as is common in the judicial domain.

---

[2] Mainstream ethical theory has been criticized by so-called anti-theorists for losing sight of practical application in seeking to explain ethics principles beyond where such explanation is useful. [9].

[3] This quotation is often attributed to Voltaire, but was actually written by a biographer, Evelyn Beatrice Hall to illustrate his ideas on freedom of speech. [12].

[4] That is to say that they cannot be measured on the same scale as they are qualitatively different and irreducible.

Organisational Level: Administration theorist Hendrik Wagenaar has advocated a practice-based approach where practitioners "deal with" value conflicts using their experience and intuition, rather than "resolving" them [22, 23]. The implication here is that organisations ought to foster an environment that facilitates the virtues of wisdom and courage, and engenders learning from experience.

Michael Spicer also considers organisational implications and makes the important point that power relations within the organisational structure need consideration. Power relations are a potential factor in the context of decisions made by people in an organisation, therefore a value pluralist "... approach should begin ... with a recognition that the application of power can narrow the bounds of administrative and political discourse and, in doing so, can serve to restrict the range of values brought to bear in such discourse" [17]. Dissent must be acceptable and contrary opinions considered.

Individual Level: Spicer argues that value pluralism has implications for the cultivation of virtues as does Paul Nieuwenberg, claiming that facing up to the agony of choice requires the cultivation of the virtues of honesty, truthfulness and courage:

What a moral life incorporating this understanding requires, then, are certain dispositions—dispositions enabling us to endure conflict and its agonies. These dispositions are nothing but virtues: more specifically, the classical virtues of honesty, truthfulness, and even courage [16].

4   State of Exception Theory

Human rights law experts Evan Criddle and Evan Fox-Decent explain that "In common parlance, the 'state of exception[5]' denotes "a legal regime in which public institutions are vested with extraordinary powers to address existential threats to public order" [3].

The crucial question to pose is the following: How can liberal democratic values accommodate extraordinary powers and measures that are apparently illiberal? Given that liberal democracies are primarily concerned with protection and promotion of fundamental rights and separation of powers, how could prerogative powers and the derogation of human rights and civil rights be ever justifiable to these same liberal democracies?

According to Carl Schmitt, the only juridical subject endowed the right to proclaim a state of emergency (and accordingly suspend the constitutional provisions) is the executive power itself in its various forms: king, president, prime minister, etc.[6] Leaders can be inevitably tempted to exaggerate the peril in order to justify their emergency declarations.

Schmitt, along with many other proponents of the state of exception rationale, also pointed at the undeniable evidence that democratic systems generally take a lot of time to deliberate and produce a political decision.

---

[5] For the purposes of this paper the terms "state of exception" and "state of emergency" are used interchangeably.

[6] Carl Schmitt, a major intellectual figure in 20th century legal, political and constitutional theory, is unquestionably recognized as the "outstanding legal theorist of the notion of exception". [7] citing [4].

While a number of commentators portray the state of exception as inherently prone to generating abuses of power, others highlight the fact that national emergencies are not exempted from legal oversight or scrutiny.

In her book, N. C. Lazar argues that during national emergencies heads of states or governments are not exempted from political accountability: their actions are always subject to adversarial review by the courts of law, the legislative body, the larger political community and a free media [13]. On a similar note, Peter Swan's study details how during national emergencies, the rule of law of liberal democracy does not "willingly abdicate its role to a state of exception" and more often than not "continues to act as an obstacle to the arbitrary authority of the executive branch" [19].

From an international human rights law perspective, the state of exception bears important consequences for the mechanism of derogation. The leading international and regional human rights covenants endeavoured to regulate states' entry, conduct and accountability before, during and after the state of emergency. The "cornerstone" of these covenants are their derogation clauses, which permit states to restrict some human rights in exceptional times - but only where this is strictly necessary to address serious threats to the life, independence or security of the nation and its members. The suspension of those human rights is subject to a carefully calibrated system of limitations, safeguards, notifications, and review procedures.

Recognizing the dangers attached to a period of national emergency, international human rights law limits the circumstances under which states may legally derogate from their international obligations to respect, protect, and fulfil civil and political rights. Each of the leading international and regional conventions on civil and political rights deploys the following criteria and guidelines to evaluate the lawfulness of the derogation processes initiated by state members: [7]

As far the derogation mechanism is concerned, one has to keep in mind an important caveat, which is founded on a qualitative discrimination between "non-peremptory" and "peremptory" human rights.

During national crises, state governments may derogate from "non-peremptory" human rights norms such as the freedoms of expression, movement, and peaceable assembly. In keeping with international human rights law, however, state governments are never permitted to derogate from peremptory norms because under no circumstances could the violation of these norms be consistent with states' legal and ethical obligations towards their citizens.

4.1   Justification and Strict Necessity

All derogations from human rights will be legally permissible only where "genuine public emergencies undermine the institutional prerequisites for the enjoyment of human

---

[7] The ICCPR, African Charter on Human Rights, American Convention on Human Rights (ACHR), Arab Charter on Human Rights (Arab Charter) and European Convention on Human Rights (ECHR).

rights by imperilling the 'life', 'independence', or 'security of the state'" [3].[8] A state's failure to provide a reasoned justification for particular emergency measures renders those measures unlawful, as the UN Human Rights Committee has recognized.[9]

4.2   Last Resort

Even under such extraordinary circumstances, however, the state still has an obligation to show that it cannot adequately address the crisis with ordinary measures and applicable laws. In other words, derogating from its non-peremptory human rights obligations must represent the last resort.

4.3   Proportionality

The influential document "Siracusa Principles on the Limitation and Derogation Provisions" suggests that "any measures a state undertakes to restrict or suspend non-peremptory human rights during emergencies must be supported by a principles of proportionality", requiring states to use "only those measures that minimally restrict the freedoms ordinarily protected by the suspended treaty rights" [21].

4.4   Notification and Monitoring

Furthermore, to ensure that international human rights law restrictions on the commencement of the derogation are taken seriously, each of the leading covenants on civil and political rights obliges states to notify the international community promptly, either directly or through an intermediary, when they suspend their human rights obligations during national crises. Traditionally, "notification requirements have been understood primarily as devices to facilitate international monitoring; when states provide notice of derogation pursuant to their treaty commitments, international and regional tribunals and other states-parties are better equipped to check human rights abuses" [3].

4.5   Temporal Scope

In their notification, states must also provide a clear timeframe (a "sunset" clause) for the state of emergency during which non-peremptory human rights are temporarily suspended. In Oren Gross and Fionnuala Ní Aoláin's words, "Only a truly extraordinary

---

[8] For instance, the European Commission on Human Rights has clarified the contours of the justification criterion, by understanding a public emergency crisis as a danger that is (1) present or imminent, (2) exceptional, (3) concerns the entire population, and (4) constitutes a 'threat to the organised life of the community'.

[9] "If the respondent Government does not furnish the required justification itself, as it is required to do under article 4.2 of the Optional Protocol and article 4.3 of the Covenant, the Human Rights Committee cannot conclude that valid reasons exist to legitimize a departure from the normal legal regime prescribed by the Covenant". [3, n. 90].

crisis that lasts for a relatively brief period of time can be a derogation-justifying emergency" [8]. Permanent or institutionalized states of emergency would represent an anathema to the principles undergirding international human rights law.

4.6 Contestation

In addition to the obligation to demonstrate justification of the necessity of declaring a state of emergency, it is crucial that, when public officials derogate from ordinary human rights, their decisions are open to public contestation to ensure that emergency powers are not held or abused so as to dominate the state's subjects.

5 Value Pluralism, State of Exception and the Slándáil System

What is desirable under value pluralism is a society structured to protect the ability of people to live out their cultural and ethical identities fruitfully.

The most pertinent implications of value pluralism for a system such as Slándáil relate to how it is used, particularly situations when decisions which involve conflicting values have to be promptly made. For example the need to protect the life and health of emergency responders can come into conflict with their duty to help and potentially save the lives of civilians. Value pluralism recognises the difficulty, even painfulness of such decisions and gives a place of priority to experience, precedent and virtue, acknowledging the courage and integrity required to put oneself at risk to protect the rights and liberty of others. It understands that, in practice, value conflicts are not "resolved", but "dealt with" through intuition and experience, in concrete and varying practical settings. Sara Geale lists "[t]he cardinal virtues of disaster response [as] prudence, courage, justice, stewardship, vigilance, resilience, self-effacing charity and communication" [6].

State of Exception doctrine has implications for a system like Slándáil primarily in its treatment of sensitive data in the exceptional circumstances of disaster response where normal ethical priorities do not pertain due to the imminent risks to life and property. In such circumstances there are strong ethical arguments to suspend normal provisions (such as privacy and data protection measures) constraining the use of personal data if necessary to save lives. State of Exception doctrine outlines the extent and scope of such constraints and therefore the provisions that must be made in the design of the system in order to implement these constraints.

The purpose of this theoretical analysis was to inform the development of an ethical framework to oversee the design, use and governance of the Slándáil system. To this end, the end users of the system were consulted on an ongoing basis to ensure that the framework accounted for their *modus operandi*, workshops were organised to discuss the proposed framework with them and the other project beneficiaries and scenario analyses were undertaken. This work highlighted the importance of consideration of ethical implications not only for the *human stakeholders* but also for the treatment of *information* contained in the Slándáil data that has been gathered from social media sources.

6   Ethical Implications for the Slándáil System

The potential ethical benefits and risks arising from use of the system were considered in the light of this theoretical research and the ethical implications were crystallised into an ethical framework. This framework set out explicit measures to be followed in terms of technical design, end-user practices (at the various phases of emergency management), licencing and administration of the Slándáil system. Naturally, some of these measures could have been (and have been in other disaster management systems) arrived at through other means; nevertheless it is useful to demonstrate their grounding in robust ethical deliberation.

The framework is structured in three sections, concerning the ethical implications for (a) the design, (b) the use and (c) the governance of the Slándáil system. In terms of the technical design, the main implications concerned data security, access control and authentication, data accuracy, anonymisation, data expiry and journaling. With regard to end user practice, information verification, triage protocols, attention to the effects of organisational power relations and adhering to specified use constraints were the main areas of ethical concern. Finally, issues relating to governance, including the ownership and licencing of the system and its associated intellectual property were assessed.

6.1   Ethical Implications for the Design of the Slándáil System

Implications for the technical design of the Slándáil system entail constraints in both its configuration and logical functioning, primarily derived from State of Exception considerations and related to the integrity and security of the data accessed by and information generated by the system.

Implications Concerning System Data
Security of the Data. Security of the system data is of primary concern. In order to respect the dignity and privacy of the people who could potentially be identified it is imperative that databases be secured to defend against hacking or any other unauthorised access.

Messages to emergency response personnel "in the field" should be encrypted, unquestionably if they contain potentially identifying data.

The physical location of the servers storing the system data and running the system's code must be considered to ensure that it cannot be accessed by external governments or agencies of other states. In addition, the legal context is affected by the physical location of the servers as even within the EU, for example, the Data Protection directive is implemented slightly differently in each state.

Access Control and Authentication. In order to ensure access to the data is only available to authorised persons the system will require user authentication and access control functionality.

User authentication will determine who can "log on" to the system. Access control permissions will need to be designed so that access to various parts of the system can be configured for each user dependent on their role and the current phase of emergency management. For example, certain data which is personally identifiable should only be accessible during the response phase of emergency management.[10]

Implications Concerning Public Protection

Data Accuracy. The phenomena of hoaxes and viral spreading of misinformation makes the task of verifying the accuracy of information especially difficult [18]. If the Slándáil system can give some measure of confidence or otherwise in the accuracy of the data it provides it would be extremely valuable for the end users and for the utility of the system as a whole.

Anonymisation. The task of emergency response personnel would be greatly facilitated by automated anonymisation of the data, whilst recognising that complete anonymisation is impossible. It is almost always possible to retrospectively disaggregate or re-nonymise data should it fall into the wrong hands [15]. Ethically speaking, it is highly desirable that the Slándáil system incorporate anonymisation measures as this would diminish the risk of infringements of privacy and dignity.

Data Expiry. A further step that is ethically desirable, and possibly legally required, is that of data expiry dependent on the phase of emergency management. In order to respect the temporal scope criterion of the state of exception doctrine it should be possible to define rules which govern the expiry of data that has been gathered or processed by the Slándáil system.[11]

Implications Concerning Slándáil End Users

Journaling. The incorporation of a journaling function that records management history as well as a journal of transactions, for the purposes of review, simulation and training is, ethically speaking, a double-edged sword. There is a risk that end-users' decision making could be influenced by the knowledge that every action taken on the system is recorded. Nevertheless, on the other side of the coin, the fact that there *is* a record of every action taken by each end user enables decisions to be retrospectively reviewed and evaluated should they be found to have been sub-optimal in the extant circumstances. Such a record also mitigates the risk of scapegoating in such circumstances.

6.2 Ethical Implications for the Use of the Slándáil System

Discussion of the ethical implications for the individuals using the Slándáil system is best structured along the phases of emergency management.[12]

---

[10] To be clear: the Slándáil system itself is to be used at all phases of emergency management but certain data (personal data) should be masked (anonymised) at phases other than the response phase.

[11] It may be ethically justifiable that the data be used post-response phase in order to facilitate debriefing and ascertaining learnings which can be used to improve response to future disasters.

[12] The UN-SPIDER glossary gives the following as the phases of disaster response: prevention, mitigation, preparedness, response, rehabilitation, reconstruction and recovery. The most relevant ones for Slándáil are mitigation, preparedness and response. Post-response, debrief and review are necessary but do not fit particularly well into the UN_SPIDER phases. [20].

Phases of Emergency Management: Mitigation and Preparedness

The main ethical implications here entail taking existing vulnerabilities and inequalities into account.

In the context of ethical considerations related to Slándáil, vulnerability of mobile internet infrastructure is a key consideration and a geospatial analysis of likely infrastructural damage would inform disaster response as there is a likelihood that areas susceptible to infrastructural damage would be under-represented in social media data.

Inequality in access to information technology and communications, the digital divide, would also lead to under-representation in the data. Again, geospatial analysis at the planning phase of the existing distribution of access to and use of social media technology would alert emergency response personnel to such inequalities which could then be accounted for in subsequent response.

Inequality in vulnerability needs to be integrated into disaster planning. These inequalities are likely to be reflected in social media use. Over-reliance on social media data may thus exacerbate them.

Another aspect of planning is training. The relevant emergency response personnel clearly need to be adequately trained in the use of the Slándáil system and in the manner in which its use is to be integrated into the overall disaster response strategy.

Phases of Emergency Management: Response

Verification. The importance of information verification has already been stressed and whilst it is anticipated that Slándáil will have means to assess the validity of information there nevertheless remains an ethical obligation on the part of the end users to seek to verify information by other means if possible, be that via traditional media, reports of emergency services personnel on the ground or interaction over social media with people on the ground.

Triage. The response to a disaster is essentially a triage operation at several levels, depending on the scale of the disaster. At each level decisions are made concerning the distribution of emergency response resources. The Slándáil system is intended to support decision making by providing information that would otherwise be unavailable. Nevertheless, such decisions are difficult as resources are not infinite and therefore sometimes will not be sufficient to meet need. In such circumstances a triage operation is undertaken and a decision made as to where there is the most need or where there will be the most benefit from deployment of limited resources.[13]

---

[13] Geale outlines the distinctions between triage in an emergency room situation and a disaster response situation: *"In day-to-day [A&E] triage, the common sense rule is to serve persons whose condition requires immediate attention and defer care to those who are more stable and can afford to wait; however, all patients will eventually get care. The process helps to ensure that no one is lost, and all get care appropriate to their needs. In a disaster involving multiple victims, and resources are completely overwhelmed, new protocols come into play. Disaster triage allows that the most seriously injured are left to the end – and may even remain untreated – so that those who can be saved can be cared for. This approach is one of the few instances where the utilitarian rule applies in health care. The greater good rule can be justified because of the clear necessity for allocation of resources to benefit the most people."* [6].

Value pluralism recognises the difficulty of such decisions and that experience and certain character virtues enable people to make the best choices. Therefore, as noted earlier, a culture supportive of unencumbered decision making should be fostered which has respect for stakeholder needs, desires, self-abnegation, courage and integrity. Aristotelian virtues also come into play in the decision not to treat in a disaster. It takes courage to make an ethical decision that a patient cannot be saved and that the resources both in manpower and equipment are better used in some other area [6].

Again, given considerations such as the digital divide and unequal vulnerability to disaster, the Slándáil system should not be the only means of triage in disaster response.

No personally identifying data, or data that identifies the ethnicity, sexuality or other potentially categorising data of people should have any effect on decisions of emergency response personnel. In other words, social sorting is unethical as it infringes the principle of justice as fairness.

Power. Issues around power are particularly pertinent when the emergency response personnel do not share the culture (and/or values) of the affected population. In any case response personnel have power based on their role of authority and their knowledge in the circumstances of disaster response, and Slándáil is a part of that.

Attention to the power relations inherent in the circumstances of disaster response demonstrates the danger of objectifying the "disaster victim" and essentialising the affected population, highlighting the necessity of respect for the dignity and worth of each individual, as is espoused by the principles of value pluralism and the absolute priority given to the protection of (all) human life by the emergency services.

The power of the Slándáil system itself to gather data which could be misused, renders it imperative that Slándáil data not be used for surveillance. Not only would this infringe on people's dignity through their right to privacy but it would also undermine the beneficence of the Slándáil system by undermining public trust in it, thus potentially putting lives at risk in future disaster situations.

Data Protection and Specified Use. End users have an ethical and legal obligation to respect privacy and anonymity of members of the public by using personal data only for the specified purpose (of emergency response) and for the period of the emergency itself. In communications with the public, as Watson et al. state:

"It is essential that those organizations involved in sharing material such as photos of disaster sites, take the appropriate measures to ensure the privacy of the public is upheld (e.g., masking faces and vehicle number plates), and where required, ensure that permission is gained from people to ensure their anonymity is protected" [24].

Legislation recognises that consent for the use of data is not always possible in a state of emergency, however, publicising personal data is a separate consideration which should respect privacy and anonymity rights.

Phases of Emergency Management: Post-response

Post-response phases of emergency management are not so closely related to the use of the Slándáil system, which is primarily intended as a decision-support tool. There remains, however, a question as to the ethical justification of using Slándáil data in the situation that a potential criminal offence becomes apparent during emergency response.

Ethically speaking, this could undermine trust in the system, as well as risking its use for purposes of surveillance should such "function-creep" be permissible. Legally speaking, derogations from human rights laws do apply for the purposes of criminal investigation, but may fall foul in this case as the specified use of the data is emergency response, not criminal investigation.

More straightforward ethically is the use of the system for debrief and review. The question is over the time-period of derogation: can it be said to include post-disaster review and learning? Certainly there is a strong ethical argument that review is an integral part of disaster response as it has the potential to improve future operations and therefore pertains to the principle of beneficence as it increases the system utility.

6.3   Ethical Implications for the Governance of the Slándáil System

Principles of beneficence and respect for human dignity entail further implications for the use of the Slándáil system that do not relate to the end users in a situation of disaster response but more to the uses to which the technology is put.

Firstly, responsibility for its governance in each state should be vested in an appropriate authority which has exclusive rights to the technology within the territory of the state, in order to prevent misuse for nefarious purposes by third parties. Responsibilities of this authority would include monitoring for and detecting ethical violations in the use of the system. Ownership of intellectual property must also be vested in an appropriate (European-level?) authority which can licence it out to the relevant national bodies to use in emergency response.

Secondly the terms of the end-user licence must ensure that its use is according to legal and ethical standards and in a transparent and accountable manner.

Finally, each emergency response organisation which uses the system will, under the terms of the licence, have to sign a document which specifies the legal and ethical constraints and terms governing the manner of its use so that its use at all times respects the ethical principles outlined in this document as well as the legal context in which it is deployed.

7   Conclusion

The large scale use of publically-available social media has great potential to inform decision making and improve disaster response efficiency. The Slándáil system is intended to achieve this in an ethically sound manner by harvesting social media data related to natural disaster, aggregating this data and providing informational outputs to emergency managers that identify vulnerable areas.

To this end the ethical the traditions of value pluralism and state of exception have been adopted to assess potential benefits and risks of the system. This has resulted in a practical and robust ethical framework which will inform the development, use and governance of the system to minimize the potential for undesirable consequences from its use.

References

1. Ashktorab, Z., et al.: Tweedr: Mining twitter to inform disaster response. In: Proceedings of the 11th International ISCRAM Conference (2014)
2. Berlin, I.: Two concepts of liberty. In: Hardy, H. (ed.) Liberty: Incorporating Four Essays on Liberty, pp. 166–217. Oxford University Press, Oxford (2002)
3. Criddle, E.J., Fox-Decent, E.: Human rights, emergencies, and the rule of law. Hum. Rights Q. **34**(1), 39–87 (2012)
4. Diner, D., Stolleis, M.: Hans Kelsen and Carl Schmitt: A Juxtaposition. Bleicher, Gerlingen (1999)
5. Galston, W.A.: What value pluralism means for legal-constitutional orders. San Diego Law Rev. **47**(2), 803–818 (2010)
6. Geale, S.K.: The ethics of disaster management. Disaster Prev. Manag. **21**(4), 445–462 (2012)
7. Gross, O.: Normless and exceptionless exception: Carl Schmitt's theory of emergency powers and the norm-exception Dichotomy. Cardozo Law Rev. **21**, 1825 (1999)
8. Gross, O., Ní Aoláin, F.: From discretion to scrutiny: revisiting the application of the margin of appreciation doctrine in the context of article 15 of the European convention on human rights. Hum. Rights Q. **23**(3), 625–649 (2001)
9. van den Hoven, J.: The use of normative theories in computer ethics. In: Floridi, L. (ed.) The Cambridge Handbook of Information and Computer Ethics, pp. 59–76. Cambridge University Press, Cambridge (2010)
10. Imran, M., et al.: AIDR: artificial intelligence for disaster response. In: Proceedings of the Companion Publication of the 23rd International Conference on World Wide Web Companion, pp. 159–162. International World Wide Web Conferences Steering Committee (2014)
11. Imran, M., et al.: Extracting information nuggets from disaster-related messages in social media. In: Proceedings of the 10th International ISCRAM Conference (2013)
12. Kinne, B.: Voltaire never said it! Mod. Lang. Notes. **58**(7), 534–535 (1943)
13. Lazar, N.C.: States of Emergency in Liberal Democracies. Cambridge University Press, Cambridge (2013)
14. Middleton, S.E., et al.: Real-time crisis mapping of natural disasters using social media. IEEE Intell. Syst. **29**(2), 9–17 (2014)
15. Narayanan, A., Shmatikov, V.: Robust de-anonymization of large sparse datasets. In: IEEE Symposium on Security and Privacy, SP 2008, pp. 111–125 (2008)
16. Nieuwenburg, P.: The agony of choice Isaiah Berlin and the phenomenology of conflict. Adm. Soc. **35**(6), 683–700 (2004)
17. Spicer, M.W.: Value pluralism and its implications for American public administration. Adm. Theor. Prax. **23**(4), 507–528 (2001)
18. Starbird, K., et al.: Rumors, false flags, and digital vigilantes: misinformation on twitter after the 2013 Boston Marathon bombing. Presented at the 1 March 2014
19. Swan, P.: American empire or empires: alternative juridifications of the new world order. In: Bartholomew, A. (ed.) Empire's Law: The American Imperial Project and the "War to Remake the World", pp. 137–160. Pluto Press, Ann Arbor, London, Toronto (2006)
20. United Nations: Disaster Management Cycle (2014). http://www.un-spider.org/glossary/disaster-management-cycle
21. United Nations, Economic and Social Council: Siracusa Principles on the Limitation and Derogation Provisions in the International Covenant on Civil and Political Rights (1985)
22. Wagenaar, H.: The necessity of value pluralism in administrative practice a reply to overeem. Adm. Soc. **46**(8), 1020–1028 (2014)

23. Wagenaar, H.: Value pluralism in public administration. Adm. Theor. Prax. **21**(4), 441–449 (1999)
24. Watson, H., et al.: Citizen (in)security?: Social media, citizen journalism and crisis response. Presented at the ISCRAM 2014 Conference Proceedings - 11th International Conference on Information Systems for Crisis Response and Management (2014)
25. Wright, D., et al.: Ethical dilemma scenarios and emerging technologies. Technol. Forecast. Soc. Change **87**, 325–336 (2014)
26. Yin, J., et al.: Using social media to enhance emergency situation awareness. IEEE Intell. Syst. **27**(6), 52–59 (2012)

Decision Support Systems and Collaboration

Towards a Support to Stakeholders' Collaboration During a Loire River Major Flooding

Audrey Fertier[1], Anne-Marie Barthe-Delanoë[1(✉)], Johan Manceau[2],
Sébastien Truptil[1], and Frédérick Bénaben[1]

[1] Mines Albi — University of Toulouse, Route de Teillet, 81013 Albi, France
{audrey.fertier,anne-marie.barthe,sebastien.truptil,
frederick.benaben}@mines-albi.fr
[2] CEREMA - Direction territoriale Ouest, 9 rue René Viviani, 44262 Nantes, France
johan.manceau@cerema.fr

Abstract. Major flood of the Loire (longest river in France) is the third feared natural disaster in France. As the Loire flows through major cities and that four nuclear plants are located on its banks, flooding risk increases the vulnerability of critical backbone infrastructures of the West area of France, such as road, energy and communication networks. Crisis response involves numerous and heterogeneous stakeholders, and their services, into a collaborative network to coordinate their actions. Moreover, effectiveness of the crisis response depends on the aforesaid backbone networks. To address these issues, the French funded project GéNéPi aims to provide a Mediation Information System to support the coordination of the stakeholders and to enhance data retrieval, information analysis and knowledge gathering among the responders. It will aggregate data collected from the field of operations into information and then filter and exploit this information into knowledge, usable for the decision makers.

Keywords: Loire river · Collaboration · Flood · Crisis response · Network

1 Introduction

In France, crisis situation management is an issue falling within the governmental functions of the state, through its institutions. Emergency plans, doctrines and rules are officially defined. But it appears that even if the stakeholders and their capabilities are relevant regarding the crisis situation to deal with, the main issue is the coordination of their actions. This problem appears clearly in the context of the flooding of the Loire River area, as underlined by the feedback on past floods and training exercises [1]. To both protect the impacted civilians (and goods) and the backbone networks (roads, energy, communication), the coordination of people and goods is critical. Some constraints challenge even more this need of coordination, like the timeline of the flood, the geographic scope or the networks' interdependence.

To address these issues, the French funded project GéNéPi aims to provide a Mediation Information System to support:

N. Bellamine Ben Saoud et al. (Eds.): ISCRAM-med 2015, LNBIP 233, pp. 183–193, 2015.
DOI: 10.1007/978-3-319-24399-3_16

- The coordination between the responders, on the field of operations,
- The coordination between the several levels of decision-making.

To achieve these purposes, the system will enhance the data retrieval, the aggregation of these data into information and the analysis of this information. This final part has been made possible thanks to the knowledge gathered among the responders. Finally, the system will adapt itself to the inherent contingencies of the crisis. The aim of this article is to present the major issues faced by the crisis management unit actors during a response to a major flood of the Loire River, and to propose a way to support collaboration during such a situation.

This article is organized as follows: Sect. 2 presents the context of the Loire River area, considering the timeline of the events in case of flooding and the networks' vulnerabilities during such a natural disaster. Based on the necessities of the described situation, it will also highlight the major issues faced by the stakeholders to work in a collaborative manner. Then it presents, in Sect. 3, a solution to support the collaborative behavior and share information efficiently, before concluding in Sect. 4.

2   Complexity and Vulnerabilities of Actors and Backbone Networks

In this section, we will describe the ins and outs of a major flood on the Loire River. Then, we will focus on (i) the actors involved into crisis management and on (ii) the four major backbone networks existing in the area and which may be severely disrupted by the described flood.

We will present a brief description of a 1/50 per year flood on the Loire River. The Loire, the longest river in France, rises in the southeastern part of the Massif Central called the Cévennes. It flows northward for over 1,000 km through Nevers to Orléans, and then West through Tours and Nantes until it reaches the Atlantic Ocean at St Nazaire. Massive rainfalls in the Cévennes happened from October 20th until October 27th. These meteorological phenomena result in an important flood all along the Loire River.

The use case focuses on the Middle Loire area (450 km), between Nevers and Angers, which is split into five vals [2]: Vals Amont, Val d'Orleans, Val de Blois, Val de Tours, Val d'Authion, as shown on Fig. 1. A val is an area protected by dikes from flooding by relatively small floods. The system of vals will work in such a way that gradually the vals will be inundated in case of a flood flow on the Loire [3].

2.1   Forecast Events

Six days before the flood (D−6), Meteo France (the French weather forecast service) forecasts rainfalls in the Cévennes in the following week. At D−4, the forecasts are refined and used to estimate the water level of the Loire. At D−2, waterfalls occur at the rise of the Loire and the 48 h forecasts project a major flood on the Middle Loire area.

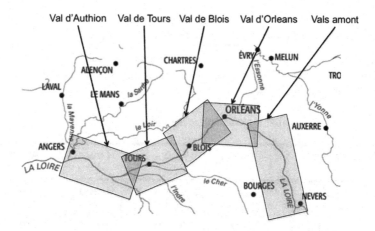

Fig. 1. The five vals of the Middle Loire area (based on [2]).

2.2 Flood Events

Table 1 presents the evolution of the alerts in the five vals, starting to D-day, two days after the rainfalls began. The French early warning system for floods uses a color code matching with warning levels (matching increasing severity of water level and threats), in yellow, orange and red, while green means no warning situation.

For example, at D−1, the five vals have a green code status (no alert). At D−0, the Vals Amont switches to yellow alert and the lower districts of Gien (a city located between Nevers and Orléans) are evacuated. If the other vals are still in green status, the Val d'Orléans and Val de Blois prepare to switch on yellow alert up to the next 24 h (water level will be likely to rise up over 3.5 m). At D + 5, the water level begins to decrease in the Vals Amont and Val d'Orléans, while Val de Blois, Tour and Authion are still facing a very high water level (up to 6 m). As shown in this table, there is a cascading effect of the flooding, and a gap between the moments when the flood impacts cities.

2.3 Various and Heterogeneous Actors

In the case of a flood in the Middle Loire area, crisis response involves 23 kinds of actors in the crisis management unit [4], including institutions, government representatives, public and private organizations like:

- State services and agencies, such as DREAL (regional agency for environment and housing management, under the umbrella of the Ministry of Ecology, Sustainable Development and Energy and the Ministry of Housing), DIR (regional road network management), DDT (territory management and natural risk prevention) and ARS (support evacuation of health and medico-social institutions), police, etc.,
- Forecast services: Meteo France (weather forecasting), Service de Prévision des Crues (flood forecasting), local early warning systems,
- Emergency services: SAMU (Urgent Medical Aid Service), SDIS (fire brigade),

- Local actors and other organizations: mayors, regional councils, water/power/communication/road network managers, civil security, etc.

These actors are from various hierarchical levels (local, departmental, zonal, regional, national) of the French civil protection structure and at either decisional, operational or support levels [4].

Table 1. Evolution of the alert in each val.

Vals	Amont	Orléans	Blois	Tours	Authion
D-0	Yellow	Green	Green	Green	Green
D+1	Orange	Yellow	Yellow	Green	Green
D+2	Orange	Orange	Yellow	Green	Yellow
D+3	Orange	Orange	Orange	Green	Yellow
D+4	Orange	Orange	Orange	Yellow	Orange
D+5	Yellow	Yellow	Orange	Yellow	Orange
D+6	Green	Yellow	Yellow	Yellow	Orange
D+7	Green	Green	Green	Green	Yellow
D+8	Green	Green	Green	Green	Green

From these levels, two main dimensions (orthogonal with each other) have been considered by the research project GéNéPi to define crisis management points of view, as illustrated by Fig. 2:

- Horizontal dimension: it focuses on the operational distribution of the stakeholders, considering their abilities, capacities and missions,
- Vertical dimension: it is about the management granularity, especially at the decision level (local, county, zonal and national levels).

2.4 Backbone Networks

In the Middle Loire area, power is mainly produced by four nuclear plants. They were built on areas which are (normally) non-affected by the historical floods. The transmission of electricity is made through the electricity grids, which are composed of very high

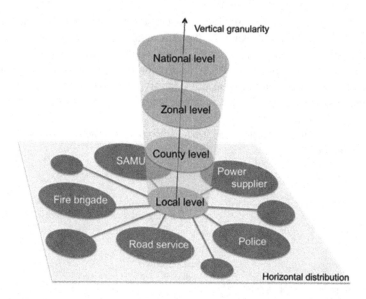

Fig. 2. Horizontal and vertical points of view of crisis management in France.

voltage power lines, high voltage power lines and transformer substations. Twelve of such substations are located in areas liable to flooding, and some power lines cross the Loire River [5]. Electricity distribution is ensured by middle and low voltage lines and transformer substations (4000 substations are located in flood-prone areas).

The road network is very vulnerable to floods. Thus, there is an issue to link both banks of the Loire River as soon as the water level reaches the front of average floods. This issue can be a major one in case of severe floods, causing hundreds of kilometers where crossing the Loire is impossible. This is mainly due to the submersion of the roads to the bridges. As road network is crucial to support crisis management (evacuation of people, transport of emergency means, etc.) and to on-site service for other backbone networks (power grid, telecommunications, drinking water), this issue is particularly serious.

The fixed line telecommunications network is subdivided into four networks: wide area, sectoral, regional and local networks. These networks are composed of wires splitters, routing centers and distribution frames. During a flood, the splitters are the most vulnerable part of the network: they are numerous, part of the non-meshed network and sometimes built on exposed areas. In the countryside, flooding causes landslides that threat the poles supporting the wires.

During a flood, the main issue is the halting of drinking water production mainly due to (i) the loss of power supply, and/or (ii) the poor quality of pumped water (as a consequence of the extraction from the Loire or from a submerged well). The catchments are particularly vulnerable because they are often located on the edge of watercourse and they do not have necessarily auxiliary generators.

In addition to the inherent vulnerabilities of these major networks, resilience is also challenged by the interdependence of the networks. The report made by French regional authorities [5] underlines the vulnerabilities caused by these interdependencies (as summed up into Table 2). For example, the telecommunications network relies on the power grid to ensure its proper functioning. The road network is also necessary in case of on-site service (to repair facilities) or to provide mobile stations to support crisis management telecommunications. On the contrary, the loss of all (or a part) of the drinking water system has no effect on the telecommunications network.

Table 2. Synthesis of the major interdependencies among technical networks in the Middle Loire area (adapted from [5]).

	Power	Telecommunications (Telco)	Road	Drinking water
Power		Necessary during crisis response management (for early warning and communication)	Needed in case of on-site service	None
Telco	Necessary for the proper functioning of the telecommunication exchange and routing of signals		Necessary in case of on-site service on impacted sites, and for crisis management (providing mobile stations and human resources where required)	None
Road	Necessary for traffic regulation and tolls (cities, motorways)	Necessary to communicate with the crisis management unit and on-site stakeholders (vehicles are not always equipped with radio)		None
Drinking water	Highly vulnerable to power loss for pumping, cleaning and supply activities	Necessary during crisis response management (for early warning and communication). Also necessary for remote alarms and management systems of some water treatment plants	Needed in case of on-site service (water sampling, repairs)	

Thus, networks are considered as structuring parts of the territory and necessary to ensure its proper functioning, especially in the context of a crisis situation. Now, adding the temporal dynamics of the flood to the interdependencies of the networks, and thereby of the stakeholders in charge of them, shows the need for effective coordination of tasks and information sharing, especially during a crisis situation. How to coordinate actions and allocate resources, and how to allow exchange between stakeholders?

3 Supporting the Crisis Response

To answer the two questions raised in Sect. 2, the proposed solution will have to manage the numerous actors, considering their heterogeneity, their interdependencies through the networks and the timeline of the flood, and will have to deal with the evolution of the crisis situation and occurrence of new threats.

3.1 An Interoperability Issue...

Supporting the collaborative behavior of the crisis management unit is a major gap in crisis response management, as underlined by the European project ACRIMAS [6]. In the case of the Middle Loire flooding, the French hierarchical organization of the crisis management unit challenges the coordination of the actors at several levels:

- Information is shared across several channels among the crisis management unit. If redundancy could be seen as a way to ensure information sharing whatever happens, the feedback shows that at a given instant t, information is not necessary consistent across the collaborative network [1],
- The amount of available data is increasing due to the digitation of the space, through connected objects, social networks, etc.,
- The software tools used to support the responders are heterogeneous (e.g. at the local level, some mayors use OSIRIS software to support decision making about evacuation of the population of their villages [7]).

The number and variety of involved stakeholders make it difficult to exchange the right information at the right moment: data loss, complexity of the information, many heterogeneous data formats, lack of visibility about the data sources, etc. In other words, the crisis management unit is facing an interoperability issue.

3.2 ... and an Agility Issue...

As shown in Sect. 2, the crisis response execution and accuracy can be threatened by the dynamics of the flood (actors have to face more and more flooded areas as the front moves forward on the Loire river) and by the vulnerability of the networks. In other words, the collaborative situation is subject to evolutions.

According to [8], these evolutions can be classified under three categories:

- Evolution of context: the collaboration's environment differs from the one taken into account to define the collaborative processes (i.e. the crisis response in the considered case),

- Evolution of network: this evolution concerns the stakeholders, their abilities and their resources. For instance, the departure of the stakeholder from the crisis management unit is considered as an evolution of the network,
- Failure: one or several activities do not lead to the expected results. This can be due to an incomplete initial definition of the collaborative processes or an improper execution of them.

By the nature of crisis, these evolutions are not necessarily planned or expected (even if the preparation phase of the crisis management intends to identify risks). It is therefore necessary to take into account the possible evolutions that can challenge the networks and so the crisis response, in order to change the collaborative behavior on-the-fly if needed. Considering these requirements, the issue is to provide agility to the crisis response (i.e. to the collaborative processes) to ensure its accuracy (and the resilience of the networks).

3.3   ...Solved at the Information System Level

According to the International Virtual Laboratory for Enterprise Interoperability, interoperability is "the ability of a system or a product to work with other systems or products without special effort from the customer or user" [9]. Considering that actors involved in crisis management can generally be considered as fully relevant and capable, they have to remain autonomous for their deployment (in terms of means and realization of their activities). So the point is to support the collaborative processes, i.e. the processes defined and executed among the actors (and not those inherent to each actor). According to Morley [10], Information System (IS) can be seen as a set of interacting workflows, services and data, and so it is the visible part of an organization. The point is to tackle organizations' collaboration issue through ISs interoperability satisfying the business requirements (considering their heterogeneity).

The GéNéPi project proposes a Mediation Information System, which is in charge of supporting ISs interoperability in the context of a crisis situation in France. The main functions of such a MIS are (as illustrated by Fig. 3):

- Business level: this first level deals with knowledge gathering (regarding the crisis itself, the partners capabilities, the risk pools, the doctrinal elements and rules, etc.) and knowledge management to deduce collaborative processes (dedicated to solve the crisis situation, according to both the mobilizable partners and the specificities of the impacted perimeter).
- Technical level: this second level concerns the orchestration and the steering of the collaborative processes defined at business level. The main goal is to orchestrate technically the business collaborative processes (deduced at business level) by (i) connecting with existing ISs and tools of the involved partners, and (ii) generating interfaces to support human tasks of the business processes.
- Agility management level: this last level concerns situation awareness through the monitoring of both the current crisis situation (to get a "picture" of the real status of the system) and the process orchestration (to maintain a "composite picture" of the expected status of the system deducted from the activities states). By comparing both

these "pictures" and analyzing their differences, it is possible to (i) detect any potential need for adaptation and (ii) give advice regarding the required adaptation. Consequently, such an agility principle can deal with the kinetics of crisis situation and adaptation of the response to ensure resilience.

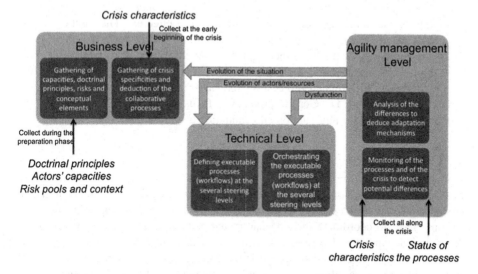

Fig. 3. Conceptual architecture of the mediation information system.

At the technical level, the MIS architecture relies on both Service Oriented Architecture (SOA) and Event-Driven Architecture (EDA) principles. This mixed ED-SOA architecture allows (i) a very high level of low coupling among the tools used by the stakeholders (meeting the interoperability and agility issues), (ii) gathering, filtering and analyzing amounts of data in real-time through events and Complex Event Processing (CEP) [11]. Data, information and knowledge collection to assess the situation (from both field and processes points of view) can be made not only with classical means but also by exploiting the Internet of Things.

For example, an ERDF team (stakeholder in charge of the power network) has to go on-site to check a substation. On their way to the substation, they have to stop as the road in flooded. Their GPS cannot find an alternative route nearby. They decide to go to the substation across the fields, as they are equipped with all-road capability vehicles. We can imagine that the embedded GPS registers the new route and is able to automatically share it with the MIS on the fly. In the meantime, a fire brigade has also to go on a site located near the substation. Through the MIS, they automatically know that the ERDF team changed their route after a while to reach the substation and so, it should be more relevant to choose another route or to have a vehicle with all-road capability (to go across the fields). Moreover, a message is automatically sent to alert the partner in charge of the road network. This partner will be aware of this new danger and can then ask to a team to close the concerned road properly.

One may wonder how the crisis management unit may accept such a solution. To support these research works in the frame of the GéNéPi project, the same stakeholders as those described in Sect. 2 take part into the project consortium. For instance, this conglomerate gathers the DREAL, ERDF, the Ministry of Ecology, Sustainable Development and Energy, the Prefecture of the Loiret department among many others. They validate all the steps of the project, so the crisis management unit will accept the proposed Mediation Information System when it will be effective. The solution is now at its early stages, but it inherits some results from past successful research projects: (i) ISyCri (French ANR funded project) for the characterization of collaboration in the context of crisis management [12]; (ii) SocEDA (French ANR funded project) and PLAY (European FP7 funded project) for the EDA and CEP approach to ensure the context awareness [13]. The GéNéPi project will focus on the vertical dimension of the collaboration and on the aggregation and validation of information.

4 Conclusion

The Loire River flood use-case presented in this paper underlines two major issues in French crisis management: (i) the heterogeneous stakeholders involved in the crisis response have to coordinate their decisions and actions on numerous flooded areas, (ii) the interdependence of the networks that can challenge their own resilience and their ability to support the crisis response. It is therefore necessary to support the share of information and the coordination of the actions among the actors of the crisis management unit.

A Mediation Information System, as proposed by the GéNéPi project, can solve this interoperability issue through the implementation of an ED-SOA architecture. This MIS will also propose capabilities to aggregate and filter information in order to support decision-making. This MIS is currently under development and will be assessed with a realistic scenario about a major flood of the Loire River (validated by practitioners involved in such a crisis situation). Two main limitations can be identified: (i) the dependency on the technical network as we are based on organizations' ISs, (ii) the trust into collected data/information/knowledge and the levels of dissemination. Concerning limitation (i), hardware security measures should be taken to protect the physical network. Limitation (ii) can be overcome by ensuring the governance of the data collection.

Acknowledgements. This work has been partially funded by the French Research Agency (ANR) regarding the research project GéNéPi (Granularité des Niveaux de Pilotage en Gestion de Crise) (Grant ANR-14-CE28-0029). The authors would like to thank the project partners for their advices regarding this work.

References

1. Minister of the Interior: Synthese RETEX 2013 (2013). http://www.interieur.gouv.fr/content/download/68180/495663/file/Synthese_RETEX_2013.pdf

2. Equipe pluridisciplinaire plan Loire Grandeur Nature: Etude de la propagation des crues et des risques d'inondation en Loire Moyenne (2004)
3. Dijkman, J., Maaten, R.: Flood management for the middle loire; an outsiders' perspective. Delft Hydraulics (2006)
4. Centre Européen de Prévention du Risque d'Inondation: L'évacuation massive des populations - Les territoires face à l'inondation (2014). http://www.cepri.net/Evacuation_massive_des_populations.html
5. Etablissement Public Loire, Agence de l'eau Loire-Bretagne: Etude préalable à la réduction de la vulnérabilité des réseaux liée aux inondations en Loire moyenne (2006)
6. Hamrin, M.: Aftermath crisis management system-of-systems demonstration - D4.2 Gap analysis report., Stockholm, Sweden (2011)
7. Hissel, F., Morel, G., Pescaroli, G., Graaff, H., Felts, D., Pietrantoni, L.: Early warning and mass evacuation in coastal cities. Coast. Eng. **87**, 193–204 (2014)
8. Pingaud, H.: Prospective de recherches en interopérabilité: vers un art de la médiation ? In: Actes du 8ème Congrès International de Génie Industriel., Tarbes, France (2009)
9. Konstantas, D., Bourrieres, J.-P., Leonard, M., Boudjlida, N.: Interoperability of Enterprise Software and Applications. Springer, London (2006)
10. Morley, C., Hugues, J., Leblanc, B.: UML pour l'analyse d'un système d'information. Le cahier des charges du maître d'ouvrage. DUNOD (2010)
11. Etzion, O., Niblett, P.: Event Processing in Action. Manning Publications Co., Greenwich (2010)
12. Truptil, S., Bénaben, F., Pingaud, H.: A mediation information system to help to coordinate the response to a crisis. In: Camarinha-Matos, L.M., Boucher, X., Afsarmanesh, H. (eds.) PRO-VE 2010. IFIP AICT, vol. 336, pp. 173–180. Springer, Heidelberg (2010)
13. Verginadis, Y., Apostolou, D., Barthe-Delanoe, A.-M., Benaben, F.: Addressing agility in collaborative processes: a comparative study. In: 2013 7th IEEE International Conference on Digital Ecosystems and Technologies (DEST), pp. 120–125 (2013)

On the Literature Divergences
of the Humanitarian Supply Chain

Hossein Baharmand[1](✉), Laura Laguna Salvadó[1,2], Tina Comes[1],
and Matthieu Lauras[2]

[1] Centre for Integrated Emergency Management, Department of ICT,
University of Agder, 4879 Grimstad, Norway
{hossein.baharmand,tina.comes}@uia.no,
[2] Mines d'Albi (University of Toulouse), 81000 Albi, France
matthieu.lauras@mines-albi.fr,
laura.lagunasalvado@mines-albi.fr

Abstract. The field of humanitarian logistics has evolved rapidly over the past decade, drawing on contributions from the areas of operations research, business engineering, supply chain management, information systems, and computer sciences. Even more varied are the specific problems that are modeled and addressed, ranging monitoring of the supply chain as a whole to decision support for specific sourcing or distribution decisions. While recently, few studies have presented taxonomies and identified research gaps, there is to this date not yet a clear understanding of how the different methodologies and domains shall be combined to achieve a consistent mix of methods and tools. In this paper, we present a start towards this aim comparing two distinct perspectives and related research approaches, methods and tools: business engineering and operations research. Our findings indicate that there are real opportunities for interdisciplinary research to improve the overall performance of the humanitarian supply chain.

Keywords: Humanitarian supply chain · Operational research · Business engineering · Literature review

1 Introduction

There has been a remarkable raise on the numbers of humanitarian disasters during the last decade. Despite the increase of funding [1] still there is a significant gap between appeals and what is provided, hence the need for more effective and efficient response [2]. Humanitarian disaster management (HDM) is characterised by complexity, e.g., uncertainty, time pressure, or the large number of heterogeneous actors. Humanitarian supply chain (HSC) management plays a key role in disaster response and is recognized as a field of research [3]. Several literature reviews have been done to identify the gaps that research should address [4, 5], and different approaches applied to deal with the challenges raised [6, 7].

Although the performance of the response is contingent to meaningful knowledge integration across disciplines [8], research in the humanitarian field has often been

© Springer International Publishing Switzerland 2015
N. Bellamine Ben Saoud et al. (Eds.): ISCRAM-med 2015, LNBIP 233, pp. 194–204, 2015.
DOI: 10.1007/978-3-319-24399-3_17

limited to a disciplinary approach (e.g. operations research in humanitarian logistics). However, a multi- or interdisciplinary perspective can bring new insights, models and theories dedicated to the interplay of factors in real-world environments that are suitable for conceptual, analytical, empirical, and applied research [9].

The authors' backgrounds allowed us to review the HSC literature from two scientific angles: business-engineering science (BS) and operations research (OR). While BS aims at keeping track and aligning all processes in a supply chain, OR requires decomposing the supply chain into units that can be captured in abstract models [10]. We limited our study on four fundamental topics (HSC structure, flow control, time frames, and dynamic uncertainty) frequently addressed in literature. Our objective is to address the following research questions:

- What is the state of the art in HSC referring to those topics by focusing on BS and OR literature?
- What are future research directions in those topics according to BS and OR?

The novelty of this paper is this twofold focus on literature, which is illustrated by Fig. 1. This survey aims to contribute to the multi-disciplinary study of HSCs.

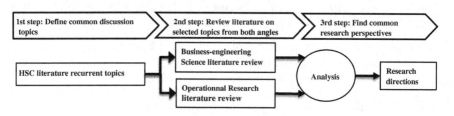

Fig. 1. Research Methodology

The rest of the paper is organized as follows: Sect. 2 discusses the research methodology; literature is reviewed in Sect. 3 by focusing on four specific topics; Sect. 4 provides the research needs; and the paper ends with conclusion at Sect. 5 by a summary of key findings.

2 Research Methodology

Following the well-known disaster management cycle, this review is dedicated to the response phase. Instead of conducting an exhaustive review, we conducted an exploratory study focusing on key publications in the areas of BS and OR. We start from identifying fundamental common topics to classify the literature in them.

BS focuses on a holistic view of the HSC. It looks at different flows and business processes that form the value chain: information, materials, financial, people (man power) and knowledge & skills [11]. OR pursuits to accomplish its contribution by focusing on detailed quantitative simulations and modeling [7]. While OR is more focused on logistics aspects, BS mainly focuses on relationships among the actors and organizational or management aspects.

To develop a classification we reviewed post-disaster HSC literature from both the BS and OR angle. In addition, we reviewed recent survey papers [4–7], to select a set of keywords to define our search chain, which was executed in GoogleScholar to ensure that a broad set of papers was covered. Our initial review revealed four joint areas of interest: HSC structure, flow control mechanisms, time frames, and dynamic uncertainty. The final selection was done on the basis of relevance of the articles to two scientific angles by reviewing their abstracts, findings and conclusions.

3   Literature Review

3.1   HSC Structure

According to the Council of Supply Chain Management Professionals, *"supply chain management integrates supply and demand management within and across companies."* HSC is not a series of discrete events in a linear process. According to a typical HSC shown by Fig. 2, it encompasses all activities involved in sourcing and procurement, conversion, and almost all logistics operations [12]. For more than a decade now, authors have tried to provide directions to advance HSC technology [13–15]. Following Hellingrath, Link and Widera [16], the main humanitarian-specific attributes are:

- Highly responsive (effective) instead of efficient (cost effective) processes,
- Uncertain and unpredictable demand,
- The role of donors as buyers and beneficiaries as end users,
- A highly volatile environment,
- Partly temporary and unknown supply chain design,
- Focus on procurement and distribution within the logistics value chain.

Mays, Racadio and Gugerty [15] insist that ignoring the differences can raise the risk of too focus on efficiency aims (e.g. operation cost) which may lead to less effective humanitarian efforts or divert from their stated mission and values. They suggest that academics should better contribute to HSC by a 'ground up' research design like the recent study of Chan and Comes [17].

However, HSC still suffers from key problems. In comparison to commercial supply chains (CSC), the process modeling of HSC is in its infancy [18]. The aim of process modeling is to help decision makers to optimize the processes by enabling a rapid visualization of HSC tasks. Although there are several successful approaches for CSCs, the applicability of existing solutions from the corporate world to the humanitarian sector is limited [19, 20].

Looking at the HSC mathematical models, previous surveys confirm that literature mainly focuses on a specific part of HSC [6, 7, 9]. Typically, simulations and modeling approaches are classified in three categories: facility location problems, distribution problems and inventory decision problems. Further investigation in each category reveals that also the focus on specific subproblems did not lead to much progress: Galindo and Batta [7] surveyed the existing literature of disaster operations management comparing to the similar work of Altay and Green [10] and didn't find any major change. Holguín-Veras, Jaller, Van Wassenhove, Pérez and Wachtendorf [9] highlight the urgency in

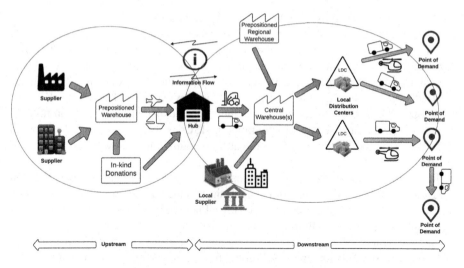

Fig. 2. A Typical HSC

understanding the specific HSC aspects like the decision making process. Similar literature review by Caunhye, Nie and Pokharel [21] depicted that research on transportation,
like casualty transportation, is still limited. Luis, Dolinskaya and Smilowitz [22] pointed
out that multi-period routing has not been modelled in the relief routing literature. Similar
to Kunz and Reiner [23] findings, our review revealed that attention is dedicated mostly
to the post-disaster, and specifically to distribution problems. There are a few common
assumptions, which are frequently repeated in mathematical models. Realistic or not, these
assumptions and constraints leave the field still interesting for further research. Several
authors have also proposed solutions to solve humanitarian case-specific processes, or
reference models transposable to several organizations [24].

Blecken [18] developed a reference model framework that is composed of two
dimensions; hierarchical and structural. This framework can be used combined with the
modeling language BPMN (bussiness process model and notation), as suggested by
Blecken and then used by Franke, Widera, Charoy, Hellingrath and Ulmer [25] and
Hellingrath, Link and Widera [16] among others. Furthermore, recent research suggest
to take a step forward towards the use of simulation tools to evaluate modifications of
the HSC network [16]. In the same way, Hofmann, Betke and Sackmann [26] propose
a theoretical workflow management system to support a semi-automated analyses and
adapting of ongoing disaster response processes.

3.2 Flow Control

The HSC networks, support essentially three different flows: Material, Information and
Financial. The initial flow of material reflects the immediate reaction of actors according
to the information transmitted [27]. It is necessary to provide accurate and timely information on what supplies are needed, what supplies was delivered to beneficiaries and

where [28]. However, most NGOs manage the response processes mainly based on experience, and the concept of flow control, or performance, is poorly understood [29].

Improved information flow is also necessary for performance management [4]. There are only few publications on performance measurement systems (PMSs). Key performance indicators (KPIs) are a way to 'control the flow' of HSC [29, 30], yet this field is still in its early steps. A recent review by Abidi, de Leeuw and Klumpp [4] indicates that while there are some theoretical considerations, the number of contributions that deal with real situations in HSCs is low. In addition, there is no convergence on which performance indicator or evaluation framework is suitable for specific situations.

Information systems have been developed to support HSC management. Blecken and Hellingrath [31] did a comparative analysis concluding that currently, no software system responds to all requirements of HSC: Planning; Documentation; Reporting; Cross-linking of systems; Offline use & Synchronization; Modularity & Adaptability; Tracking & Tracing; User friendliness, Training; Software costs and Hardware costs. They suggest to use commercial solutions that are better developed e.g. OpenERP (UniField) by MSF [32].

Another approach is Value Stream Analysis. Taylor and Pettit [33] did a theoretical study of the use of such a Lean Management approach and raised some challenges for the use of this "commercial" approach: 1) the transitory nature of HSCs; 2) HSCs should operate effectively from the start; 3) there is a need to improve the performance in real time as well as after the response.

In comparison to BS which mainly looks for monitoring indicators to establish flow control, OR primarily focus on network flow models with the objective of optimizing the flow of supplies through these networks. It discusses different modes of flow in distribution plan problems in time dependent approaches and models the commodity flow in distinct distribution network styles, for instance dynamic network [34] and static network [35], or sometimes in resource allocation [9].

In mathematical models, typically, relief goods, equipment, and personnel "flow" in almost zero lead-time from the source to the beneficiary using ad-hoc distribution facilities and networks [36]. This approach might work if suppliers comply to provision of specific items or services in a prearranged time frame. It is also unrealistic to develop models based on reliable commodity flow. Sometimes, assumptions are also affected by political instability, infrastructure, topography, and the limited (or non-existent) transportation capacity in the affected area [37].

Furthermore, material convergence—the spontaneous flow of supplies, donations, and equipment to a disaster area— is a poorly understood phenomenon and comprises three groups [38]: 1. High-priority supplies for immediate distribution and consumption, 2. Low-priority supplies that are not immediately needed but could be useful later, and 3. Non-priority supplies that are not of any use. To prevent losses (or diversions) and convergences, and ensure a more efficient use of resources, one idea could be to track the supplies and establish controls to indicate what types of supplies have been mobilized, in what quantity, and condition. They could also identify the parties that have intervened in the process.

3.3   Time Frames

A large amount of literature HSC management focuses on the response phase of a disaster [39]. This could be influenced by: (1) the significant role of logistics in this phase; (2) the key objective of saving lives during response phase; and (3) the huge amount of media coverage in comparison to other phases.

The response phase covers all actions to be carried out after an initiating hazard event. Regardless of crisis nature, humanitarian operations can be classified in distinct time frames: ramp-up, mature/sustain, and ramp-down [40]. Ramp-up is equivalent to the "immediate-response" which is defined by Cozzolino [41]. During this stage, supplies are pushed to the disaster location [12], and there is a priority on effectiveness. The transition to the sustain and ramp-down phases involves a shift in HSC management focus from speed to cost reduction in terms of operational performance [40], or from agile to lean principles.

The paradigm between leanness and agility has been discussed a few times (i.e. by Cozzolino [41] and Heckmann, Comes and Nickel [42]). However, this transition can be also seen in the HSC stream relating to the choice of *decoupling points*. We found some literature concerning the hybrid *leagile* HSC, suggesting the combination of lean and agile approaches [43]. First impressions are pointing to support IT developments for adopting such strategies.

The changing environment is an important challenge requiring a flexible HSC. To deal with the issue of flexibility, there are several research addressing problems in single time periods [44], a few contributions have struggled with multi period modelling [39], neglecting the fact that the deployed network is usually temporary and needs to be flexible to accommodate the demand's variation in different time frames. Moreover, in a multi-period planning horizon, site's costs and capacities may impact the decisions, turning the selection of appropriate time step in multi period modelling into a significant factor that can dramatically affect the performance of time-space networks [34]. In short: to keep the problem manageable, it is favourable to have longer time steps but shorter time steps will improve the accuracy of modelling the emergency response operations. Beyond these response related issues, Kunz and Reiner [23] concluded that more attention needs to be paid to the logistics operations with longer-term considerations, spanning into the development phase.

Considering the OR's literature on multi period modeling, specifically in distribution plans, nearly 50 % of contributions on logistics networks aim to minimize cost. In the transportation problems the objectives focus more on the speed or the satisfaction of demand. All of the abovemention as well as social costs and priority are recognized as key objectives in OR literature, and monodimensional problems are considered as limited and unrealistic [6]. To be as close as possible to reality, distributions plans (or models) not only should work in multi periods, their objective function should include a combination of objectives at the same time to reflect the complexity of decision making.

3.4   Dynamic Uncertainty

HSC involves a large numbers of actors and stakeholders (beneficiaries, host governments, local and international relief organizations, donors, etc.) and operates in highly unpredictable, dynamic environments. Hence, disaster response activities vary widely and are driven by numerous factors depending on each situation. Lack of efficiency and misalignment of the response with the real situation are common implications of uncertainty. These difficulties are linked to considerations of time frame (and pressure to make decisions) and flow control (information), the integration of uncertainty is a separate step.

From the BS point of view, uncertainty has makes long-term planning difficult and prevents supply chains from reaching a stable equilibrium. This suggests a few research challenges: (1) short term forecast and prediction of patterns could be made; (2) the chaos can be reduced if the focus is on the beneficiaries' needs and (3) the simulation of the HSC system and dynamics analysis of key parameters can help to prevent chaos (inspired on Wilding [45]).

Upon severe uncertainty, the order quantity determines the quantity delivered by a supplier which is a random variable. Quite contrary in capacity uncertainty, the delivery capacity is a random variable that is typically independent of the order quantity. Lead-time uncertainty is a stochastic element in the order lead time and input cost uncertainty represents stochasticity in the procurement prices [46]. To face these uncertainties appropriately, decision support systems could be developed to enable decision makers to have a clear vision of the on-going situation (real-time) as well as future of demand (predictive management).

Dynamic uncertainty in the aftermath of disasters may result in the need to move or relocate facilities such as shelter, warehouse and distribution centres. HSC may face an updated dynamic problem according to the new scenarios of catastrophe. Trends in using static data modelling reveals that stochastic and dynamic models are harder to solve. However, stochastic and scenario-based data modelling can help the decision makers to represent the uncertainty related to the process of the impact's estimation; closer to the chaotic circumstances of disasters.

Significant effort is still needed to efficiently solve these kinds of models; appropriate solutions must generate good relief plans in a short time. Therefore, we suggest an integrated perspective that includes the analysis of the interrelation between decision levels [6]. Literature shows that many contributions have been made on one stage or the other, but the integrated approaches are still rare.

4   Research Directions

HSC management still has many open issues and is therefore relevant for mathematical modeling, actual applications, and multidisciplinary perspectives to get a holistic analysis in the decision-making process [47]. Looking at the literature of HSC from different angles, BS and OR, we found that there are common topics: structure, flow control, time frame and dynamic uncertainty. In the following paragraphs, as summarized by Fig. 3, we will highlight research directions for each of these dimension.

HSC Structure. Literature shows the demand for grounded research design for better understanding the real challenges practitioners face. It is not sufficient to bring limited CSC solutions to the HSC as long as they do not fulfil the user requirements. Reviewed papers in OR indicate that research focuses on specific parts of HSC like distribution

Topics	Business-engineering Science	Operational Research
Structure	- Need of ground up research design - Applicability of existing CSC solutions to the HSC is limited - Simulation tools to help decision makers to evaluate network changes	- Reviewed papers are mainly focused on a specific part HSC - Distribution plans in decision making process are important - Unrealistic assumptions and constraints for optimization models and also insufficient objectives
Flow control	- Insufficient information for decision making - Importance of change management to use PMS (still in early stage at the field) - Need of Performance indicator for specific situations - VSA (lean) approach (challenges /opportunities) to optimise processes	- To find a way to consider facility ability in OR - The problem of material convergence at primary hubs and bottlenecks
Time frames	- Need of a DSS to combine the concepts of agility and lean to find a hybrid leagile management system that suits each time-frame.	- Multy-periods modelling to deal with changing environment - Multy-objectives modelling at same time - Modelling evolving to short time frames
Dynamic uncertainty	- Need of a clear vision of the HSC (real-time) - Use of predictive management to face dynamic uncertainity	- Reflecting uncertainty by stochastic/dynamic modelling - Need of efficient solving methods - Testing different scenarios to anticipate

Research Directions

-Development of "practitioners-friendly" PMS (real-time), which include the identification of supplies status (OR) through various stages of HSC (BS).

- Converge on the definition of time frames to facilitate vertical integration of BS and OR approaches.

- Development of stochastic (predictive) approaches to support decision makers in uncertainty.

- Development of a DSS to support leagile strategy to deal with efficiency vs. effectiveness paradigm.

Fig. 3. Synthesis of the litterature review

plans. However, to develop more realistic models, OR researchers have to avoid unrealistic assumptions and constraints. In this context, BS also suggests more use of simulation tools to evaluate modifications of HSC network.

Flow Control. BS literature suggests that there is insufficient information to assist decision makers. The common approach of developing PMSs is immature and change management has an important impact on PMS establishment. By concentrating on specific situations, literature lacks convergence on specific performance indicators. The newly introduced approach of VSA is still struggling with challenges in controlling processes. While field experts are suffering from material convergence at primary hubs and bottlenecks, OR has not yet found a way to reflect these challenges in mathematical models. Hence, developing a PMS which can also identify the status of supplies through various stages of HSC can be a step forward for both BS and OR.

Time Frames. Due to the importance of response phase and the transition from rapidity to cost optimisation in HSC during response time frames, BS suggests to find a hybrid *leagile* management system. OR follows its recent trend toward developing models on the basis of shorter time frames to better reflect dynamics. To show the temporal network, these multi period models need to be flexible enough to capture variations during response. Furthermore, literature asks for multi-objective contributions to reflect the complexity of decision making.

Dynamic Uncertainty. The relief organisations have tried to develop agile HSCs, but practitioners still deal with significant misalignments. BS insists on improving real time assessment as well as developing predictive DSS to reduce this unbalancing. From the other angle, when OR concentrates to address dynamic uncertainty, it refers to the merits (or demerits) of stochastic/dynamic models in comparison to deterministic ones.

Since there is not much efficient solving methods for these kinds of models, OR asks for further research in this area; which will ease the way through developing integrated models to reflect real situations better.

5   Conclusion

Our investigation reveals that both BS and OR have common interests in HSC. Both of them are trying to develop a PMS (in their own research area) and they need more improvement in related simulation systems. While OR is searching for an optimised time scale for its dynamic models, BS is also looking for a time-period to use its indicators on real-time basis. Furthermore, both BS discussion about predictive management and OR attempt in reflecting uncertainty in models by including probability (stochastic modelling), can contribute in developing an integrated stochastic approach. This approach can lead to a decision support system which considers different scenarios to assist in facing dynamic uncertainty.

This research tried to address the state of the art in four common frequently repeated topics of both sciences in HSC. However, there are other areas which can be added to our list for future like collaborative networks and virtual organizations. Literature review depicts some research directions, shown by Fig. 3, which ask for further study. As the outcome, authors are currently working on these directions and believe that cooperation between their research areas in the mentioned topics can result in more efficient and effective HSC.

Acknowledgments. The authors are gratefull to the anonymous reviewers for their helpful comments and suggested improvements.

References

1. UNOCHA: Global Humanitarian Overview 2015 (2014)
2. Comes, T., Schätter, F., Schultmann, F.: Building robust supply networks for effective and efficient disaster response. In: Proceedings of ISCRAM (2013)
3. Charles, A., Lauras, M.: An enterprise modelling approach for better optimisation modelling: application to the humanitarian relief chain coordination problem. OR Spectrum 33, 815–841 (2011)
4. Abidi, H., de Leeuw, S., Klumpp, M.: Humanitarian supply chain performance management: a systematic literature review. Int. J. Supply Chain Manag. 19, 592–608 (2014)
5. Manopiniwes, W., Irohara, T.: A review of relief supply chain optimization. Ind. Eng. Manag. Syst. 13, 1–14 (2014)
6. Anaya-Arenas, A.M., Renaud, J., Ruiz, A.: Relief distribution networks: a systematic review. Ann. Oper. Res. 223, 53–79 (2014)
7. Galindo, G., Batta, R.: Review of recent developments in OR/MS research in disaster operations management. Eur. J. Oper. Res. 230, 201–211 (2013)
8. Faraj, S., Xiao, Y.: Coordination in fast-response organizations. Manage. Sci. 52, 1155–1169 (2006)

9. Holguín-Veras, J., Jaller, M., Van Wassenhove, L.N., Pérez, N., Wachtendorf, T.: On the unique features of post-disaster humanitarian logistics. J. Oper. Manag. **30**, 494–506 (2012)
10. Altay, N., Green, W.G.: OR/MS research in disaster operations management. Eur. J. Oper. Res. **175**, 475–493 (2006)
11. Tomasini, R.M., Van Wassenhove, L.: Humanitarian Logistics. Palgrave Macmillan, Basingstoke (2009)
12. Kovacs, G., Spens, K.M.: Relief supply chain management for disasters: humanitarian aid and emergency logistics. Information Science Reference (2012)
13. Van Wassenhove, L.N.: Humanitarian aid logistics: supply chain management in high gear†. J. Oper. Res. Soc. **57**, 475–489 (2006)
14. Tatham, P., Pettit, S., Charles, A., Lauras, M., Van Wassenhove, L.: A model to define and assess the agility of supply chains: building on humanitarian experience. Int. J. Phys. Distrib. Logistics Manag. **40**, 722–741 (2010)
15. Mays, R.E., Racadio, R., Gugerty, M.K.: Competing constraints: the operational mismatch between business logistics and humanitarian effectiveness. In: Global Humanitarian Technology Conference (GHTC), 2012 IEEE, pp. 132–137. IEEE (2012)
16. Hellingrath, B., Link, D., Widera, A. (eds.): Managing Humanitarian Supply Chains: Strategies, Practices and Research (1st ed.). Literature Series, vol. Economics and Logistics. DVV Media Group GmbH, Bremen/Germany (2013)
17. Chan, J., Comes, T.: Innovative research design–A journey into the information typhoon. Procedia Eng. **78**, 52–58 (2014)
18. Blecken, A.: Logistics in the context of humanitarian operations. In: Dangelmaier, W., Blecken, A., Delius, R., Klöpfer, S. (eds.) Advanced Manufacturing and Sustainable Logistics, vol. 46, pp. 85–93. Springer, Heidelberg (2010)
19. Beamon, B.M.: Humanitarian relief chains: issues and challenges. In: Proceedings of the 34th International Conference on Computers and Industrial Engineering, pp. 77–82. University of Washington Seattle, WA (2004)
20. Charles, A., Lauras, M., Tomasini, R.: Collaboration networks involving humanitarian organisations-particular problems for a particular sector. In: Camarinha-Matos, L.M., Boucher, X., Afsarmanesh, H. (eds.) Collaborative Networks for a Sustainable World, vol. 336, pp. 157–165. Springer, Heidelberg (2010)
21. Caunhye, A.M., Nie, X., Pokharel, S.: Optimization models in emergency logistics: a literature review. Socio-Economic Plann. Sci. **46**, 4–13 (2012)
22. Luis, E., Dolinskaya, I.S., Smilowitz, K.R.: Disaster relief routing: Integrating research and practice. Socio-economic plann. sci. **46**, 88–97 (2012)
23. Kunz, N., Reiner, G.: A meta-analysis of humanitarian logistics research. J. Humanitarian Logistics Supply Chain Manag. **2**, 116–147 (2012)
24. Charles, A.: Improving the design and management of agile supply chains: feedback and application in the context of humanitarian aid. Ph.D Thesis, Toulouse University, France (2010)
25. Franke, J., Widera, A., Charoy, F., Hellingrath, B., Ulmer, C.: Reference process models and systems for inter-organizational ad-hoc coordination-supply chain management in humanitarian operations. In: 8th International Conference on Information Systems for Crisis Response and Management (ISCRAM 2011) (2011)
26. Hofmann, M., Betke, H., Sackmann, S.: Automated analysis and adaptation of disaster response processes with place-related restrictions. In: The 12th International Conference on Information Systems for Crisis Response and Management (ISCRAM 2015) (2015)
27. Restrepo, H.E., Málaga, H.: Promoción de la salud: cómo construir vida saludable. Pan American Health Organization (2001)

28. Coppola, D.P.: Introduction to International Disaster Management. Butterworth-Heinemann, Oxford (2006)
29. Rongier, C., Galasso, F., Lauras, M., Gourc, D.: A method to define a performance indicator system for the control of a crisis. In: 8th International Conference of Modelling and Simulation (MOSIM 2010) (2010)
30. Balcik, B., Beamon, B.M.: Facility location in humanitarian relief. Int. J. Logistics **11**, 101–121 (2008)
31. Blecken, A., Hellingrath, B.: Supply chain management software for humanitarian operations: review and assessment of current tools. In: Proceedings of the 5th ISCRAM (2008)
32. Salvadó, L.L., Lauras, M., Comes, T., Van de Walle, B.: Towards More Relevant Research on Humanitarian Disaster Management Coordination. In: The 12th International Conference on Information Systems for Crisis Response and Management ISCRAM 2015 (2015)
33. Taylor, D., Pettit, S.: A consideration of the relevance of lean supply chain concepts for humanitarian aid provision. Int. J. Serv. Technol. Manag. **12**, 430–444 (2009)
34. Afshar, A., Haghani, A.: Modeling integrated supply chain logistics in real-time large-scale disaster relief operations. Socio-Economic Plann. Sci. **46**, 327–338 (2012)
35. Özdamar, L., Demir, O.: A hierarchical clustering and routing procedure for large scale disaster relief logistics planning. Transp. Res. E Logistics Transp. Rev. **48**, 591–602 (2012)
36. Ertem, M.A., Buyurgan, N.: A procurement auctions-based framework for coordinating platforms in humanitarian logistics. In: Zeimpekis, V., Ichoua, S., Minis, I. (eds.) Humanitarian and Relief Logistics, vol. 54, pp. 111–127. Springer, New York (2013)
37. Holguín-Veras, J., Pérez, N., Ukkusuri, S., Wachtendorf, T., Brown, B.: Emergency logistics issues affecting the response to Katrina: a synthesis and preliminary suggestions for improvement. Transp. Res. Rec. J. Transp. Res. Board **2022**, 76–82 (2007)
38. Holguín-Veras, J., Jaller, M., Van Wassenhove, L.N., Pérez, N., Wachtendorf, T.: Material convergence: Important and understudied disaster phenomenon. Nat. Hazards Rev. **15**, 1–12 (2012)
39. Özdamar, L., Ertem, M.A.: Models, solutions and enabling technologies in humanitarian logistics. Eur. J. Oper. Res. **244**, 55–65 (2015)
40. Tomasini, R.M., Van Wassenhove, L.N.: From preparedness to partnerships: case study research on humanitarian logistics. Int. Trans. Oper. Res. **16**, 549–559 (2009)
41. Cozzolino, A.: Humanitarian logistics and supply chain management. humanitarian logistics, pp. 5–16. Springer, Heidelberg (2012)
42. Heckmann, I., Comes, T., Nickel, S.: A critical review on supply chain risk–Definition, measure and modeling. Omega **52**, 119–132 (2015)
43. Tatham, P., Pettit, S., Scholten, K., Sharkey Scott, P., Fynes, B.: (Le) agility in humanitarian aid (NGO) supply chains. Int. J. Phys. Distrib. Logistics Manag. **40**, 623–635 (2010)
44. Huang, M., Smilowitz, K.R., Balcik, B.: A continuous approximation approach for assessment routing in disaster relief. Transp. Res. B Methodol. **50**, 20–41 (2013)
45. Wilding, R.: The supply chain complexity triangle: uncertainty generation in the supply chain. Int. J. Phys. Distrib. Logistics Manag. **28**, 599–616 (1998)
46. Snyder, L.V., Atan, Z., Peng, P., Rong, Y., Schmitt, A.J., Sinsoysal, B.: OR/MS models for supply chain disruptions: a review (2012). SSRN 1689882
47. Leiras, A., de Brito, Jr., I., Peres, E.Q., Bertazzo, T.R., Yoshizaki, H.T.Y.: Literature review of humanitarian logistics research: trends and challenges. J. Humanitarian Logistics Supply Chain Manag. **4**, 95–130 (2014)

A Position Paper on Improving Preparedness and Response of Health Services in Major Crises

Aggelos Liapis[1(✉)], Antonis Kostaridis[2], Antonis Ramfos[1], Ian Hall[3],
Andrea DeGaetano[4], Nickolaos Koutras[5], Nina Dobrinkova[6], George Leventakis[7],
Andrej Olunczek[8], Geert Seynaeve[9], and George Boustras[10]

[1] INTRASOFT International SA, Peania, Greece
{aggelos.liapis,Antonis.ramfos}@intrasoft-intl.com
[2] Satways - Proionta Kai Ypiresies Tilematikis Diktyakon Kai Tilepikinoniakon
Efarmogon Limited, Chalandri, Greece
a.kostaridis@satways.net
[3] Department of Health, London, UK
Ian.Hall@phe.gov.uk
[4] Consiglio Nazionale delle Ricerche, Rome, Italy
andrea.degaetano@biomatematica.it
[5] ADITESS, Advanced Intergrated Technology Solutions & Services Limited, Athens, Greece
management@aditess.gr
[6] Institute of Information and Communication Technologies, Sofia, Bulgaria
ninabox2002@gmail.com
[7] Center For Security Studies - KEMEA, Athens, Greece
gleventakis@kemea.gr
[8] Fraunhofer-Gesellschaft zur Foerderung der Angewandten Forschung E.V, Dresden, Germany
andrej.olunczek@ivi.fraunhofer.de
[9] Ecomed bvba, Brussel, Belgium
geert.seynaeve@attentia.be
[10] AS Cyprus College Limited, Nicosia, Cyprus
g.boustras@euc.ac.cy

Abstract. There exists a huge variety in the occurrence and characteristics of major incidents. Incident management stakeholders and in particular emergency health service providers have to deal with two basic challenges: The disproportion between the needs and the available human/material resources in the response capacity and the inherent time constraints of an emergency. These critical factors play a seminal role in the decision-making process during a crisis event, which affects all levels of command & control (strategic, operational, and tactical). The drawback with current health emergency management systems lies with the command & control operations that should coordinate the actions of the separate services and turn them into an effective, multi-faceted crisis response mechanism. IMPRESS improves the efficiency of decision making in emergency health operations, which has a direct impact on the quality of services provided to citizens. Furthermore it provides a consolidated concept of operations, to effectively manage medical resources, prepare and coordinate response activities, supported by a Decision Support System, using data from multiple heterogeneous sources. The proposed solution facilitates communication between Health Services

© Springer International Publishing Switzerland 2015
N. Bellamine Ben Saoud et al. (Eds.): ISCRAM-med 2015, LNBIP 233, pp. 205–216, 2015.
DOI: 10.1007/978-3-319-24399-3_18

(and Emergency Responders) at all levels of response and the crisis cycle with the necessary health care systems support, supervision and management of participating organizations. It will assist health services in becoming more proactive, better prepared and interoperable with other emergency response organizations.

Keywords: Incident management · Emergency health services · First responders · Decision support systems · Crisis management

1   Introduction

Countries are facing major challenges to protect their populations from an increasing number of potential health threats in the future. Preparedness and prevention plays a significant role in ensuring an efficient response to national and international crises. Emergency Medical Services (EMS) systems form an integral part of any public health care system: their primary function is to deliver emergency medical care in all emergencies, including disasters and crises. It is widely recognized that an effective disaster response is heavily dependent on pre-existing local system capacity and capabilities than on external assistance. In the early stages of a health crisis, the ability to respond depends on the level of preparedness of the local community (citizens and volunteers) and health services. An efficient and well-structured EMS system ensures the achievement and maintenance of the skills necessary to deal with disasters, while disaster preparedness doesn't help to identify organizational gaps (WHO 2008) but in many cases helps to minimize the consequences of a hazardous event so mitigate the risk and avoid potential crises.

Between 1990 and 2010 approximately 47 million people in the WHO European Region were directly affected by natural disasters that resulted in over 132 000 fatalities. This does not include the wars and violent conflicts that have killed over 300 000 people in the Region over the last 20 years. Other severe events of the recent past include the Chernobyl (former Soviet Union) nuclear power plant accident in 1986, which affected several million people according to United Nations estimates, and the Marmara earthquake (NW Turkey) that killed nearly 18 000 people and injured close to 45 000 people in Turkey in 1999 (WHO 2012). During the same year (1999), a big earthquake (magnitude 5.9) struck Athens, Greece, revealing its disrupting potential in terms of residential structural damages, injuries, social effects and financial consequences. This disastrous event and the subsequent crisis have stressed again the importance of prevention and preparedness actions in aim to enhance interoperability and coordination among the public Emergency Services including Health Services (e.g. EMS). Another relevant incident is the Japanese earthquake and subsequent nuclear reactor crisis, which provided us with a catastrophic scenario that would present formidable public health and healthcare challenges to the EU, if such an incident occurred here. Moreover, the 2009 H1N1 pandemic, though mild in comparison to the anticipated morbidity and mortality of a H5N1 pandemic, stressed the interdependence of the public health, pre- and post-hospital care, primary care, and hospital care systems (US Department of

Health and Human Services 2011). The ongoing – since 2014 – Ebola outbreak in West Africa although mostly confined in three countries (Liberia, Sierra Leone and Guinea), stressed the medical and health care systems of many countries in two continents (North America/US and Europe/Spain-Italy-UK-Germany-Denmark).

Although all examples mentioned above were natural disasters and accidents or combinations we must also consider the Tokyo subway sarin incident (1995) that had an enormous impact on the Japanese megapolis, despite the small number of lives lost. It was the first and so far the only chemical warfare agents' release in urban environment during peace time worldwide. The 2001 anthrax letters' scare that caused certain deaths in the US is still a threat that occasionally tests national preparedness and response in various countries' around the globe.

1.1 Background

There exists a huge variety in the occurrence and characteristics of major incidents. In general, an adequate major incident management has to deal with two basic challenges. First, there is a disproportion between the needs and the available human and material resources: limitations in the response capacity (coordination, triage teams, search & rescue, Advanced Life Support and transportation squads, ground vehicles, and other health and psycho-social interventions), not only with respect to the number of people affected (quantity) and the time constraints (emergency), but also concerning the nature of the needs (quality). In disasters, characterized by disruption of infrastructure, facilities and/or services, this imbalance is even more serious and long-lasting. Secondly, very often there is inadequate information, low levels of risk perception and possibly scientific uncertainty or public concern and awareness with respect to the causes, nature and extent of the health issues involved and the risks that may represent. The field on which this situation is more dramatic is that of medical rescues, where every minute of delay means death and suffering for numerous victims. In a society, that regularly reminds us of the vulnerability of man in the face of natural or man-made events, one of the major tasks for governments and crisis managers is to ensure attentive prevention and an appropriate response to disasters. On the other side of the spectrum, the critical factors are more related to analysis and decision-making. A situation e.g. where there is an actual or potential risk of a major exposure to an unusual serious health hazard for a community (or which is perceived as such) can result in a public health crisis.

A Decision Support Tool (DST) needs to be capable to deal with the whole scope of health emergencies, from a single accident, over multi-casualty and mass-casualty situations to the most complex disasters. For health professionals to be able to use this tool in extra-ordinary situations, they must have experience in using its functionalities in daily practice. The extra-ordinary approach and special arrangements, does not only relate to the emergency response, but must be implemented for all phases of the management cycle.

All types of emergency situations require – from a health perspective - extra-ordinary competencies, skills and attitudes, and thus specific education and training, the broader scope of which is commonly called 'disaster health'. Mass emergencies, like major accidents and classical disaster, must be dealt by a structured mobilization of additional or specialized material and teams, combined with a more efficient use of the available resources (e.g. using methods of noria and triage, improved coordination, etc.). Public health crises require surveillance with early detection and early warning, extra-ordinary (often cross-border) decision making and control strategies, follow-up research & structural measures, all of which relies on timely (pro-active) and adequate exchange of information and communication. The EUSDEM consensus approach is to logically link terminology with the scope and conceptual framework of major incident and emergency situations (Archer and Seynaeve 2007; Seynaeve 2003; Seynaeve 2008). There exists of course an enormous variety in the occurrence and characteristics of major incidents. It is obvious that understanding the pathogenesis of major incidents, the pathway and mechanisms leading to health emergencies, contributes to better preparedness and response. Although every disaster is unique and always has specific characteristics, it is possible to develop a generic conceptual framework explaining in general the health impact of extraordinary events and how it can be mitigated by certain measures. Also, after a major emergency it is essential to provide on-going assistance, restore key services and infrastructure, organize socio-economic recovery, reconstruction and development as well as integrate lessons learned in future risk management and preparedness. In a nutshell, previous incidents confirmed the need for a "whole of community" approach in planning and responding to a disaster, and confirmed that a healthcare preparedness program must address the entire healthcare community in its preparedness activities. Regardless of the threat, an effective medical surge response begins with robust hospital-based systems and effective Healthcare Networks to facilitate preparedness planning and response at the local level. Simply put, strong and resilient Healthcare Networks are the key to an effective state and local emergency response to an event-driven medical surge. In addition, trauma Centers, Hospitals, and Healthcare Systems face multiple challenges daily in addition to the growing list of man-made and natural threats. Emergency department overcrowding, the rising uninsured, and an aging population all inhibit the healthcare system's ability to respond effectively.

1.2   Use of Decision Support Tools in Emergency Situations

In an emergency situation, organization leadership and management needs clear, accurate real-time information about the effect of the disaster upon human resources and the readiness status of the organization. One of the key IT elements for emergency response is the availability of decision support tools (Graves 2004). Today, the decision support in emergency situations represents a current issue that is being researched in various fields. The complexity of the problem and the corresponding incident resolution approaches, methodologies and support tools ask for intertwining knowledge out of fields such as computer science, psychology, sociology, medicine, biology, chemistry and knowledge engineering. Currently, there is neither an integrated plan nor a complex set of procedures that would unite principles, rules and regulations for emergency response operations.

1.3   Tools and Procedures for Preparedness of Emergency Health Services

Traditionally, crises have been conceptualized as having pre-impact, impact, post-impact and recovery phases. In most studies of crises, the following simplified sequence uses the terms pre-event, event and post-event/long-term recover. Pre-event activities include risk assessments, mitigation and preparedness. The event may be either static, as a single point in time, or dynamic, evolving over time. Response and recovery occur during the post-event. Preparedness behavior includes a variety of actions taken by families, households, communities, governments and emergency responders to get ready for a disaster. Preparedness activities may include devising disaster plans, gathering emergency supplies, training response teams, and educating residents about a potential disaster (Mileti 1999).

Preparedness is the phase of crisis management, which refers to activities, programs and systems existing prior to a crisis that are used to support and enhance emergency response. They actually mitigate the risks and inhibit the threatening events to become crises. The crisis managers prepare resources including staff and equipment and develop plans of action and procedures for use when the crisis strikes, i.e. planning to provide the capability to deal with emergencies, and preparedness is the discipline, which ensures an organization, or community's readiness to respond to a crisis in a coordinated, timely, and effective manner. The crisis preparedness includes information and public awareness campaigns, education, exercises and training, early warning and emergency plans.

1.4   Interoperability of Health Services in Emergency Situations

The post-impact, emergency response stage of a disaster is characterized as the immediate aftermath of a disaster, typically including the first hours or days, perhaps up to one week, depending on the event. In a disaster or emergency situation, there is a need for EMS and hospitals to be able to communicate with each other and with other members of the emergency response community. The ability to exchange data regarding hospitals' bed availability, status, services, and capacity enables both hospitals and other emergency agencies to respond to emergencies and disaster situations with greater efficiency and speed. In particular, it allows emergency dispatchers and managers to make reliable logistics decisions - where to route victims, which hospitals have the ability to provide the needed service. Some hospitals have expressed the need for, and indeed are currently using, commercial or self-developed information technology that allows them to publish this information to other hospitals in a region, as well as EOCs, 9-1-1 centers, and EMS responders via a Web-based tool. The fact is that most of the systems that are available today do not record or present data in a standardized format, creating a serious barrier to data sharing between hospitals and emergency response groups. Without data standards, parties of various kinds are unable to view data from hospitals in a state or region that uses a different system – unless a specialized interface is developed. Alternatively, such officials must get special user accounts and toggle between web pages to get a full picture. Other local emergency responders are unable to get the data imported into the emergency IT tools they use (e.g. a 9-1-1 computer-aided dispatch system. They too must get a user account and visit the appropriate web page. This is very inefficient. A uniform data standard will allow different applications and systems to communicate seamlessly. Both HL7 and OASIS are dedicated to providing open standards for the exchange, integration, sharing, and retrieval of electronic information. While HL7 focuses on health information that supports clinical practice and the management, delivery and evaluation of health services, the EDXL suite of messaging standards (CAP, EDXL-SitRep, EDXL-RM, EDXL-DE, EDXL-Have, EDXL-TEP/TEC) published by OASIS focus on information that supports emergency and disaster response, management, and coordination across jurisdictions, organizations, and professions. In addition, a multi-agency, multi-discipline coordinated and timely response is needed to deal with a disaster or large-scale incident. Although first responders have the technology to help accomplish this — in this case, pre-established and pre-programmed Shared Channels/Talk-groups in their portable radios — there are no Standard Operating Procedures (SOPs) to help guide the responder interaction and provide greater coordination through enhanced communication. As a result, interoperable communication is fragmented and action is delayed. The lack of a set of interoperable communication SOPs has been identified as the primary impediment to a timely and coordinated response.

2   IMPRESS Decision Making and Response Levels

The success of every operation depends on the hierarchical structure of the organizations and units involved. The hierarchical structure allows acting quickly and responding to different situations very effectively. Therefore, the hierarchical structure of the EMS domain is based on command and control structures as well as reporting rules. Since EMS organizations do not only operate inside the limited timescale of an operation, there exists a general hierarchical structure (administration) and the hierarchical structure of the incident scene (operational structure). The general hierarchical structure differs throughout the EU in the ways the responsibilities are distributed. However, there always exist a strategic (gold), a tactical (silver) and an operational (bronze) level of command. These levels of command exist in the general hierarchical structure as well as in the hierarchical structure of the incident scene. The following paragraphs position the IMPRESS DSS functionalities at all levels of decision making.

Strategic Level. In strategic level, the main engaged organization is the National Control Center operating in the field of Health Services, which has the overall supervision of all the engaged entities (Hospitals, Critical Infrastructure, Government, Civilians, Public Safety Agencies, Volunteer Organizations, Private Sector, and Businesses) in regional or national level. IMPRESS strategic level functionalities include:

- Allow interoperability between health services operating across different regional, governmental and cross border levels.
- Information exchange will be used to optimally allocate resources in response to major disasters and also facilitate the cooperation between operating teams of different cultural and operational background.
- CECIS type of layer functionality, allowing for exchange of data between international organizations.

- Necessary tools for strategic level decisions with resource allocation, scenario analysis and definition of operational procedures.
- Post crisis module for registering, evaluating and exchanging lessons learned with all related information.

Tactical Level. At this level, a Regional Command and Control Center is operating, represented by an Incident commander who coordinates all the relevant Health Sector Agencies. IMPRESS tactical level functionalities include:

- Provide coordination layer of the Health Services that will ensure (a) cooperation with the relevant agencies and (b) the readiness of the Health Sector services according to the requirements and evolution of the envisaged incident.
- Functionality for evaluating and optimally utilizing the available resources, analyzing and predicting the evolution of the incident and providing an efficient cooperation system.
- Collect and transmit biomedical and other patient data between emergency responders and health services. Logistic component for assessing the needed stockpiles of necessary equipment, medications, vaccinations and personal protective equipment, their positioning and restocking, will be established.
- Appropriate component providing easy forms for exporting such goods for cross-border missions.
- Mathematical modeling tools will be integrated for (i) enhanced surge capacity (ii) statistical recognition of events (iii) evolution models for major crises (iv) bio-mathematical modelling and simulation of patients and first aid activity.

Operational Level. The third level to structure the EMS domain is managed by the Local Health Control Center. Vehicles in the EMS domain are distinguished by their use for example Emergency treatment and transport, Doctor Transport, Non-emergency transport, Transport of highly infective people, Command and control, etc. IMPRESS operational level functionalities include:

- Processing and entry of data into a single, appropriately structured geographic database,
- Processing and customization of map data
- Providing appropriate tools (Web Services) to exploit specialized medical functions.

2.1   IMPRESS High-Level Architecture and Main DSS Components

IMPRESS will develop and integrate into a holistic concept of operations the following distinctive components, which will expand beyond the present state of the art in response and preparedness capabilities of health services. Figure 1 shows the high-level architecture of the envisioned IMPRESS DSS in relations to these components and other auxiliary modules, which will form the solution as a whole.

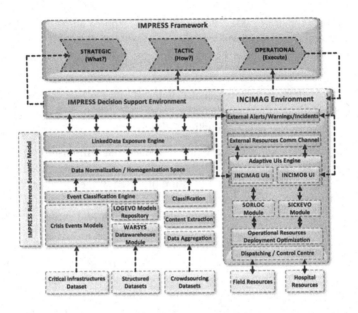

Fig. 1. IMPRESS high-level architecture

The IMPRESS architecture is divided in three main layers: The bottom layer consists of the data resources, which IMPRESS will use to facilitate the decision making process. They can be either structured or unstructured sources including data coming from the field (through crowd sourcing or first responders), data retrieved from hospital records on supplies, personnel, medical incidents and more.

The second layer consists of the core data infrastructure of IMPRESS which will form the point of collection and processing of gathered data to provide the required "intelligence" to decision makers at different levels of intervention. The **WARSYS** database structure will be developed within IMPRESS, with a view of extracting in real time medical and logistics information from available repositories (such as hospital information systems). It will be accompanied by the IMPRESS Reference Semantic Model, which will enhance this layer into a semantically enhanced data repository in order to provide more advanced knowledge management and inferring capabilities. This layer will contain DSS components, which will support the project's objectives as follows:

The SOuRce LOCation (**SORLOC**) tool will (among other functionalities) automatically interrogate hospital records and use model comparison techniques to improve on the rapidity and accuracy of contaminant source localization. The SICK patients physiological EVOlution forecast (**SICKEVO**) module, will address physiologic trajectory assessment and forecast. The main improvements that SICKEVO will present will concern the level of detail in physiology representation, and the automatic interaction with actual observations and hospital records. Finally, the **LOGEVO** suite will enable the use of models for the LOGistics EVOlution of health care resources, focusing in particular on models of hospital surge (expansion of offer with current resources). The third layer of the IMPRESS DSS will provide the decision support environment, which interfaces with the layers below through a linked data exposure engine to provide end users with the necessary information in the appropriate format. Key to this role is the INCident MAnaGement (**INCIMAG**) tool, which is an integral part of the overall IMPRESS DSS and will work in tandem with other components. It will allow an efficient response of emergency agencies by connecting them among themselves, with other emergency responders, with dispatch centers and with international relief agencies. An extension to INCIMAG is its mobile version, **INCIMOB**, which will allow live data from the field relative to e.g. structural damage to buildings, emergency calls for help, identification of deceased individuals, identification of cleared or unprocessed areas etc., to flow into the IMPRESS platform data warehouse system WARSYS. Specific needs of medical first responders (eTriage, eVitalSigns) will be contemplated by INCIMOB. INCIMOB will also allow volunteers and affected people to submit data that will be used for crowd sourcing. This part of INCIMOB is strictly separated from the part for medical personnel and allows a more or less structured communication between the incident management and the public.

3   IMPRESS Use Cases

3.1   Use Case 1 – Cross-Border Perspective (Greece-Bulgaria)

The particular use case involves all the planning and deployment required to create the necessary conditions for the Greek-Bulgarian crisis validation scenario: Earthquake scenario at E79 motorway near Greek-Bulgarian border, with two impacts: Firstly an overflow of the river Strimona causing a landslide of the side of the road and secondly a sliding of large stones in the street. All the above caused a large number of injured drivers and passengers in urgent need of medical attention and transportation to nearby hospitals triggering essentially a cross-border emergency operation, which will initiate the full scale of the IMPRESS solution. The collapse of E79 motorway is caused due to a large earthquake. The effects of this natural phenomenon is both the overflow of the Strimonas river which flows parallel to the road and secondly several rock-falls phenomena causing damages to the road. The overflow caused a landslide of the side of the road, so a land mass collapsing into the river together with parts of the lane, sweeping away several vehicles and colliding with each other, resulting in many passengers to be injured. The landslide also blocked a tunnel at some point of the road network, causing damages to vehicles while falling on them or due to collisions between the vehicles trying to avoid the rocks and a truck have skidded. The collapse of E79 motorway is caused due to a large earthquake. The effects of this natural phenomenon is both the overflow of the Strimonas river which flows parallel to the road and secondly several rock-falls phenomena causing damages to the road. The overflow caused a landslide of the side of the road, so a land mass collapsing into the river together with parts of the lane, sweeping away several vehicles and colliding with each other, resulting in many passengers to be injured. The landslide also blocked a tunnel at some point of the road network, causing damages to vehicles while falling on them or due to collisions between the vehicles trying to avoid the rocks and a truck have skidded. All the above caused a large number of injured drivers and passengers in urgent need of medical attention and transportation to nearby hospitals.

A cross-border perspective is attributed to this emergency medical operation due to the fact that the overall incident is located near the Greek- Bulgarian borders and the injured passengers will be carried both in Greek and Bulgarian hospitals in order to have more efficient response. IMPRESS DSS aims to reduce the time of providing pre-hospital medical services, enhancing the coordination of Emergency Responders (Dispatch centers and ambulances) from both engaged countries and by fully integrating all medical units to the response operating environment of the hosting nation. Moreover, IMPRESS will provide a valuable tool for Field Units and Incident Commander by providing them a channel of communication and exchange of medical information (e.g. surge capacity, availability of personnel, tracking of patients, examination information) and resource allocation (availability of beds, medicines, medical equipment, etc.). So the most appropriate unit, concerning the medical equipment and the knowledge of the personnel needed, will deal with each incident and each injured person will be routed to the most appropriate hospital, regarding the type and availability of medical staff, equipment and resources not only needed but also exists inside each Hospital or Clinique.

3.2   Use Case 2 – Palermo Use Case

The work on the Palermo scenario is divided into two logical segments, a preparation phase A (partially historical, partially live) and a simulation phase B. This scenario concept moves from the availability of actual data from a historical fire, which developed in the Palermo waste dump of Bellolampo between July 29 and August 7, 2012. The fire released a variety of toxic compounds, but it turned out that during a fire in a waste dump relatively low levels are produced of those toxicants (nitrogen oxides, sulphur oxides) which may represent an acute threat to the neighboring population. In these cases there is typically the liberation of compounds (like dioxin), which enters the food chain (through deposition in pastures etc.) and which produces chronic intoxication with increased frequencies of tumors. These however do not seem very interesting for an acute crisis scenario.

However, in an industrial fire accident many of the same compounds are released as in a waste dump fire, only at higher concentration levels (able to induce acute respiratory embarrassment and possibly death). The possibility therefore exists to model the spread of these toxicants (nitrogen and sulphur oxides), given their volatility and tendency to be absorbed by the vegetation etc., match the model against available Palermo waste dump fire data and then extrapolate the model to (possibly cross-border) industrial site fire scenarios. The Palermo scenario therefore will simulate the sudden liberation of high concentrations of toxic compounds from a tank fire developing on-board a ship moored in the Palermo harbor. The relevance of the simulation to potential cross-border situations in Europe is immediate, if one thinks about the Mediterranean coast of France (e.g. the Nice-Genova area), or the Baltic. The advantage of developing the entire analysis in Palermo stems from the possibility of characterizing in detail the geography over an area where actual historical data of toxicant diffusion are available.

Phase A will consist of two simultaneous activities. In activity A1, the sensor archives will be interrogated and data on toxicant concentrations will be aggregated in appropriate Analysis Data Sets (ADSs), together with geolocation data. Also, a map of the relevant Sicilian area will be digitized and relevant diffusion parameters will be associated to homogeneous subareas in it. In activity A2, a number of logistic parameters (transfer times between structures and locations as dependent over variations of the traffic density over the day, number of the police force patrolling the city again at different times of the day etc.) will be measured.

Phase B will consist of the development of the spread and contamination model and of the population reaction model as they pertain to the specific geographic area of the Palermo harbor. Both models will be intrinsically stochastic and will accept parameterized input, so that several (thousand) runs of the combined models will allow the determination of a distribution of possible responses given the same basic scenario. These will then be available for further analysis comparing different strategies and their expected effectiveness over a range of possible scenarios.

By allowing obtaining scenario results in the presence and absence of IMPRESS procedures and methodologies, and with incorporation or exclusion of the effects of the IMPRESS incident management tool, the Palermo testbed will allow the demonstration of the main features of the IMPRESS-solution against a historically validated, geographically realistic situation.

4   Limitations

The IMPRESS concept is by itself a self-standing medical DSS that would allow emergency medical services to be able to fully cope with different types of emergencies ranging from large-scale mass events to multiple incidents. Such large-scale systems have many fine points that need to be fully accounted for in order to maximize its benefit to the community.

- The interoperability of IMPRESS with legacy systems at all crisis governance levels is critical to its success. Therefore, prompt considerations of the existing DSS or its modular components must be taken into consideration.
- IMPRESS DSS has been designed to receive real time sensor and emergency resource operational data from the incident and presents this information to medical personnel at the time and place that they need it to enable more effective patient management. The number of sensors is currently limited to fit to the needs and requirements of the existing components, although its expansion is something to be discussed in the future.
- A potential limitation is that software components will have trouble to communicate or being impractical to integrate or that are unable to deliver the required functionality on time due to various factors (such as loosely defined and/or changing requirements, inaccurate estimation of the time and resources needed for the development, etc.).
- Specific care must be given to the cultural and ethical dimension of the emergency responders and the victims. This has to be portrayed in a medical DSS, so that responders are fully aware of the procedures needed to be applied in such situations.

5   Conclusions

This paper describes the conceptual framework for the development of a holistic emergency medical DSS that has started to be implemented in the framework of the FP7-project IMPRESS. It aspires to be a major step forward over current health emergency management systems in terms of command & control operations that should coordinate the actions of the separate services and turn them into an effective, multi-faceted crisis response mechanism. The proposed solution aims to improve the efficiency of decision making in emergency health operations, which will have a direct impact on the quality of services provided to citizens, by providing a consolidated concept of operations, to effectively manage medical resources, prepare and coordinate response activities, supported by a Decision Support System, using data from multiple heterogeneous sources.

Acknowledgments. This work has been partially funded by the EC in the 7th Framework Programme, (SEC-2013.4.1-4: Development of decision support tools for improving preparedness and response of Health Services involved in emergency situations) under grant number FP7-SEC-2013–608078 - IMproving Preparedness and Response of HEalth Services in major criseS (IMPRESS).

References

Archer, F., Seynaeve, G.: International guidelines and standards for education and training to reduce the consequences of events that may threaten the health status of a community. Prehospital Disaster Med. **22**(2), 120–130 (2007)

Seynaeve, G.: The 1999 dioxin and Coca Cola crisis. A case study in Public Health Crises. Ecomed, Brussels, Belgium (2003)

Seynaeve, G.: Education and disaster risk reduction. Prehospital Disaster Med. **23**(4), 309–313 (2008)

US Department of Health and Human Services: From Hospitals to Healthcare Coalitions: Transforming Health Preparedness and Response in Our Communities, US Department of Health and Human Services (2011)

WHO: Emergency Medical Services Systems, Report of an assessment project co-ordinated by the World Health Organization. WHO (2008)

WHO: Health security in the WHO European Region. Assessment of Health-System Crisis Preparedness. WHO, May 2012

Graves, R.: Key technologies for emergency response. In: Proceedings of ISCRAM 2004, Brussels, Belgium, pp. 133–138 (2004)

Mileti, D.S.: Disasters by Design: A Reassessment of Natural Hazards in the United States. Joseph Henry Press, Washington D.C (1999)

Author Index

Printed in the United States
By Bookmasters